The King Danced
In the Marketplace

. . . and then in sign of great
rejoicing and celebration,
the king danced in the marketplace
with the valiant
and stouthearted Mexicans . . .

Tezozomoc, *Crónica Mexicana*, p. 309

THE KING DANCED
in the marketplace

FRANCES GILLMOR

Illustrated by Carolyn Huff Kinsey

UNIVERSITY OF UTAH PRESS
Salt Lake City 1977

L.C. Card Catalog No. 63-11970

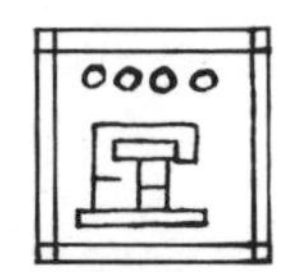

Reprint edition by the University of Utah Press,
Salt Lake City, Utah 84112.

International Standard Book Number 0-87480-148-6.

Printed in the United States of America.

Contents

Descriptions and sources of the decorative drawings, adapted by Carolyn Huff Kinsey from various codices, are briefly given with chapters where they appear.

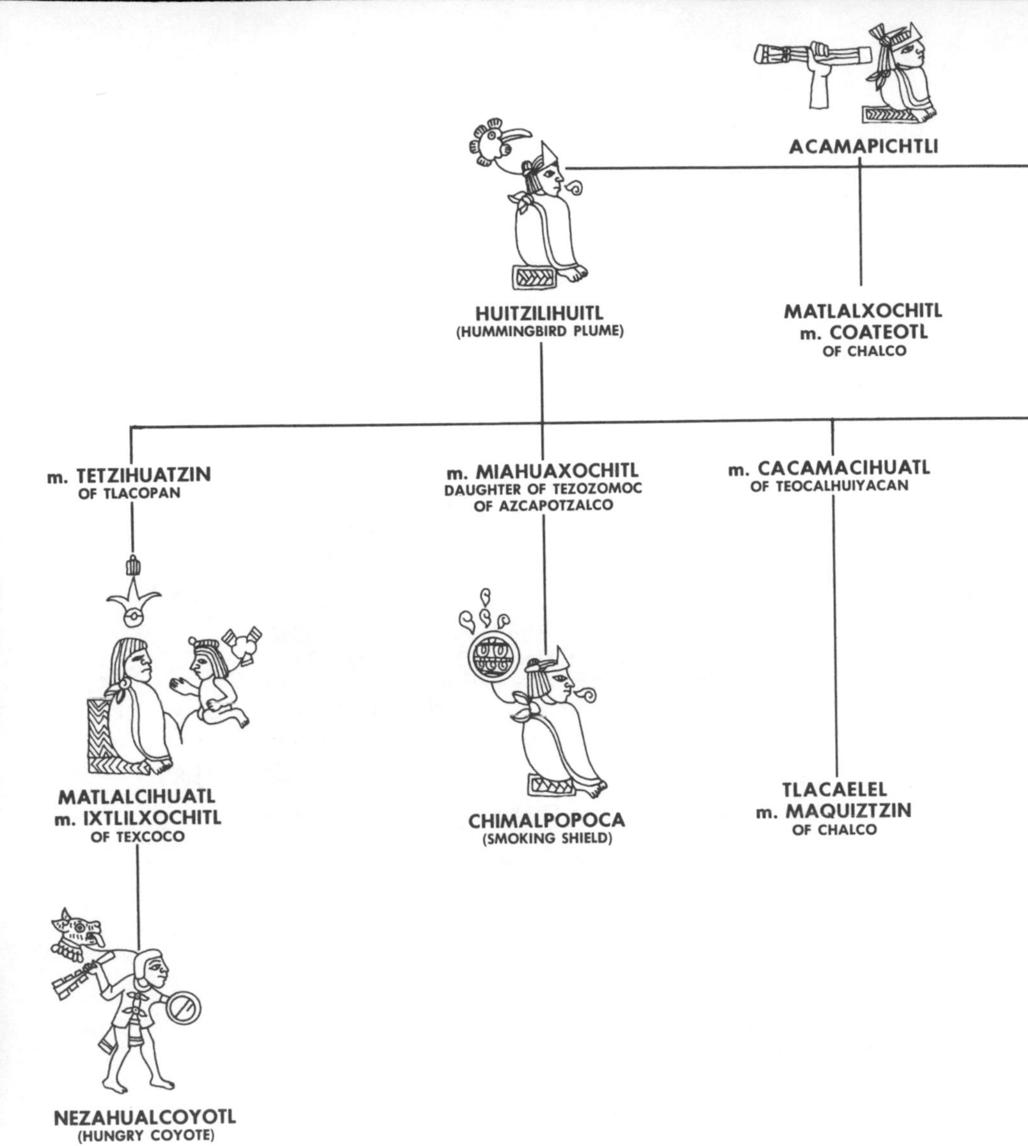

MAIN FAMILY RELATIONSHIPS OF HUEHUE MOTECZUMA ILHUICAMINA

selected and compiled from codices and chronicles

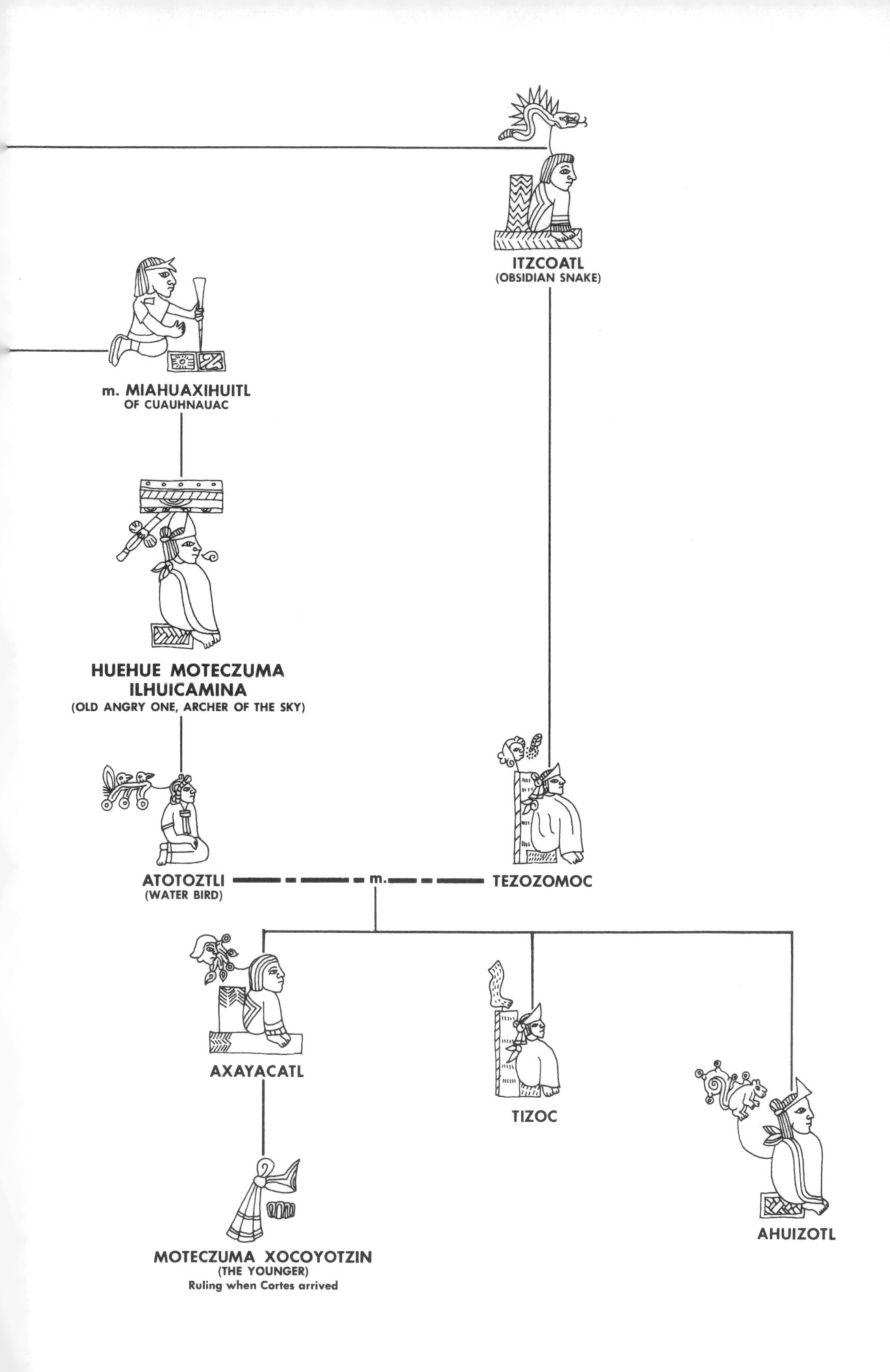
ITZCOATL
(OBSIDIAN SNAKE)
m. MIAHUAXIHUITL
OF CUAUHNAUAC
HUEHUE MOTECZUMA
ILHUICAMINA
(OLD ANGRY ONE, ARCHER OF THE SKY)
ATOTOZTLI
(WATER BIRD)
m.
TEZOZOMOC
AXAYACATL
TIZOC
AHUIZOTL
MOTECZUMA XOCOYOTZIN
(THE YOUNGER)
Ruling when Cortes arrived

The years of Huehue Moteczuma Ilhuicamina's life

1398—1468

10 Rabbit—2 Stone

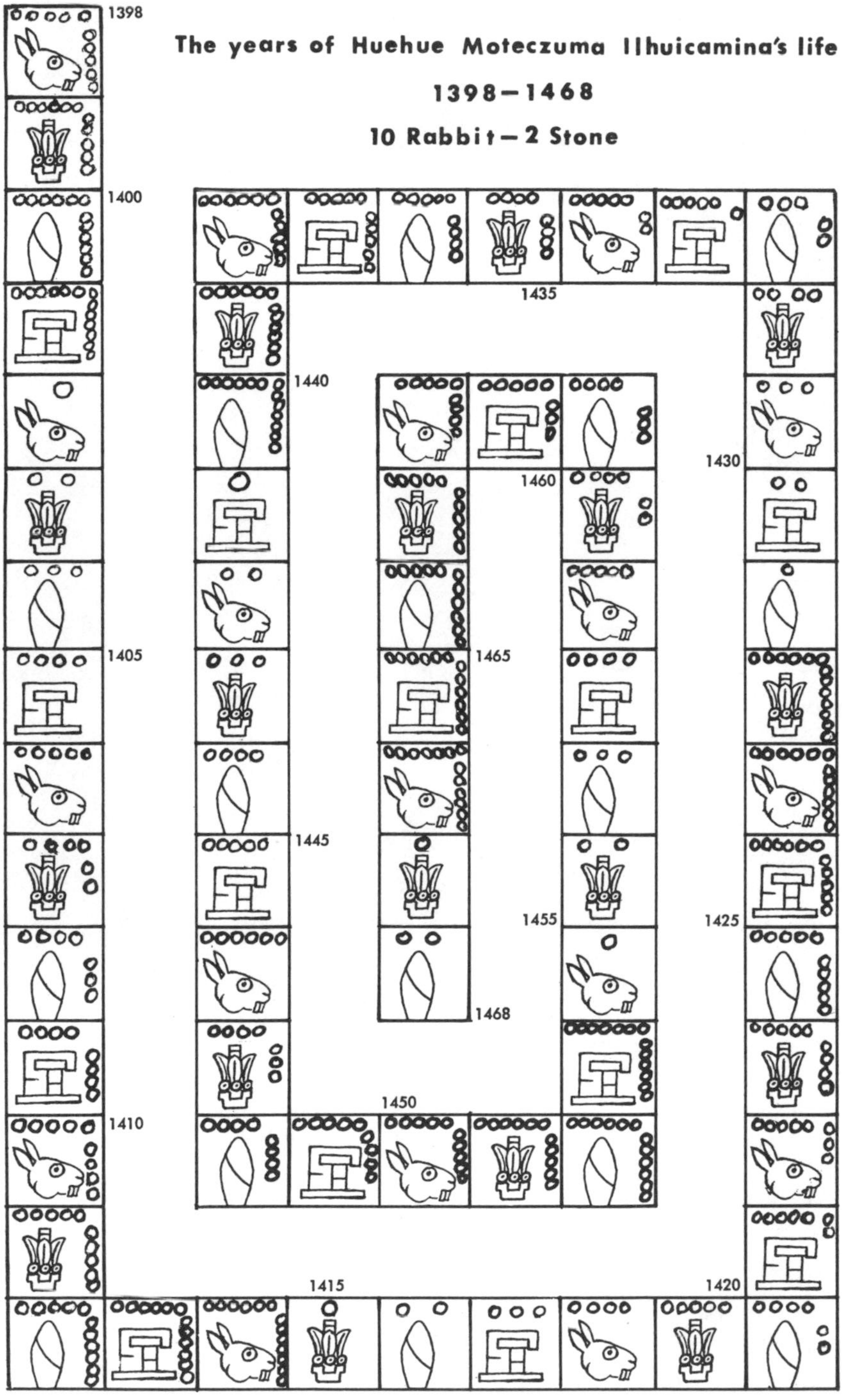

1398
1400
1405
1410
1415
1420
1425
1430
1435
1440
1445
1450
1455
1460
1465
1468

Foreword

THE MOTECZUMA who is the subject of this biography should not be confused with his great-grandson who was ruling when the Spaniards arrived. To distinguish Moteczuma the First, under whose rule the tribute area of the central Aztec alliance first spread outward from the Valley of Mexico, from Moteczuma the Second, under whose rule the break-up came, later Nahuatl-speaking people applied to him the adjective *huehue*—old. The name Moteczuma itself has many variations in spelling according to the way the Spaniards heard it. English-speaking people usually say Montezuma. Mexicans often say Moctezuma. Longer forms of the name are Moteuczoma or Motecuzoma—he who grows angry from within his stomach. A name more distinctively his and most frequently used was Ilhuicamina, Archer of the Sky. When he became the Tlatoani—the speaker-ruler—of Tenochtitlan, now Mexico City, the people who saw his riches from far off added another name—Chalchiuhtlatonac, He Who Shines Like Jade. He lived from 1398 to 1468—from 10 Rabbit to 2 Stone—and when Cortez arrived in 1519 there were old men still living—Xicotencatl in Tlaxcala, for instance—who had known him.

We seek him as a person across the centuries. We look for the human moments, few of which were recorded in that stern time, which make us realize that he and his contemporaries were men and women whom we may understand a little in spite of the wide areas that separate our cultures and our ways of thinking.

It was difficult even for his contemporaries to bridge the gap between themselves and Moteczuma Ilhuicamina. He was a militarist, an expansionist, a dictator. He had the reputation of cruelty, of having established the sacrifices of the skinned god and victim, in Tenochtitlan. He hides as an individual behind the great events of that period of expansion of the power of the alliance. The emphasis of command in his own city is divided between him and his half-brother Tlacaelel. The emphasis of authority in the alliance is divided between him and Nezahualcoyotl of Texcoco. But little by little as one studies the many sources which have preserved the record of his activities, there stands forth from the mist of the centuries a simple man, caught in the rhythm of the dance of power and expanding commerce, of the social and religious organization, which forced him into the role of dictator. It should surprise us that we know so many aspects of his character as an individual — for example, the love for the Cuernavaca country from which his mother came, a tie which was never broken; the failure of his love for the tall widow, whom we may now call by her name—Wreath of Cacao Flowers; the tragedies which accompanied his friendship for Nezahualcoyotl of Texcoco and Coateotl of Chalco. He learned that indeed rulers of many people eat the bread of sorrow. He did not wish his sons to share that rule and that sorrow, but to learn trades and crafts. Contented, he could talk with the men who worked with skilled hands building his city, though in general his people feared to look at him as he passed by.

One comes to feel pity for this cruel and austere ruler of Tenochtitlan. His success was his tragedy. By his military and political operations he extended the power of his city to the "neighbors of the Sea of the Sky"—which today we call the Gulf of Mexico. He gave food to his people through trade and tribute, and removed the fear of new years of hunger like those in the 1450's. But in the Speaker-Ruler, the man was lost. He danced quite literally in the market to the music of bones, of war, and of sacrifice. He danced to the rhythmic outward march and return of traders and fighters. He danced to the balanced pattern of powers within the alliance and within his own city.

Since the truth of history exists in all its relations, it is worth looking from the perspective of modern wars and dictators at this ancient stage on which was played out the drama of a people and a man, in their self-realization and their tragedy, in their dance increasingly stylized by the necessities of their relationships to each other and to their philosophy.

It will be of interest to explain briefly the method employed for this biography. I try to see this ruler against the background and in terms of his culture. I use the religious symbolism employed by the tlacuilos—the painters of the preconquest and immediately post-conquest records—and of the writers of the city annals who recounted the year by year events which the pictures portrayed. Without interrupting the swiftness of the narrative for comment, I refer in the notes to the sources, and explain there problems or contradictions which may exist. To indicate the types of source material, I arrange the bibliography in classified form, with brief descriptions of each type—the picture records or codices, the annals, the chronicles, etc.—and with frequent cross references for overlapping categories.

Further indication of the source material is given in the drawings based on the codices, and in the Aztec name glyphs for persons and places which are shown on the genealogical chart and on the map. Both chart and map will aid in keeping the difficult names straight as traders and fighters march from the high Valley of Mexico to the "land of the great sun." And the pronunciation of these names will be simplified by remembering that the accent always falls on the syllable before the last.

I have considerably shortened the long traditional speeches made on particular ceremonial occasions and dictated carefully to Sahagún by his Indian informants, who even indicated the proper positions of speaker and listener and made clear that both speeches and posture were mandatory. In their shortened form, however, these speeches fill in the formal background of such occasions as the notification of Ilhuicamina of his election.

I have considerably shortened also the long conversations

given by the chroniclers. The use of conversation by the sixteenth and seventeenth century annalists and chroniclers is worth looking at for its own sake. Radin has pointed out the clear stylistic intent in placing the conversations adroitly to emphasize particular changes in policy and to relate them to the individuals initiating them. More recently Dibble has pointed out the relation of the sequence of certain drawings between the speech scrolls in the *Codex Xolotl* to conversations used by Ixtlilxochitl in which the same details are given in the same order. Since the chroniclers such as Durán and Torquemada sometimes refer to the picture manuscripts they have used and weigh the reliability of one against the other, it is probable that many of their conversations are based on picture manuscripts now lost. It is also to be noticed that the difference between direct and indirect conversation even in the same chronicler is a matter of varying preference. Ixtlilxochitl uses the conversations pictured in the *Xolotl* in one of his books as direct quotation and in another as indirect. Durán and Tezozomoc, using a common source, give to a single conversation direct form in the one case and indirect in the other.

The conversations reconstructed in this manner by the earliest sources now available to us often reveal patterns of stylization taken on in the records of this period of oral, written, and carved history. The reversal of role of Ilhuicamina and his half brother Tlacaelel found in some of the conversations given by Tezozomoc and Durán shows one of the standard changes which take place in oral transference and, added to the possible influence of twin legends on the account of these brothers, illuminates the processes which give a folk element to the records of this time-conscious, history-conscious people.

On the other hand, these reconstructed and stylized conversations often contain the key which can correct mistakes of the chroniclers themselves. The murder of Chimalpopoca, the Smoking Shield, is a case in point. The *Anales Mexicanos: México-Azcapotzalco* have Chimalpopoca say to his women:

"Come, dear ones, I will lead you on the day that Huitzilopochtli Chimalpopoca goes forth." This obscure remark, put together with Ixtlilxochitl's mention of the month of the murder, and Sahagún's description of the fiesta of that month, reveals the significance of Chimalpopoca's dance, and the meaning of his costume as shown in the *Codex Xolotl.* We know that Chimalpopoca was taking the part of the god Huitzilopochtli in the dance as only a ruler could do. We can correct Ixtlilxochitl's own interpretation of the *Xolotl* when Nezahualcoyotl brings tortillas to Chimalpopoca, knowing that they were brought not because Chimalpopoca was starving, but because the tortillas were a regular part of that fiesta. We can see how each political faction was using the procedures of the fiesta for its own ends. The brief remark accredited to the ill-fated ruler provides the link to this scattered material which makes a new understanding possible even at this late date.

This biography has served as a thesis for my *doctorado en letras* from the Universidad Nacional Autónoma de México. I wish to take advantage of this opportunity to express my profound gratitude to those who through the years have been my guides and friends on that faculty and its related Escuela Nacional de Antropología e Historia and Instituto de Historia, and who have aided and encouraged my work in the prehispanic history of Mexico: especially to Professor Wigberto Jiménez Moreno, who suggested the subject of this biography, who gave invaluable aid in chronological and geographical problems, and whose classes in Nahuatl illuminated many corners in the sources which I would have otherwise found obscure; to Dr. Alfonso Caso, who in his course on the codices many years ago started me on these complicated paths; to Dr. Ignacio Bernal, who gave me a wide perspective over the history and archaeology of pre-conquest Mexico; to Dr. Pedro Armillas whose seminar on the aspects of warfare in preconquest times aided me in treating the military organization of the alliance which Ilhuicamina directed.

I should like to pay special tribute to two distinguished and gentle scholars who often made the road of my Mexican studies easier, and whose deaths since this book was begun have brought sorrow to all who had the privilege of their friendship and direction: Dr. Pablo Martínez del Río who encouraged me to complete this life of the Archer of the Sky,. and who always had an exact and understanding appreciation of the literary and historical intentions of my Aztec biographies; and Dr. Rafael García Granados, counselor in all my study and research.

I mention with gratitude the patience and help of the Biblioteca del Museo Nacional de México, the library of the University of Arizona, and the library of the Arizona Pioneers' Historical Society.

I deeply appreciate the work of all those at the University of Arizona Press who have seen the book through the stages of design and production. Jack L. Cross, Director of the Press, and Douglas A. Peck, Production Manager, have been constant in their enthusiasm and care to detail. Carolyn Huff Kinsey's drawings, based on the codices, accent and illuminate the text. Donald M. Powell's index adds a necessary tool for scholar and traveler and general reader. It is difficult to come to an end in naming those whose ideas and skills have been intricately woven into this book. They know my gratitude.

Tucson, Arizona
December, 1963

FRANCES GILLMOR

I

Reed into the Sky

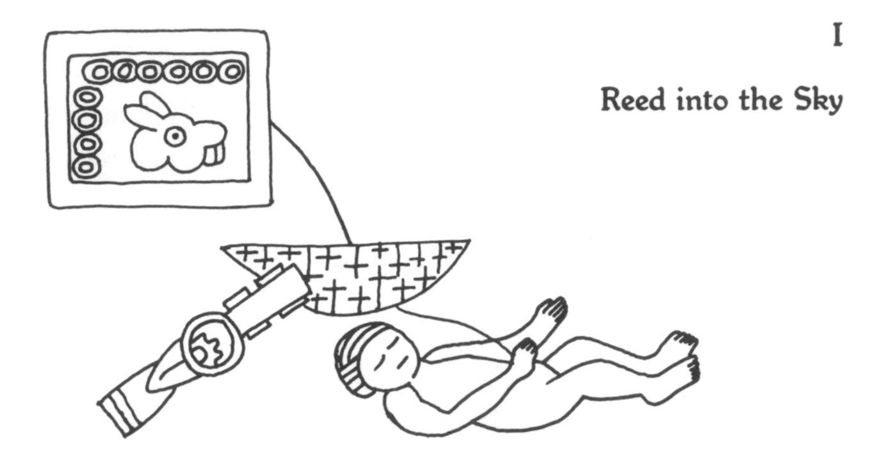

As THE PEOPLE in the high lake country among the reeds and the swamps looked back on the birth of their first Moteczuma, the mist had already dimmed the memory of it. They spoke of it in symbols. But through the mist and the symbols came the gentleness of an old love story in the green country of Cuauhnauac—and the echo of bitterness that it was a love alien to the island in the windy lake.

Over the mountains and down in the green land at the edge of the wood lived Miahuaxihuitl, Turquoise Corn Blossom, sheltered by her father, unseen by men, denied to the suitors who came even from distant towns. When Huitzilihuitl, Hummingbird Plume, turned his thoughts to her, all men warned him that his desire would be in vain. They mentioned other girls in other towns, whom he had sought and found, marriages to strengthen the ties of the poor islanders and the mainland people. But now yonder, yonder flew his heart to Cuauhnauac. So said the chronicler, using the pictures and words of the old men's telling. (They belong to us, said the old people of Mexico-Tenochtitlan—to us and not to Tlatelolco or to any other town.)[1]

A whispered command came from the god of darkness and of night as Hummingbird Plume lay thinking of the girl in Cuauhnauac. He obeyed and sent the marriage makers over the mountains.

The father of the hidden girl did not give the hoped for answers. He did not say, as was proper, "The girl is not ready for marriage, nor is she worthy of such a man." He did not say, as would have been only polite, "I do not understand how this young man can be so deceived, for she is worth nothing—she is a little fool." He did not say, as he should have said finally, "Good, it is settled. The young man must be content to marry her although he may have to endure poverty and work, since it appears that he has fixed upon this girl who knows nothing of womanly skills."[2]

Instead, the ruler of Cuauhnauac said bluntly to the marriage makers, "What can he offer my daughter? She wears cotton. She eats the fruits of this valley. These things do not grow in your marshes."

Huitzilihuitl knew that the words were true. His own father, though he had ruled the Tenochca, had once had barely enough to eat and had died mourning that he had not been able to free his people from paying hard tribute to the shore city of Azcapotzalco. When he himself had been enthroned on the straw icpalli, his people had said to him, "We give you not rest but work—we have nothing else to give you."[3]

Now he had nothing to reply to the word the marriage makers brought back from the rich valley of cotton and fruit. To the father of Turquoise Corn Blossom, tribute came from many towns where macehuales worked the land for him. He was rich and he was wise. He knew magic, it was said, and could take the form and mask of an animal, and call the flying and crawling things of the hot country—the snakes, the centipedes, the scorpions, the bats, and the spiders—and command them to guard his daughter from any man who might approach her. A man walked in danger who came near.[4] She lived secure in the courtyard of her house in the green valley. And on the lake island in the high country,

Huitzilihuitl, Hummingbird Plume, slept and dreamed of her.

Again the whisper came to him from Yoalli—god of night and dimness. Was it the voice of Tonacatecuhtli, giver of life and sustenance, Ometecuhtli, one yet two-fold, who had lived in a cave near Cuauhnauac, creator of life? Or was it the whisper from Tezcatlipoca, the Smoking Mirror of darkness and terror? Out of the night the sleeping king heard the word of life and terror.[5]

"Take a weapon of judgment, and a carrying net for travelling, and a straight reed painted. Put in the reed a precious green chalchihuitl stone. Go to Cuauhnauac—and the girl shall be ours."

The king heard the dark whisper and obeyed. With his net and his weapon, his painted reed and precious green jade, he went over the mountains to the forbidden edge of the woods. He shot the painted reed holding the chalchihuitl stone high toward the sky like an arrow, and it fell, as he had aimed it, into a courtyard.

The girl picked up the reed and marvelled at the painted design. She held it in her hand a long time, and turned it, looking at the colors in the sun. Finally she opened it and found the green stone within.

And Miahuaxihuitl, Turquoise Blossom and Spike of Corn, swallowed the precious chalchihuitl stone.

It was so that they told the story later there on the lake island. (This is our story and it does not belong to anyone else.) They knew what they meant when they talked of the chalchihuitl as symbol of rain, of life-giving substance, of fertility for earth and men and gods; when they recounted how Xochiquetzal—Flower Feather, Chimalman—lying on the shield of earth, had swallowed the chalchihuitl and become the mother of Quetzalcoatl;[6] when they drew in the painted books footprints from the creating gods, a quetzal feather, and a chalchihuitl necklace to say that a child had been conceived[7]—a child who at birth would be described by the old men in their congratulatory speeches as a rich plume and a precious stone;[8] when they sang in the rituals to Xipe, god of fertility, Drinker of Night,

"Like the chalchihuitl is my heart,
 The tender ear of corn hidden within me;"[9]

and again,

"My heart is chalchihuitl.
 My heart will grow cold: the man will grow,
 A warrior will have been born."[10]

A warrior would be born from that hour when the green stone fell from the sky into the courtyard of the hidden girl in Cuauhnauac. This too the tellers of the tale knew, remembering that the precious green stone, symbol of life, was symbol also of death, of the blood of sacrifice which gave life to the gods through the death of a warrior. Twofold this symbolism of the precious thing. Twofold the joy and terror of this hour in the courtyard at Cuauhnauac.

But the girl who had been guarded from all men took the reed and the chalchihuitl, took the man who was called the Hummingbird Plume.

The child who was born came to have the name Moteczuma, the offended one, the angry one, for Huitzilihuitl his father knew that the Mexica would not wish this younger son of his to rule them, child as he was of an alien mother from beyond the mountains.[11] Nor would Cuauhnauac want him, child of the man who had entered the forbidden courtyard.

It would be many years, however, before this little crying Angry One need worry that his father's heart had gone yonder, yonder, over the mountains to find his mother. Now the new alliance seemed to bring only good. Now the islanders had white cotton clothes. Traders ventured beyond the mountains, busy with a commerce that in this child's lifetime would bring up to the high country riches so fabulous that another name would be given him—Chalchiuhtlatonac—He Who Shines Like Jade.[12]

But the name that went with him from birth to death was Ilhuicamina, Archer of the Sky—a name and a glyph in the painted books whose meaning reached beyond himself. The rectangular sky glyph was banded with color. The arrow pierced the blue band of blue rain and blue east—ruled by the gods of windy air and rain. The next band was jagged red for fire and for the south ruled over by the fire god. There too was the eye of the morning star, the Lord of the House of Red Dawning, flanked by the two half-eyes of the Smoking Mirror, god of north and south and darkness. The next band was green for growth and for the west, ruled by the earth goddess, with the Skirt of Snakes. Then came the band of yellow for drought and for the north ruled by the Lord of the Dead. Finally another band of blue, with nine white spots, represented the nine united heavens, abode of Flower Feather, goddess of love.[13]

Blue rain and red fire, green growth and yellow drought, death and love, creation and the wideness of the world directions, an arrow into the sky—all these were in the glyph, with echo and with promise.

Huehue Moteczuma Ilhuicamina Chalchiuhtlatonac—the Elder Angry One, Archer of the Sky, Who Glowed like Jade.

According to the chroniclers this child with his many names and his later fame was born at sunrise one day in the year Ten Rabbit.[14] The Fire God, Lord of the Turquoise

Year, Lord of the South, was patron of that sunrise hour.[15]

But they did not mention the day name which the child must also have carried for his own. (Note carefully this history of the old ones, you who are our child, you who are Mexica, you who are Tenochca.) And so we do not know the patron of the day, nor what the priests read in the painted books when they sought his future there and set the compensating day for his dedication to the goddess of water—of the Skirt of Jade.[16] Nevertheless he had names enough. And they sounded the overtones of his life as the chroniclers heard them later among the lake reeds.

II

Out of the Lake Mist

IN THOSE DAYS the movement in the lake town was silent —bare feet on the damp earth, dip of paddles and lapping of water against the hollowed-out canoes.

Men who were poor and often hungry took with dipnets what fish they could find in the narrow channels among the reeds or out in the open lake. They spread long nets above the surface of the water to catch the low flying night birds, and at daybreak waded far out into the shallow water to find what they had caught. They plucked the marsh grass whitened with the eggs of the waterflies, and dried it in the sun, until they could shake off the white eggs and make a paste for spreading and cooking. They learned to set bunches of marsh grass in shallow water for the waterflies to lay their eggs, and took them up when they were ready for drying and scraping. They found they could eat the waterflies themselves, and the green substance that floated upon the water.[1]

They took reeds and wove them into mats to sleep on, or into an icpalli, fit for a king to sit on and for the picture makers to paint in the folded books. Sometimes a slave representing Napatecuhtli—lord of the four directions and god of those who worked with reeds—walked among them sprinkling them with water from a green gourd vessel, sprinkling rain from a green branch before he should die for the god.

And the reed workers danced to adore the god and shook out the reed mats before his image.[2]

The lake mist covered the king's sons—the Archer of the Skies, born of the girl from Cuauhnauac; and another about whom a tale was told, like far music, like distant counterpoint, that he had been born of a girl in Teocalhuiyacan, on the same day at the same sunrise hour—Tlacaelel, the unhappy, the dispossessed, the cruel.[3]

Only the son who was the child of the Tepanecan mother from Azcapotzalco, grandson of the tyrant Tezozomoc, was noted by the islanders these days, and his name was in men's mouths—Chimalpopoca, the Smoking Shield. Because of him the old tyrant's hand had lightened, and the yearly tribute had become no more than a token—two ducks and a few fish and frogs and waterflies.

"Let them rest now,"[4] Tezozomoc had said.

At last there was time and strength to build new land slowly, to tow lengths of tangled and matted water plants to chosen spots on the lake shore and let them serve as slowly settling foundations for layer upon layer of mud. And on the new chinampa garden plots the careful sequence of planting began, from beans to the life-giving corn.[5] The islanders came to own corn stored across the lake at Chalco, the fertile and ancient place of the rich green chalchihuitl, where farmers knew how the old ones had grown corn in Tula, where lines of friendship were established anciently with the people of Huexotzinco and Tlaxcala, and with Cuauhnauac.

It was a time of peace. But faintly in these childhood years of the Archer of the Sky the war song could be heard, as if half remembered from the days when the Tenochca had moved into this highland valley singing. The song of Huitzilopochtli, Hummingbird God of sun and war, Hummingbird on the Left, sounded below the slapping of lake waves on wooden canoes:

"Mexica, behold your charge and duty. Here you will wait and hope, and conquer the four parts of the world. It will cost you sweat and work and blood to reach the fine green chalchihuitl stones, the gold and silver and feather work, the cacao and fragrant flowers and sweet fruits."[6]

In Two Reed when the young Archer of the Skies was five years old, the Mexica wrecked the canoes of the people of the chinampa at Mixquic and Cuitlahuac. In Six Reed when he was nine they accused the custodians of the corn in Chalco of dishonesty and demanded their death.[7]

"Is there not yet a little earth?" replied the frightened Chalca, and fled to find it.

"The Chalca have been our protectors when the Mexica were scarcely heard of. Let the Mexicans come to us with shields and arrows," challenged the other garden towns.

In Mexico-Tenochtitlan, by order of the Speaker-king himself, boys and men were trained in the making of bows and became skilled in the handling of boats for war.[8]

But the threat of war passed by. Itzcoatl, Obsidian Serpent, half brother of Huitzilihuitl, and his tlacatecatl in these days,[9] with astute caution extended the trade and influence of the islanders to the shore towns without open clash with Tezozomoc's extending power. The tyrant of Azcapotzalco had arranged marriages and position and power in fifteen towns for his children—but the beloved grandchild was in Mexico-Tenochtitlan.[10]

There no support was forthcoming for the first movements of independence in Texcoco, no recognition of the crowning of Ixtlilxochitl as Great Chichimecatl and his son Nezahualcoyotl as heir, though the boy was grandson of Huitzilihuitl, the Hummingbird Plume.[11]

The ties with Azcapotzalco grew firmer with the death of Huitzilihuitl.[12] From his sons Chimalpopoca was chosen to succeed him—The Smoking Shield, the beloved grandson of Tezozomoc. The child of the strange woman from beyond the mountains was not spoken of, though now he had reached young manhood—Moteczuma Ilhuicamina, the Offended One, the Archer of the Skies. Men trusted for continued freedom from tribute and for peace to the Smoking Shield who could speak for them to Azcapotzalco, the great city where the people boiled up like ants. They leaned on the careful experience and direction he could draw upon from Itzcoatl, the Obsidian Serpent, still tlacatecatl.[13] They worked in their chinampa garden plots, and maneuvered their narrow dugout canoes on the lake, welcoming the east wind that blew from the green paradise of Tlaloc and stirred up no squalls.[14] Slowly stone houses began to replace their thatched reed huts.[15]

From the prospering islanders at last a request went to the old ruler of Azcapotzalco, carried by his beloved grandson.[16]

"Now many boats move through our canals. We are making chinampas from the marshes. We are drinking stirred and dirty water. Let us have sweet water from Chapultepec, the Hill of the Grasshopper."

Maxtla of Coyohuacan, the son of the tyrant, heard the far music of the war god in this request. But the old man listened to his favorite grandson, and gave him water rights in the cold springs of Chapultepec.

As they worked on the conduit the sun-baked clay and sod washed out. A new request went to the tyrant of Azcapotzalco, again carried by the Smoking Shield.

"We need stone and men to help build a stronger aqueduct," said Chimalpopoca to his grandfather.

Maxtla of Coyohuacan, his father's counsellor, heard the war music growing stronger.

"Shall we pay tribute to this rebellious people?" he protested.

"Let them have help to build the channel," said old Tezozomoc, feeble with years, gentle with his daughter's son.

Now workmen from Azcapotzalco labored for the tribute town of Mexico-Tenochtitlan, labored as if they were not of the ruling city of a wide valley, rich in treasure and people. The murmur grew among them.

Perhaps Chimalpopoca had not realized the challenge in the message he had carried to his grandfather. Perhaps, though a man, he had asked like a child who had always received. But there were men in Mexico-Tenochtitlan, a tlacatecatl and a council, who knew what they did. What had they meant by their requests for water and stone and labor?

"We should fight the Mexica," Maxtla urged.

The old man, troubled and torn, said,

"Then let my grandson be brought here to live with me, out of danger."

But still the surface of peace remained unbroken. The Mexica came untroubled to the markets of Azcapotzalco and Coyohuacan. The corn supplies stored in Chalco grew. Traders went back and forth over the mountains to Cuauhnauac, bearing fruits and cotton to the high valley.

Azcapotzalco, still at peace with Mexico-Tenochtitlan, laid its hand heavily on Texcoco and sent cotton to be woven into blankets.

"We will make it into quilted armor," said the angry Texcocans.

Chimalpopoca had supported the demand, allied with his grandfather who had given sweet water to his city.[17]

War flared around the lake. The great Chichimecatl of Texcoco, unrecognized in his claim to power, fled with his son Nezahualcoyotl, and in a hidden thicket waited death at the hands of his pursuers.

"Remember that you are now the Great Chichimecatl recovering your icpalli of command," he said to his son.

The boy with the future heavy upon him watched his father die, watched the flames rise from his lonely funeral pyre.

And now out of the mist of the lake in the year Four Rabbit, Moteczuma Ilhuicamina, the Angry One, Archer of the Sky moves for the first time—clear on the record, clear in his allegiances.

In the dark night, a young man of twenty, with sure skill

and knowledge of the channels, he dipped his oar quietly and drew closer to the shore. He and his companions listened.

A voice spoke in hushed tones from the land questioningly.

"Brothers—"

They waited, still silent.

"Brothers—is it you?"

They answered then, cautiously, repeating the word of kinship. In a moment, still hidden in night, they asked a question of the man on shore.—

"Are you Coyohua?"

"I am, brothers."

They avoided the important names that would tell too much.

"Have the children died?" they asked anxiously.

The voice from shore spoke with equal caution.

"They live, but this night cost their father high."

Dimly the speakers could see each other at last. Now they spoke freely.

"The children are over here. I will bring them," said Coyohua, the loyal Texcocan.

"It is good," came the voice from the boat. "Itzcoatl sent us to seek them."

In the faint light before day, the children of the Texcocan king stood on the shore. Nezahualcoyotl, a boy of sixteen, stepped into the boat where the Archer of the Sky awaited him.

The two boys were together as the oars dipped again, and the boat from Mexico-Tenochtitlan, protected by order of Itzcoatl, pushed out into the lake.[18]

Again Ilhuicamina comes out of the mist of lake and marsh, eight years older now, and again with Nezahualcoyotl, as in the year Twelve Rabbit they join those who came from the Aztec towns to bring the ordered tribute of ceremony and songs and gifts to the funeral of Tezozomoc, tyrant of Azcapotzalco.[19]

So long had tribute poured in to the old king that many could not remember a time when his calculating hand had not guided the life of the towns where he had placed his governors and where his sons and daughters had married. But now he had been warmed for the last time by the fires at the head and foot of his bed, carried for the last time by his servants into the sun.[20] The mask that had been placed during his last illness over the face of Tezcatlipoca, the Smoking Mirror, god of night and darkness, had been removed, for the end was known.[21] Ahead of him was the journey across the Plain of the Wind of Knives, over the river to the final place of the dead.[22]

His body lay upon a woven reed mat for four days, and the ceremonies took place in their order. He was bathed in water made fragrant with flowers and herbs. He was dressed in rich garments and jewels. And he who had shivered beside his fires in the chill of his great age was wrapped in seventeen blankets with only the wizened face looking out.[23] Into his mouth was placed the chalchihuitl, the precious jade, the precious life at the heart of death.[24] And over his face was laid the turquoise mask of a king.[25]

The procession moved slowly forward to the temple enclosure where the funeral pyre was waiting. To the right and left of the dead king marched a double line of mourners,[26] each testing the temper of the new alignments that would come now in the Aztec towns, each accepting for the moment the ordered ceremonial which paid tribute to great age and death beyond the enmity of life.

Moteczuma Ilhuicamina who in the night mist had already taken his stand against Tezozomoc and even against Chimalpopoca, looked across at his young friend Nezahualcoyotl, the Hungry Coyote of Texcoco, who, though a fugitive, had come openly to this funeral of his enemy. He waited for a chance to speak to him under cover of the funeral songs. And he watched Chimalpopoca, the beloved grandchild, truly mourning.

He himself was between the two who would be rivals for the vacant place of the old king. Behind him was Tayatzin, the son whom the old man had chosen to succeed him; ahead of him marched Maxtla of Coyohuacan, the son whose reach for power had set him high in the councils of Azcapotzalco, the enemy of the rising Mexica and of the beloved grandson who had been given too much.

The procession moved forward, and with it those who would die on the funeral pyre. The slave who had lighted the lamps and fires before the gods in the great house of the king walked ready for the sacrifice,[27] going into the dark with the old man. Hunchbacks and dwarfs marched too—those whose shed blood would give life to the gods. And a little red dog went with them to help his dead master across the river.[28]

The mourners walked with jewels and feathers. They sang of Tezozomoc:

"With tears of flowers of sadness . . .
I remember the princes
Those who were broken like a vessel of clay
Those who went to be enslaved in the region where
everyone goes . . .[29]
For Tezozomoc I sing my sorrowful song . . ."[30]

Under the cover of the songs of death Ilhuicamina at last found his opportunity He spoke quietly to Nezahualcoyotl.[31]

"They are planning to kill you."

In the courtyard of the temple the body of the old king was placed on a fire of pitch pine, and the incense of copal rose around him, and the slaves hearts were torn out and thrown into the flames, and a little dog was killed.

When all was done, Moteczuma Ilhuicamina saw that his warning had been heeded. Nezahualcoyotl was gone.

Nor was he there the day following when Ilhuicamina watched the old king's ashes gathered into a box and placed beside the altar of the Smoking Mirror, nor for the final ceremonial detail when over the box was set a wooden mask inlaid with the precious chalchihuitl stones.[32]

III

Death of the Smoking Shield

HARDLY WAS THE FUNERAL of Tezozomoc over when Maxtla claimed his father's place.[1]

"Otherwise my followers will level all the land and leave it to parch in the sun," he threatened.

For the sake of peace, though the sun might live by the blood of warriors, the Tepaneca of Azcapotzalco reversed the decision of old Tezozomoc. Not his younger son Tayatzin but his older son Maxtla would rule over them.

One hundred and five days went by[2] and it was the month of Tecuilhuitontli, the little feast of the lords. The salt goddess who was to die danced with golden earrings, her skirt embroidered with waves and clouds and her sandals with designs of foam. And the women sang for her with voices like birds and like little bells.[3]

Afterward there was feasting and drinking in the houses of the nobles. Chimalpopoca spoke freely to his guest and uncle Tayatzin.[4]

"Why are you content with the rule of Coyohuacan when your father chose you as his heir in Azcapotzalco?" he demanded.

"For the sake of peace," said Tayatzin.

"There is a way," suggested Chimalpopoca. "You could build a thatched house[5] quickly, and invite Maxtla to the housewarming. You could welcome him with a rope of flowers around his neck and bind the rope tighter, and tighter."

A dwarf listened. He had been brought up in the household of Maxtla. That night he fled to him with the warning.

"This is important enough to awaken him," he urged.

Maxtla listened. Afterward he called his counsellor.

"Why should the younger one inherit, when, according to all the laws of Xolotl our ancestor, the oldest is heir? Why should my younger brother plot my death with Chimalpopoca? Should he not die?"[6]

Maxtla gave permission graciously when workmen from Tayatzin's town of Coyohuacan and two foremen from Chimalpopoca's town of Mexico-Tenochtitlan came to start the building. He offered more men and materials to rush it to completion. Within a few days the house was finished.

Then Maxtla was ready to turn the plot upon its inventors. He himself issued the invitation to the housewarming, sending messages to Tayatzin and to Chimalpopoca.

Chimalpopoca drew back from the moment of action. He regretted that he could not be present. He was occupied with plans for the festival and the sacrifice.

Tayatzin came trustingly, with his original intent. Around his neck the rope of flowers was placed in welcome, and tightened, and tightened again.

In Mexico-Tenochtitlan Chimalpopoca heard, and knew that the plot had been discovered. His enemy Maxtla now ruled without opposition and his own plot now seemed about to precipitate the war that as beloved grandchild of the old king he had prevented so long. Fear came upon him.

"Where shall we go?" he cried. "The Tecpanecatl is our enemy."[7]

In this month of the little feast of the lords when the women sang for the salt goddess, the concubines of the principal lords of the city were permitted to walk abroad on the streets and in places of recreation. They talked to other girls, who belonged to other men. They wore wreaths of flowers on their hair and bright embroidered skirts, and the young men laughed and called to them as they passed. But the girls were guarded and protected by older women in order that the holiday laughter and flirting might not go beyond bounds and that nothing might cloud this day of sun and blossom and freedom.[8]

The women from the household of Chimalpopoca went over the road across the marshes. They went happily in skirts of black and red, adorned for the outing.[9]

And in the fields of Azcapotzalco they were found and brought to Maxtla. He had no respect for them or for the day.

"Chimalpopoca's women are mine," he said.

Afterward he sent them back to Chimalpopoca with a a threat.

"Your men go hidden in our fields—I will see that Chimalpopoca and all the Mexica die."

They came weeping to Chimalpopoca.

"We have heard the terrible word in Azcapotzalco," they told him. "It is said that the blood of the Mexica will be exterminated. The birds will be hunted even to their nests, and our gardens will float in pieces over the water."[10]

Chimalpopoca cringed before the insult to his women and the threat to his city. More troubles piled upon him. Word came from the Chalca, who had made carved canoes from the timber of the mountainsides and who had stored grain for the Mexica, that they could no longer serve the island city. Five islanders were dead, and three canoes broken on the water. The meaning was clear.[11]

Chimalpopoca, who had never had to face open enmity, felt hatred closing around him and was helpless. He called his son and counsellor Tecuhtlehuacatzin to him.[12] Pitifully he spoke his bewilderment—"Where shall we go?" And he said frankly, "I had thought to be able to take refuge in Azcapotzalco if the Tenochca turned against me, and in Mexico-Tenochtitlan if the Tepaneca of Azcapotzalco became my enemies."[13]

He thought of the coming festival, and the offering to the gods.

"It is best to die," he suggested doubtfully. "We will sacrifice ourselves."[14]

Perhaps in his city some would remember the times when he had brought peace even from angry conferences, so that now the islanders had sweet water from the woods of Chapultepec, and a road across the marshes to the market of Azcapotzalco. Perhaps they would stop him short of the deed.[15]

The month of the great feast of the lords opened in joy with the thought of sacrifice still far off. The poor came in great numbers to fill their pitchers with a cool drink mixed in canoes and sweetened with honey. They picnicked in groups on the ground and at noon were given green corn tamales, some made with fruit, or corn blossoms, or honey. The children were fed carefully and shared in the gladness of the day. Only when food ran out were some left sad, and their words echoed unconsciously those of their Speaker-king.

"What shall we do? Evilly has the feast day come."[16]

Every day there was feasting and toward evening fires

were lighted in braziers and the dancing began.

Then Chimalpopoca went into the festival group.

"Come, appear before the people," he said to Tecuhtlehuacatzin.

And to his women he said,

"Come, dear ones. I will lead you on the day that Huitzilopochtli Chimalpopoca goes forth."[17]

The Smoking Shield, fearful and desperate, whose way had been a way of peace, went forth, a warrior representing the war god, as those go forth to dance and to die in the sacrifice.[18] He wore the black stripe of face paint, the head plumes of quetzal feathers like corn silk, the great feather devices on his shoulders, and deer hooves tied with deer skin thongs on his legs.[19]

His women went in skirts of black and red.[20] And the harlots came from the house of song where the women lived who gave pleasure to the young warriors. They too came in bright skirts—some of plain rich colors and fine weave, some embroidered in designs of smoke, or leaves, or the hearts with the precious blood that would be sacrificed to the gods. Warriors and nobles danced, and each chose the girl who would come to him secretly in the night.

A whisper went around among the people.

"It is said that Chimalpopoca will die at midnight."

And one answered.

"Tecuhlehuacatzin has already died, but his father still dances."[21]

"No, they both dance still. It is Acamapichtli who has been killed and they dance around his body, shooting arrows into the temple."[22]

They peered at the king fearfully as he danced with his arrows and his shield and the blackened face-stripe of the festival. In the flickering light from the braziers the rumor of his mad intent spread. But no one stopped him as he danced.

Then through the dark lines of dancing figures, stately in their order between the flaming braziers, a figure moved.

It was Moteczuma Ilhuicamina, breathing hard in anger. He faced the king.

"The dance must stop," he told him.[23]

But the mad king ready for the sacrifice danced on.

Swift council in the shadows—and the Angry One, Archer of the Sky, had left the dancers and the rhythmic clash of pared deer hooves on swinging thongs, had disappeared along the causeway through the marshes, across the quiet lake.

If Chimalpopoca were to die, it must not be this way, which might look like a way of courage. Nor should the people of Mexico-Tenochtitlan move to stop him, to choose him as their man of peace. Let Maxtla be the open enemy, and war the only way.

He came in the night to the Ant Hill City, and to its ruler Maxtla. His request seemed reasonable—to save the mad king from himself. And should not Azcapotzalco take authority over a tribute town?

It did not seem strange in Mexico-Tenochtitlan the next day that men from Azcapotzalco should be in numbers at the fiesta. Always they came to aid in the feasting and drinking when the warriors were honored.[24]

Nor did it seem strange that Chimalpopoca's mother's brother had saved him from the sacrifice that would have been suicide. From the city where he had been the beloved grandchild had come the firm order that had stopped the desperate lonely dancer, that had put him for his own safety into the prison cage.

For his safety—or for his death? Here lay the real uncertainty. For the Tepaneca from Azcapotzalco had put the Speaker-king of Tenochtitlan into a cage where in that festival of the lords a sacrificial victim was put to be guarded against flight until the moment of sacrifice.[25] Did they mean that he could not escape from the way of death he had chosen? Who now might lead him to the sacrifice?

Across the lake in Texcoco Nezahualcoyotl heard only

that Chimalpopoca had been imprisoned by the Tepaneca of Azcapotzalco, knew only that in Chimalpopoca's city he had found friends and help and support in a lonely exiled boyhood.

He hurried to Maxtla.

"Chimalpopoca was like a plume on your head that you have thrown away, like a necklace of precious stones that you have taken off. Let him go from his prison."

"Do not be sad," said Maxtla smoothly. "Chimalpopoca is not dead. I took him into custody because of the disturbance and unrest he was creating."[26]

Nezahualcoyotl hurried on to Tenochtitlan and stood at last in front of the cage. The imprisoned Speaker-king looked out at him pitifully, and spoke of those who he thought were his friends.

"You will be next," he warned. "Ally yourself with Ilhuicamina and with Itzcoatl. Fight against Maxtla, the tyrant."[27]

Nezahuacoyotl spoke what comfort he could.

"You are imprisoned in the city of your fathers, and all your people mourn you, afflicted," he said.

But none came to release him from the cage and the guards. And Nezahualcoyotl went alone out from the city to Chimalpopoca's own cornfields and got from his farmers the tamales of the fiesta to give to the imprisoned man.[28]

Again Nezahualcoyotl hurried across the causeway to consult with Maxtla. This time he found Chimalpopoca's concubines sitting beside their captor. Maxtla turned his head aside from the young man and did not speak.[29]

Over in Tenochtitlan the brooding sense of disaster lightened. Word came that the imprisoned ruler could be released. Evidently the danger was over, whatever that danger had been. Evidently the Smoking Shield, quiet and weary now, no longer intended to sacrifice himself, and the Tepaneca from the lake shore no longer intended to hold him now that their right to do so had been asserted. It was not clear just what the situation had been or would be.

For Chimalpopoca himself there was now only the aftermath of that high moment when out of his despair he would have sacrificed himself to the gods, giving blood that was not in war. He had not fulfilled the sacrifice. He had not found support among his own people. The tecpanecatl was still his enemy. The concubines that Maxtla had once dishonored, and who had danced among the harlots of the House of Song, were now in Azcapotzalco.

Helpless, Chimalpopoca went into the thatched Calmecac.[30] Apart from the people he waited. He watched the sculptors work on the image of a god.[31]

Again the council met. And again Moteczuma Ilhuicamina went as messenger to the shore towns—this time to Tlacopan, whose Tepanecan people like those of Azcapotzalco would be glad to find an excuse to intervene in Mexico-Tenochtitlan. He carried word from Itzcoatl.

"What has Chimalpopoca done? Is perhaps the care of the city in our charge now? We need your clear judgment in deciding what is to become of him."[32]

The ruler of Tlacopan understood.

"You deserve help," he said briefly.

He called two of his men to take greetings to Chimalpopoca. He gave them oars, and arrows, and ointment for the dead.

Together the messengers went to Mexico-Tenochtitlan and into the temple school for warriors, the house of the corridors.

"Where is the Señor?" they asked. When they received no answer they put the question in different terms. "Where is the priest?"

They found him at last among the sculptors.

"What do you do here?" they asked him.

They had led him into another room called the Huitzcalli. Here the ministers of the Huitznahuac served with incense.[33] Now indeed he was to be Huitzilopochtli Chimalpopoca, for they gave him gifts and they bathed him in the darkness as the young men bathed Huitzilopochtli in this room once a year in the middle of the night—coming with torches and dancing, with one impersonating the god.[34]

The gifts they gave him were of war and death.

"Receive these gifts," they told him, "from your friends and brothers."

And he heard them name the men who had been on the Tepanecan council which had opposed the beloved grandchild from the beginning.[35] Old enemies—and now allied with them an enemy brother.

They burned incense before him, as for one to be sacrificed. They put a blanket around his shoulders like a cape, and under it a rope.

They left the deed to the Tepaneca. One seized his hands. The other tightened the rope. They spoke to him with a final challenge of war mockingly.

"Despoil us of our land! Conquer us!"

At this moment the war parties of the Tepaneca and the Tenochca had won their victory. There remained only the public confirmation that the paths of peace had been left behind.

They went out quietly.

"He is sleeping," they said to the priests.[36]

The priests entered with pine torches and found him. The shout arose.

"Mexica! They have killed your king."

They went to Itzcoatl to tell him.

"Be calm—the Tepaneca have come from Tlacopan to kill Chimpalpopoca. Give us the order to pursue them and to avenge him."

Itzcoatl was entirely calm. He gave his order—it would be known in Tenochtitlan that he had given it.

"Make haste. Pursue them," he said quietly.

But the assassins from Tlacopan were gone.

Now the two festivals of the lords were over. The grim young Mexicatl, Moteczuma Ilhuicamina, had followed his orders in night and torchlight. Unnamed by the chroniclers a girl had been sacrificed as the Salt Goddess, her heart torn out by the sword of a swordfish in the hands of the priests. The women who had sung like birds and like little bells were silent. The young goddess of corn had gone in chilli-red sandals to her death. The last disciplines had been imposed on the drunkards, and at the end of the festival the people had gone away. The place where they had been had become calm. So the Mexica-Tenochca described the quiet aftermath of the feasts of the lords.[37]

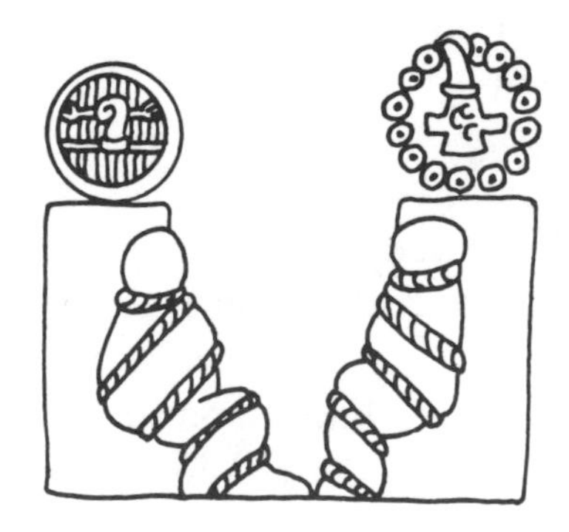

IV

Shadow of Exile

PEOPLE MOVED soft-footed beside the canals of the island town and whispered of death.

They spoke of Tecuhtlehuacatzin, the son and tlacatecatl of the Smoking Shield who had danced with him between the flaming braziers.

"He sacrificed himself," some said.

"The Tepaneca killed him sleeping beside his father," said others.[1]

They spoke of the concubines who had gone into the fields on a holiday, who had danced with the harlots from the House of Song.

"They were sacrificed by the Tepaneca," said the Tenocha fearfully.[2]

And they whispered of the son of Chimalpopoca, Xihuitl-temoc, who had been seated on the icpalli as his successor.[3] Perhaps there would still be peace.

Then after sixty days it was known that he too had died. Those who told the tale did not explain how he died. The painters of books did not paint him seated on the icpalli, nor wrapped in hs graveclothes. (It was Tenochtitlan that kept this tale—it belongs to us and not to Tlatelolco or any other town. Note it well, you who are our child.)

Only it was known that an agreement had been made that

neither son nor nephew nor grandson of Chimalpopoca should ever rule in Tenochtitlan—however great his name might be in war. No remembered heritage of a peace-loving Speaker-king should shape the councils of the islanders who had heard the charge of Hummingbird on the Left, and the war hymn sounding in the lake water against the wooden canoes.[4]

Now the formal traditional phrases sounded in the small group of electors.

"There are still men in Mexico-Tenochtitlan. Look about you. Choose. Say, 'This one I want; this one I do not want.' Consider on whom your eyes look, on whom your heart thinks. Him our god Huitzilopochtli chooses."[5]

They looked at two men, both of whom had been passed over when the Beloved Grandchild had been chosen.

Here was Moteczuma Illuicamina, the Grave One, the Archer of the Sky.

"He was the one chosen by his father," some remembered.

But the murmur rose against him which had been heard from the beginning.

"He is a child of a woman from Cuauhnauac," they pointed out.[6]

"And now he has taken a wife from his mother's people," they added.[7]

Alien from the calpulli of the island city he was still little known for achievement. A messenger through the night mists, carrying the words of Itzcoatl. A man who had stood in the dark and watched Chimalpopoca die.

Here on the other hand was Itzcoatl. Under two Speaker-kings he was the man who had dealt with the other cities.

"His mother was a slave woman, selling herbs in the market place," some murmured.[8]

But the war party could forget his mother, remembering how the independence of the Tenochca had already grown under his experienced hand, how corn was stored at Chalco. The peace party too could forget his mother—or remembering her, rejoice that she and his wife were Tepanecan, and that he could carry on negotiations with the Tepanecan cities, as had Chimalpopoca, speaking with terms of relationship.

Moteczuma Ilhuicamina, nearing thirty, ended the discussion.

"Later I can rule. I will be of my uncle's party, loyal to Itzcoatl, perhaps his tlacatecatl. I will provide to the Tenochca their water, their food, their mats, their chairs. I will hurl to the ground the people who surround us."[9]

He had taken his stand for a war of independence, of conquest of the food-producing mainland. But he had chosen the part of the messenger and warrior under orders. He had chosen still the shadow and the mist.

They named Itzcoatl, the Obsidian Snake, the Speaker-king of the island city. They charged him with the burden of rule.

"Who will come to give you strength if you faint? Do you think perhaps your valiant forebears can come again? Already they have passed by, and nothing remains but the shadow of their memory. Can you let slip from your shoulders the burden that you have taken upon them? Will you let the old man and the old woman, the orphan and the widow perish? Have pity on the creeping child. They will perish if your enemies prevail against us. The nations scoff at us. Loosen your blanket to take on your shoulders your children, who are the poor, who trust in the shelter of your blanket and your kindness. Fear neither work nor burden."[10]

The words seemed now to be for peace, now for war.

Itzcoatl, Obsidian Serpent, seated on the straw icpalli, laid down on the ground at his right hand the symbols of justice, a bow and arrows, and his first act was to pay reverence to Huitzilopochtli, god of war.[11]

Along the canals of Mexico-Tenochtitlan new whispers spread. The enemies of the Archer of the Skies were seeing him now as a rising power in the city, symbol of the alien, symbol of war. One by one those who had stood for peace had met their death. Let now their enemy die.

The warning came at last to Moteczuma Ilhuicamina.

From the highland lake, over the pine-dark mountains, down into the valley of refugees, he fled to the city of Huexotzinco.[12]

There from a distance two friends watched the mounting tensions of the lake cities. Nezahualcoyotl, free to go and come, was seen at intervals in the towns of the high country. Then back among his friends in Tlaxcala and Huexotzinco he and Moteczuma planned and waited.

As the months passed, the threads of alliance were woven, the quiet choices made.[13]

Word came that a new ruler had been chosen in Cuauhtitlan, and that he looked toward Huexotzinco, not toward Azcapotzalco. When he was installed he kept his fast as did those of Huexotzinco, wearing a band of leather around his head, a nose ring of pottery, a white blanket and a white breach clout and leather straps with tinkling bells. He and those about him even affected the accent of Huexotzinco.

Some of the Mexica too, it was said, had adopted the fashion of the city where Moteczuma Ilhuicamina and his friend Nezahualcoyotl were staying, and were dressing and speaking in the manner of that place of refuge.

Messengers from Tenochtitlan and Tlatelolco came over the mountains to speak quietly with Nezahualcoyotl, to have him arrange meetings for them with men who could speak for Tlaxcala and Huexotzinco. As sign of their treaty they laid their obsidian knives before the god Comaxtli, and they agreed that they would wear red face paint and put a rope around their heads to help them recognize each other as allies in the confusion of the battle ahead.

Maxtla sent his own envoys over the mountains.

"We do not wish to hear. We do not wish to understand," said the people of Huexotzinco.

One by one Azcapotzalco saw the towns they controlled drop away. The Acolhua turned from them to the Mexica.

"The Mexicans are building a temple to their goddess. Let us go and carry stone and water. How else can we keep our land?"

Tenayocan, remembering past injuries, followed the trend away from the Tepaneca.

And suddenly the quiet talks in the city of exile were in the open. Nezahualcoyotl, with singing plumed companies of warriors, was in the high lake country, marching on his city of Texcoco. Men from the mountain villages where he had fled as a boy and from the shore towns that chafed under Azcapotzalco were fighting for him. Even Chalco sent help. Troops from Tlaxcala were with him.[14]

Over in Tenochtitlan, Moteczuma Ilhuicamina too had come home. Openly he and his brother Tlacaelel were aiding Itzcoatl as guardians of the city.[15]

Now there were Mexica who looked to the shore and said,

"Let us conquer with valor the fields that can give us food. Let us burn the grass which covers them."[16]

And now Moteczuma Ilhuicamina could stand with them and say to Itzcoatl,

"Do not be troubled. The whole body of the Mexica will guard your forward march and protect you from the rear. Leave everything in my care."

He could watch calmly while the leaders of the peace party insisted,

"Let us go in peace and leave our tribute in Azcapotzalco."

And he could hear their report when they came back,

"Maxtla is not our friend."

Their names reflected their caution and their worry—He Who Weighs and Ponders, the Astute and Troubled One, the Moderate One. With them were the One with the Turquoise Covered Throat, and the One Who Knew the Stars Like their Twin.[17] But events rushed on while they pondered. And Maxtla had sent a gift, insulting in its low value, a few caps made from maguey fiber. The Mexica had replied with the studied formal insult to the manhood of the Tepaneca, and laid before Maxtla women's skirts and blouses and shawls of maguey fiber.

And now they fought five days and the shawls and blouses and skirts waved on a pole with defiant insult.

At the end of the battle many Mexicans lay dead. And there were Tepanecans who wept seeing the end of peace.

"To whom shall we go in the future with greetings? Whom shall we visit?"[18]

For the tribute cities of Texcoco and Tenochtitlan had separately made their initial campaign toward independence. Moteczuma and Nezahualcoyotl had come home from their exile.

V

Messengers of War and Peace

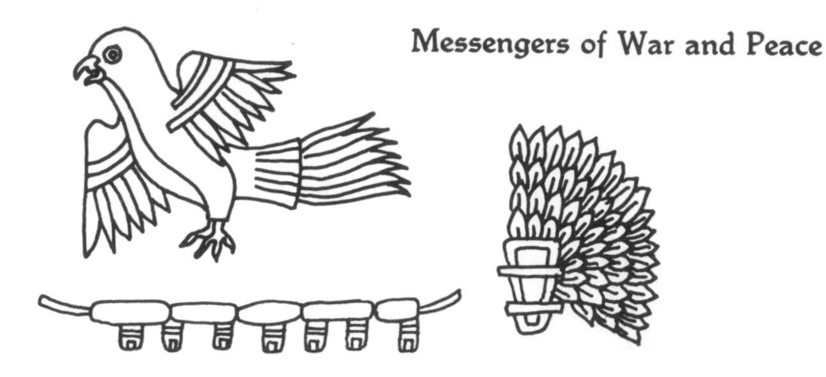

"LET US GO TO NEZAHUALCOYOTL, and ask him what he plans to do. Surely he has not lost his sense of things to come," decided the peace party in Azcapotzalco.[1]

But Moteczuma Ilhuicamina was ahead of them, and already crossing the dark lake to talk to his friend. Three young men accompanied him. One returned to his own house to get a blanket against the cold night wind, and then, confused and hurried, missed the meeting place. The Acolhua found him waiting, not at Tolpetlac, where they made reed mats, but at Tollan, where the reeds grew.

"No doubt I will die," he said. "But first tell me whether Moteczuma Ilhuicamina and his companions have come this way."

His captors pondered the well known name and stayed their hand. Instead they put the stranger into the prison cage and sent word to Nezahualcoyotl.

"Itzcoatl sends you a message asking whether you have lost your sense of things to come."

Nezahualcoyotl heard of the imprisoned messenger and replied cautiously.

"Shall I move to Mexico-Tenochtitlan, and finish my days there?"

One could speak too soon. Separately Texcoco and Tenochtitlan had made their preliminary stand against Azcapotzalco. Their campaign as allies was still ahead, and opinion divided in both cities. In Texcoco it was not forgotten that Tenochtitlan had sided once with Azcapotzalco.[2] Nezahualcoyotl waited for his friend.

Then Moteczuma was before him—also brought in as a prisoner of the Acolhua. His message was direct and open.

"We will give you our help, and we ask for yours. It is time to attack—now that you yourselves are free."

"It is because I know the quality of the messengers from Tenochtitlan that I trust you," Nezahualcoyotl replied.[3]

Quickly Moteczuma Ilhuicamina and his companions, among them Nezahualcoyotl's own brother,[4] were on their way from Texcoco to Chalco, messengers now for both Nezahualcoyotl and Itzcoatl, ready to draw into the larger alliance the city of corn and carved canoes which had supported Nezahualcoyotl's quick march.

The Chalca received them doubtfully, remembering their own past troubles with Mexico-Tenochtitlan. And around the lake the news went swiftly that Moteczuma Ilhuicamina was imprisoned in the House of Long Corridors in Chalco.

The people of Azcapotzalco were amused.

"Nezahualcoyotl has called on the Chalca to get him out of an embarrassing situation," they said. "He did not want to hold his friend a prisoner in Texcoco. The Chalca can hold him instead."[5]

And when messengers came to Maxtla from Chalco he listened to them without faith.

"We distrust an alliance between Texcoco and Tenochtitlan. We will support the Tepaneca," they told him.

"I am not deceived," he replied. "In time I will punish you with arms for your alliance with Nezahualcoyotl. As for the prisoners, they are yours. Do what you will with them. Let them go if you wish."[6]

The Chalca turned toward Huexotzinco. Perhaps there,

holding the Tenochca prisoners to prove good faith, they could find an ally against the rising power of the island city—an ally that would in turn prove good faith by sharing in condemning the prisoners to death.

While the Chalca messengers went across the mountains Moteczuma and his companions waited, listening to the shell horn sound the night hours of prayer, watching the boys in training for war follow the stern disciplines of the priests in the House of the Long Corridors.[7]

He talked sometimes with Coateotl, the singer, who had sought him out as relative and friend, recognizing the Mexican prisoner as his mother's brother's child.[8] They spoke together of the growing strength of Mexico-Tenochtitlan. They waited for the messengers to return.

At last, impatient, the Chalca decided to wait no longer.

"Let us take the prisoners to Huexotzinco. Perhaps there they will kill them—or if not, they will return them to us."

And Moteczuma Ilhuicamina took his old trail to Huexotzinco, this time as a prisoner.

There the discussions had gone on with carefully slow formality.[9]

The Chalca had begun with an offer.

"The Mexicans have been captured. If it seems good to you, they will come to your city and we will shoot them full of arrows and burn them."

They spoke in terms of the festival to Mixcoatl, Cloud Serpent, whose symbol was the arrow, image of the fire drill.[10] It was the festival of hunters on the hills and shared by both cities. In Huexotzinco, where he was known as Camaxtli, his day was the great feast of the year, and the sacrificial victim was killed by arrows.[11] The lake towns knew him too, for in Cuitlahuac, the nearest town to Chalco, legend said that he had fallen, a two-headed deer, from the sky.[12] And there the women who were the sacrificial victims were carried like deer up the pyramid steps.

"Thus they slay them as deer; they serve as the deer who thus die," it was said.

Other victims climbed the pyramid steps of their own free will, some singing, some weeping.

"And when they had died, then died Mixcoatl," it was said.

But those of Huexotzinco heard the suggestion for the feast of their god coldly. Quiet conversations had gone on between them and Moteczuma and the lake towns which the Chalca had not shared.

"It was your fortune to capture these men," they replied. We have nothing to do with it. It is of Chalco."

Then Xayacamachan, one of the leaders of Huexotzinco and a friend of Moteczuma, added with careful courtesy and equally careful ambiguity,

"Nevertheless if these important men come, we will be waiting for them."

So that there might be no misunderstanding of the situation, they called the people of Huexotzinco together.

"Listen, all of you. This is not our desire. It is an attempt of Teotzin of Chalco to put blame and responsibility on us."

When the group of prisoners from Chalco drew near, the leaders of Huexotzinco went out to meet them.

They directed their first greeting to Moteczuma Ilhuicamina.

"You have come to Huexotzinco, your home. It is a pleasure to us that you should rest here and eat a tortilla."

Moteczuma could hear in the words the welcome to a friend. His captors heard the welcome always given to a prisoner who would be sacrificed.[13]

For four days, eating the doubled tortilla and the yellow tortilla, the prisoners were honored guests. By that time the meaning of the hospitality was clear even to the Chalca. The Archer of the Sky would not be sacrificed with arrows in the town where he had lived as a fugitive. The little group started back to the highlands.

At last to Chalco came word from Mexico-Tenochtitlan. Two men spoke quietly—and clearly.

"If it comes to the point of taking the life of these Mexica, we will not object," they said to the ruler of Chalco.

Their own city had given the word, and those who had feared to make enemies of Tenochtitlan need fear no longer. The invitation went out for the day of sacrifice—this time to the Acolhua who had captured the prisoners at the beginning, to the lake towns, to places as far away as Tula and Cuauhnauac. In five days Moteczuma Ilhuicamina and his friends would die.

When news was brought to the House of Long Corridors the Angry Archer of the skies recognized the names of those who had spoken for Tenochtitlan—The Moderate One and He Who Knows the Stars Like their Twin.[14] Members of the peace party, they had gone to Azcapotzalco to offer tribute. He had fled from them once. He had opposed them in open council. He knew they did not speak for Itzcoatl. But now, helpless, he could only wait for death in the House of the Long Corridors. He could talk to Coateotl, his kinsman. He could talk to his two guards. He could watch the bright lake day end in darkness.

The waiting was over at last. Moteczuma Ilhuicamina and his companions were led out into the plaza and market place in procession, watched by the seated dignitaries of the town, prisoners about to die.

There was no haste. Little groups would be coming, one by one, from the towns to which the announcements had been sent. The morning wore on.

The leaders of the Chalca consulted among themselves. No one had come from Tlaxcala, they found. No one had come from Cuauhnauac to watch this man whose mother and wife were from the green town at the edge of the woods die by arrows and by fire. Only those from the towns of the chinampa, the gardens by the lake, had presented plumes and obsidian, and lighted fires on the plaza in memory of the time when the fallen sky had been lifted, and a road of stars put there, and life came again from the earth, and Tezcatlipoca changed into Mixcoatl, and fire came from flint.[15]

"Many have not arrived," decided the authorities. "Tomorrow everything will be done in order."

Moteczuma was led back to wait again for death.

Coateotl the singer slept restlessly that night. He thought of the increasing power of Tenochtitlan. He thought of the rebuffs Chalco had met in encouraging resistance. He remembered the talks with his kinsman. He heard in his half-waking dreams a voice which seemed to say,

"Listen, my son. You think that tomorrow all the towns will gather to watch the death of the Mexicans. But you must know these young men came only to obey, not to die."

Through the marshes they had come, bearing messages from Itzcoatl and Nezahualcoyotl, speaking not with their own authority.

The voice went on.

"Open their doors that they may go. For the empire and the blood of the Tepanecatl and of the Chalcatl draw near to their end, and that of the Mexica will increase until theirs shall be the only power that will govern and order the people of this land."

Coateotl arose from his dream and went to the guards in charge of the prisoners.

"Did you have the vision that came to me?" he asked. "The power and the blood of Azcapotzalco and Chalco draw to a close." As he spoke of Moteczuma Ilhuicamina he used the phrases of intimacy and respect. "What can we do with our child here? Open the doors and let him go. He will be our mother and our father. Instead of holding these prisoners, let them eat our double tortilla and our yellow tortilla."

The prisoners came forth quietly, unbelieving. They ate with courteous deliberation, but uneasily, the tortillas that were offered them.

"If in time to come you hear that I have died for this,

remember with gratitude the good will I bore you," said Coateotl. "And if you come into great power some day, remember my children who will be orphans for your sake."[16]

On their way at last to Mexico-Tenochtitlan the escaped prisoners could hear the alarm that had risen behind them and the shouts of the searchers. On the plaza in Chalco the representatives of twenty-five towns of the chinampa were ready to watch the sacrifice. And the victims were gone.

"Coateotl is a friend of Moteczuma," the Chalca said suspiciously.

But only the two prison guards who had opened the door were brought out to die in front of the waiting visitors on the plaza.[17] They killed them as deer near the place where the two-headed deer had fallen from the sky. They died as deer, and as the god.

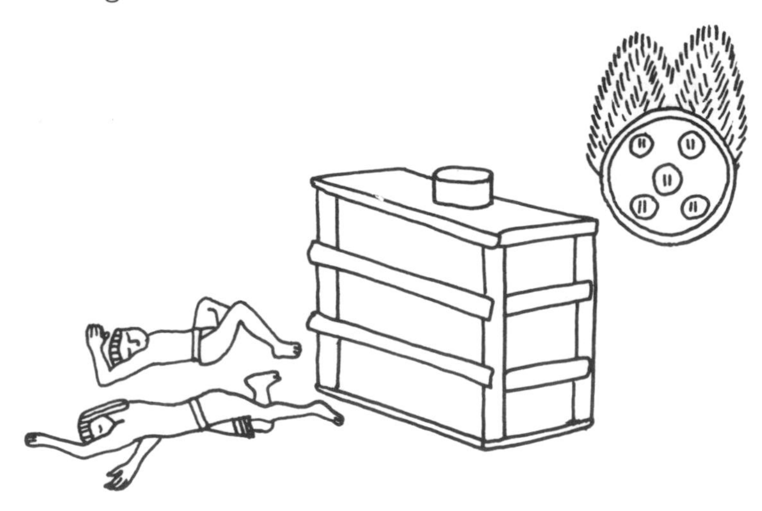

With death behind him, Moteczuma Ilhuicamina hid that day near Chimalhuacan. One of his companions brought him fresh water in a gourd, and tender green sections of nopal to eat when the thorns had been removed. Finally they saw coming toward them through the channels of the marshes a fisherman and his wife in a wooden canoe.

The young men saw their way of escape, and called a sharp command. Then in despair they knew that they would not be obeyed.

Moteczuma, the grim and angry one, had chosen the ruthless road of war and death. Death lay behind him, and now death lay ahead.

When the deed was done, they left the lifeless bodies of the fisherman and his wife there in the marshes, and in the canoe slipped through the channels into the open lake.[18]

First to Texcoco where Nezahualcoyotl welcomed his brother and the Mexica,[19] then by way of Ixtapalapa to Tenochtitlan. Moteczuma stood at last before Itzcoatl, ready with his report. The alliance with Texcoco against Azcapotzalco had been confirmed. The efforts in Chalco had failed. He told how their kinsman Coateotl had opened the doors of their prison. And he named the names of those who had come from Tenochtitlan pretending to speak for Itzcoatl.

"In Chalco we heard what they said—that no one would object when the Mexican prisoners died."

Itzcoatl heard him through.

"Let the Mexicans take up their shields," he ordered grimly.

The last minute conferences went tensely on in the lake cities. Chalco sent messengers to Texcoco.[20] Having failed to kill the leader of the war party of the Mexica, and failed to gain the support of the towns beyond the mountains, they were ready now to accept the offer of the alliance with Nezahualcoyotl which Moteczuma had brought.

"We do not want your friendship," Nezahualcoyotl replied briefly. "It will not be long before you pay for the way you received our messengers."

In Azcapotzalco itself there was division of opinion.

"Have you not settled on war?" Maxtla asked his council.

"Are you not the cause of all this? Have you not begun it?" they countered.

And members of the Azcapotzalco peace party sent messengers to Itzcoatl saying,

"Be at peace, Mexicans. Do not polish your arms."[21]

In Tenochtitlan nothing was heard of Moteczuma. A figure of controversy, a symbol of war, he was not the man to unite his own city. Instead, over in Texcoco he worked with his friend Nezahualcoyotl on the plans for the coming battle. In Tenochtitlan, his half brother Tlacaelel, like a twin, like a shadow, took up his role as opponent of the peace party, and as messenger for Itzcoatl, the Obsidian Snake.[22]

"We are few and our lands are narrow," said the old men and the common people who in each calpulli were gathering the food and weapons which would be necessary. "In our judgment it will be best to submit to the Tepaneca, and carry our god Huitzilopochtli to Azcapotzalco, and thus come freely out from the lake and establish ourselves there. That would be liberty. Let all speak what seems to them best. Lct us choose what is best."

"Are you turning cowards, Mexica?" asked Tlacaelel scornfully. "Do not be fearful of seeing as we see."

But Itzcoatl spoke tactfully.

"Let us learn where this counsel leads. Who will carry such a message?"

It was Tlacaelel who went across the causeway, past the single shield that marked the beginning of the Tepanecan lands, past the guard that challenged him.

"Do what you will with me, but do it when I return."

In the presence of Maxtla at last, he tried the message of the peace party to see where it would lead.

"Itzcoatl says he will submit to you, and you must receive him. Take pity on your Mexican people and let them all move here to your town."

Maxtla replied enigmatically.

"I know the humble and subject position of the Mexica. It is the Tepaneca who are inflamed and angry and ready for war. Have patience."

Back again in Tenochtitlan the peace party would not be able to say that the offer for peace had not been made. Tlacaelel gave his report. It seemed less kindly now that it was repeated in his own terms.

"Maxtla answered me, 'What do you wish me to do? Am I powerful enough to block the war plans of the Tepaneca?' "

The peace party made a last effort.

"Does it not stir your pity to see so many old people and children who will suffer in a war? The Tepaneca are ten to one against us. They reach even to the hills and can defend themselves in open country. On our islands we have no defenses of hill or rock or cave where we can hide the women and children and old people. Why do you not want us to go in peace and live under the dominion of the people of Azcapotzalco?"

The war party had their answer.

"If we must deliver our land to the Tepaneca, let it be with arrows and spears, and thus with courage."

"Then let this be agreed. When we see that we cannot prevail against the Tepaneca, when our numbers diminish with the loss of our wives and children and old people, we will order death for you."

"Let it be so," said the young warriors. "Eat our flesh on broken and dirty pottery. But if we come out of this battle victorious, then you will never be nobles among the Tenochca. You will be our macehuales and workers forever."

The old men agreed.

"If you defeat the Tepaneca we will give to the most valiant among you our daughters and nieces and grandchildren. According to his valor, let him have in his house two or three or four women for himself. To you who fight and win slaves in the war we will give women. For you we will carry arms on our shoulders and burdens of beans in time of war. We will receive you with pomp and festivals when you come home. We will serve you when you eat. We will sweep your houses. We will do your will."

It was a wager—and it was unity enough for action. Tlacaelel went again over the causeway, this time for the formal and final declaration of war.

"Itzcoatl sends you a gift to comfort your sadness—this war paint and these feathers, symbols of shield and arrow."

"You are welcome, Atempanecatl Tlacaeleltzin," said Maxtla.

Maxtla was anointed with ointment of the dead, and given plumes for his head and arrows in his hand.

Then he turned to Tlacaelel.

"Take this shield and war club, and see if you can go safely past the guards. I have made a hole in the wall. Pass through the opening and when you come out on the other side, do not turn around. Go bent like a hunchback. We shall not see each other again."

Disguised, Tlacaelel made his way out from the city of Azcapotzalco, and along a little used path past the guards at the border. When he was well beyond them he turned and taunted them.

"You will have good fortune. You will die, and no one will remain, not even a memory of the people of Azcapotzalco."

They pursued him across the causeway almost to Tenochtitlan before they turned back. And Tlacaelel went into the presence of the Speaker-king.

"It is done," he said. "I have anointed Maxtla, and given him the plumes and the arrows."

And the people of Tenochtitlan adorned themselves for war.

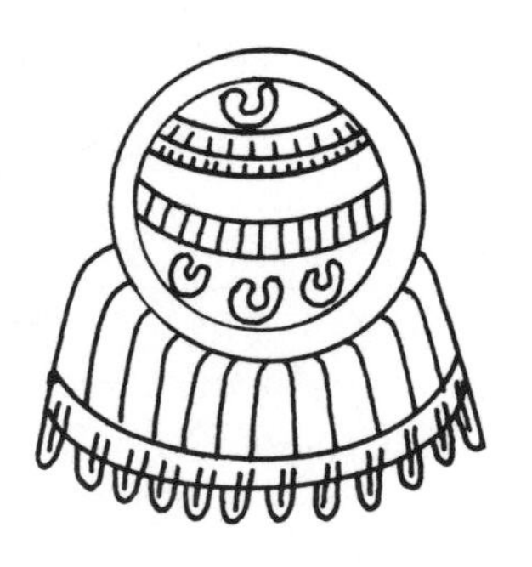

VI

By My Lance

ITZCOATL STOOD with his drum on the causeway. A signal fire flared to the northeast on the hill of Cuauhtepec. And on the causeway the waiting Mexica knew that Nezahualcoyotl and his white-clad soldiers were ready to advance. They waited only for the king's drumbeat and the orders of Tlacaelel.

The allies had assembled. The Tlaxcalteca were there, and Xayacamachan from Huexotzinco, with his fighting men, faithful to the promises made to two young men in exile.[1]

> "I have come flying. I have come here where the green-blue lake is.
> It moves, foams, boils, thunders angrily,
> While I fly, turned into a quetzal bird or into a bird the color of turquoise.
> I have come from Huexotzinco to the midst of the lake waters."[2]

Nezahualcoyotl of Texcoco, landing near Tlatelolco, had called into council Cuauhtlatoa, the Talking Eagle of Tlatelolco, and Itzcoatl of Tenochtitlan. In conference the leaders had decided on a three-part strategy.

Nezahualcoyotl chose his own position on the hills near Tepeyacac. His men, with some of the Huexotzinca and Tlaxcalteca beside them, were clad simply in white cotton armor.[3]

"Look at us beside the plumed companies of Tenochtitlan and Azcapotzalco," they complained bitterly. "The Tepaneca are clad in vermillion and blood red, yellow and white and black."

"We are like the wild flowers on the hills," replied the poet Speaker of Texcoco.

He put Moteczuma in command of the great second division with orders to take Tlacopan.[4] And beside him were the Tlatelolca under Cuauhtlatoa.[5]

The third part of the allied army was commanded by Itzcoatl, with Tlacaelel by his side. More of the Huexotzinca were assigned to him.[6]

Back of the main battle lines others were stationed. Already Cuauhtitlan and Huexotzinco had agreed that their men should wear cords around their heads so that they could know each other as allies in the confusion of battle and with combined forces close in on Azcapotzalco from the north.[7]

The Tenochca knew that Maxtla would have men in Coyohuacan and in Xochimilco. On the sides of the island toward those towns Tenochca guards were stationed ready for any attack that might come from across the lake. Nezahualcoyotl too was on guard against rebellious factions opposing the war in Texcoco and Huexotla.[8]

Knowing too that the division of mind within his own troops was not ended with their bitter contract, Tlacaelel separated the men of the war party from those of the peace party. To the men of the war party he gave his orders:

"When the drum sounds, forward!"

To the men of the peace party he gave different orders:

"Wait and be ready. When the Tepaneca begin their retreat, it will be time enough to go forward, little by little, toward Azcapotzalco."

A voice sang, rousing their courage:

"I am beating my drum, I who go in search of song
To awaken and kindle my friends
Whose hearts give no warning, in whose hearts still day does not break,
Those who in war still lie in the sleep of death
Those who glory in the night of deep shadow.
Harken to the song of the flowering dawn that once more falls like rain
In the place of the drums . . .
Those who make their souls drunk with life
Alone exist and open their petals
In the wood-thick mountains, in the steep place,
In the midst of the plain where one drinks war,
The divine liquor of combat . . ."[9]

Now in the dim light before daybreak they were in their places. Itzcoatl, Speaker-king of the islanders, spoke his last stirring words:

"Pay no attention to the numbers of our enemies stretching from the city to the wooded hills. Remember that this is your first great battle. You will make many peoples tremble."[10]

Off on the eastern hills the signal fire of Nezahualcoyotl flared. On the causeway Itzcoatl sounded his drum. Nezahualcoyotl's own drum ordered the advance of the Texcocans.[11] The day began, and the war of independence from Azcapotzalco.

It was not a test thrust along the causeway meant to end before dark. There in the high lake country the battle surged back and forth day after day, with confusion of plumed and painted and cotton-armored fighters on the causeway, on the mainland, even in boats in the marsh channels and in the open lake struggling against the day winds and against the enemy.

Now the training of boys in all the ways of the lake that had gone on through the hard days of tribute stood the Tenochca in good stead. And the song that had been a legendary murmur behind the lake winds mounted now with mourning and with promise: "It will cost you sweat and work and blood to reach the fine green chalchihuitl stones—the gold and silver and feather work."

The commanders hurried back and forth with messages, now here, now there. Xayacamachan left a young man who was tending the wounded to take authority in one section while he went to Nonohualco and Mictlantonco to confer with other Huexotzinca and with Moteczuma and Nezahualcoyotl.[12] Then hurrying back, he sent notice of another attack to Maxtla.[13]

In the despair of battle Itzcoatl cried,
"It is the end—it is the slavery of the Mexicans."
He mourned the expected help which had not come.
"Only three from Coaixtlahuaca!" he cried.[14]
Nezahualcoyotl was calm.

"They are not old men who are with us," he said.

Again the troops surged forward. Tlacaelel led the warriors on the causeway. Masks of tiger and eagle, plumes of rank, here white cotton armor, here a cord around the head—in confusion of friend and foe they sought the identifying mark, the identifying color.

Closer now to the great Ant Hill, the tyrant city of the Tepaneca. The days of sweat and struggle passed—a hundred and fifteen days until Azcapotzalco was cut off from the lake. The siege closed in.

The half-hearted Tenochca who had seen no chance to revolt against the power of Azcapotzalco saw the lines of fugitives heading to the hills. Those who had been stationed waiting until this time, came into battle now from the rear, rejoicing in the victory they had not hoped for.[15]

"There is no longer a memory of the Tepaneca," they cried. "All is ours. Now you see our valor and our strength. Victory, Mexicans!"

The combined forces swept forward.

A man in a deer mask was captured and pleaded for his life.

"Mexicans, Moteczuma is not here. Let me go find him at Acozac and tell him that the principal warriors are gone—the companies are broken and finished, the blood-colored and vermillion, the yellows and whites and blacks. Let me run and find Moteczuma."[16]

At Acozac, with his allies from Tlatelolco, Moteczuma knew victory was in the hands of his city. Out from the island to the mainland, to cornfields, to the green life of the land, and the green jewels.

Now the advance of the Tenochca was to the music of pipes and wooden teponaztli drums. Singing, the allies swept on into the city of Azcapotzalco. Rumors flew back among the dancing, singing host of warriors.

"Nezahualcoyotl has drawn Maxtla out from the sweat

bath where he was hiding," cried the Texcocoans. "Our king has killed the tyrant."[17]

"The Tepaneca themselves have killed their king so as to make peace with us," said some of the Mexicans.[18]

Through the dancing ranks of the Tlatelolca the cry of victory ran:

"Maxtla is dead. Dead by order of our own king, the Eagle Who Talks, Cuauhtlatoatzin of Tlatelolco."[19]

But Maxtla was already in flight, around the edge of the lake to the Tepanecan city of Coyohuacan.[20] Behind him the islanders who had once brought tribute of fish and lake birds from their poverty, and had considered carrying their god to Azcapotzalco in complete surrender, were burning the temple, capturing the god of the tyrant. Old God, wrinkled and ancient, great since the days of Teotihuacan, god of fire, was carried from his temple, conquered by the rising power of Huitzilopochtli.

And at his headquarters at Acozac, Moteczuma thought he heard the voice of Huitzilopochtli, great warrior god of the sun, Hummingbird on the Left:

"For this I brought you out from the House of Long Corridors at Chalco. For this I saved you from the sacrifice."[21]

The great names of the battle rang proudly in Tenochtitlan, the valiant soldiers, the conquerors of Azcapotzalco.

"They are the founders of Tenochtitlan, the place in the reeds, in the water."[22]

For they had established a new and free city, with a foothold on the mainland, and no tribute to pay—neither of fish nor frogs nor a duck on her eggs. Like a new cycle, a new sun, everything was changed. Azcapotzalco, which had once planted magueys in the conquered market place of Cuauhtitlan and moved its slave market to its own plazas, would now have only that slave market left from its glory.[23]

The names of the sons of Huitzilihuitl were praised in that victory—chief among them the half brothers, Tlacaelel and Moteczuma.[24]

The men of the peace party came humbly to those who had fought on the causeway, who had been in the forefront of battle.

"We remember our promise. Since you have fought with valor and are victors, we will serve you. We will do what you command."[25]

Tlacaelel went to Itzcoatl.

"Now the Tepaneca have promised us land. Do not forget your sons and your nephews, those who have stood the heat of battle. Let those who are named as the valiant ones have land."[26]

There was land to give at last. The Speaker-king took his own share in Azcapotzalco itself, and gave ten allotments to Tlacaelel, great among the brave. Land all the way to Tlacopan and to Popotlan was marked off and distributed, and Moteczuma's grant was large, for now his counsel of war was in disrepute no longer. He too had kept his promise and given his people food and freedom.

The calpulli also were given their assignment of additional land—the districts inhabited by the separate related units, proud of their lineage, tightly organized within themselves. They would pay their tribute to the king. From lands marked off for the purpose they would bring to the temple in their own district food for the priests. They would manage to buy the offerings of incense, of rubber-spotted paper—sulphur-yellow and blue and black—to adorn the sacrifices. But the land should be theirs forever, and the books recorded the fact for all generations. Here were the people of the calpulli, those who were the hands, those who were the feet.[27] That lineage and that land should not be confused. The lines of inheritance should be kept clear. The obligations to cultivate and use each plot should be fulfilled.

The makers of books mapped the land assignments. Carefully they laid on the fire-red paint for the king's land; the flesh-pink for the lands of the nobles who were the king's sons and nephews and brothers; clear yellow for the land of the calpulli where the macehuales would bend their backs to plant and cultivate. The painted record would stand for all generations.

And as the Tenochca took possession of their new property they could say from the Speaker-king to the simplest farmer:

"By my lance I earned it."[28]

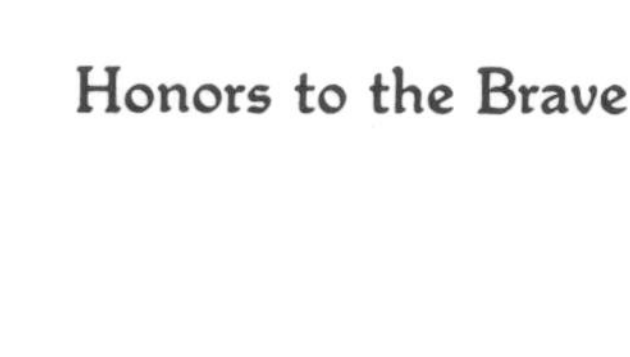

VII

Honors to the Brave

Over in Coyohuacan where Maxtla had taken refuge, the other Tepaneca contemplated his broken dream of power and the fallen glory of the city that had been like an ant hill rich in people and piled treasure.

"We too will fall, even here," they said. "The people of Azcapotzalco themselves will plan to take our land and our tribute, because now they are tributary to the Tenochca and so have become their allies. Let us go to them and urge that we fight together for our liberty."

The messengers went to the conquered city, and looked about them.

"This is the way you have given away your lands to the Tenochca and become a tribute city," they said sadly and accusingly.

"We were conquered in a just war. We gave our land as ransom for our women and children and old people, for a place in which to live."

The envoys from the Tepanecan town of Coyohuacan spoke pleadingly: "Let us turn again to the defense of our liberty. Let us call Xochimilco and the other Tepanecan towns to a right and just cause."

With the slow pacing of courteous negotiation the conquered city said,

"Come another day for your answer."

They came a second time, suggesting again a new war.

"We will find allies. We will join with Texcoco and Chalco and Cuitlahuac. Together—"

But the people of Azcapotzalco were ready with the reply.

"Did you help us during those hundred and fifteen days? Do we want to see our streets filled again with the heads and arms and entrails of the slain? Did you come when the eagle and tiger warriors swept down upon us?"

The messenger from Maxtla returned to Coyohuacan. In Azcapotzalco there was such peace as came with an ending.[1]

The fugitive king continued to send out his messengers, warning each Tepanecan town that in its turn it would fall tribute to the expanding power of the island warriors.[2] Already some of the towns tied to Azcapotzalco through the marriages of Tezozomoc's children were falling before the alliance of Texcoco and Tenochtitlan. The towns whose rebellion against Nezahualcoyotl had been the hope of the Tepaneca were being defeated. Moteczuma Ilhuicamina himself, it was reported, had met the Huexotla ruler in battle and taken him prisoner.[3]

The messengers from Coyohuacan went to two neighboring towns in the hills[4] and called on the woodsmen for help.

"Send us arms and young and valiant men who will confront the Tenochca, for they have set out to conquer all of us."

But the woodsmen of the hills replied,

"They have not troubled us. Let this be your own war."

They sent messengers then to the shore towns and the gardens among the squared channels, to the half-hidden town of Mixquic.

"Here in Mixquic," came the brief reply, "we are of the same blood as the Tenochca. Shall we be traitors to them? We will wait to see how your negotiations work out."

The messengers went to Texcoco. Perhaps now the rising power of the islanders would have aroused fear even in Nezahualcoyotl.

"Do you forget that their god fights for them?" he said.

"The Hungry Coyote knows dark and hidden things," they murmured.

"Nor will I fight against those who have done me no harm," he went on. "I will stay in my own land and let others do as they will."

Then echoing the remote acceptance of things as they would be, of wars that the Aztec gods judged, he added,

"If others defeat the Mexica, they will have no complaint from me."

Detached and silent, the allies of the two cities watched the conferences among the Tepanecan towns, saw where they were leading, and waited.

It was the ruler of Colhuacan who made a cautious suggestion at last to the messengers from Maxtla.

"Let the representatives of the towns of the chinampa gather at Chalco and discuss this thing, that whatever they decide to do they may do together."

The Chalca agreed to be hosts to the conference.

"We would rejoice in the destruction of the tyrannical Mexica," they said. "Here we await you. Here we await you."

They came from the gardens on the made land between the canals, slipping quietly through the water in the flat-bottomed chalupas, and with sandaled steps along the roadways.

"When so many gather even this quietly, the Mexica will know," the Tepaneca warned. "The time is short."

Into the streets of Chalco the envoys came—Chalco the unpredictable. They were received with the formal phrases of greeting. The long speeches of courtesy and welcome began.

Coateotl finally arose and addressed the representatives of Chalco and the other towns.[5]

"We have come together at the request of the Tepaneca. I shall not tell you what they want, but since they are here present, they may speak for themselves."

They spoke with unaccustomed brevity and haste.

"You have seen how the Mexicans are a danger to us, and unless we look ahead will become still more of a danger. It is for this that we come to ask you to join with us and encircle them and destroy them."

The others sat listening, knees drawn up, heads down.[6] There was a silence.

Coateotl spoke at last.

"There are difficulties," he suggested. "For many years the relationships between all the towns have continued until now there are few places where our daughters have not married their sons, and their daughters our sons. We are closely related to the Tenochca. That is one reason for not fighting against them."

The representatives listened quietly. What he said was true. It was just as true that nearly every town among them was related by blood to Maxtla. But they remembered that they sat in the house of Moteczuma's uncle and friend; that Tlacaelel had married a Chalco girl.[7]

"Furthermore, their god defends them," Coateotl's voice went on.

They remembered the temple at Azcapotzalco burning.

"There is another thing," continued Coateotl. "If together we should conquer the Tenochca, what then? They will come and beg for mercy. They will offer us tribute. But which of us will take it?"

He turned to man after man among them.

"Will Coyohuacan claim the victory and the tribute? No, because here in Chalco we will be sure that we won the war and that the Tenochca must serve us. Will Xochimilco and Colhuacan and Cuitlahuac claim victory and tribute? There will be only dissension among us, and more war."

Murmurs of agreement sounded in the assembly. He went on.

"Your conspiracy is in your own hands. Each of us will watch from afar. We will have no part in it."

The towns of the chinampa had chosen their way. At

midnight the delegates from Coyohuacan had heard enough. They left the house of Coateotl, and through the darkness hurried away.[8]

Now both sides waited anxiously while the pattern of war shaped itself again.

Out from Coyohuacan went Cuecuex, first among the nobles, eye and ear for the Tepaneca. He went clad richly befitting his rank, in armor of quilted cotton with shield and obsidian-toothed club, with quilted and feathered headgear that was both helmet and mask. He peered among the channels and the reeds seeking the Tenochca scouts or warriors. He reached their boundaries without seeing anyone and, returning, reported again to Maxtla.

"It is our war and ours alone," agreed Maxtla then.[9]

He took the first step to bring it to a head.

"Let us close the roads and not permit the women of Tenochtitlan to come to our market," he ordered.

From the island the women came with their lake products —fish and the eggs of the water insect scraped from the marsh grasses, and the low-flying lake birds. They came bent beneath the weight of their goods, half running with quick bird-like steps.

Suddenly a group of men fell upon them and took from them all that they had brought to the market. They fled weeping.

"Go once more," commanded Itzcoatl. "This will not happen again. In all cities there are robbers."

Again with quick feet and with shoulders bent to the weight of their burdens they went to the market of Coyohuacan. They came back robbed and dishonored and weeping.

Itzcoatl understood now.

And the trading between the markets of Tenochtitlan and Coyohuacan was ended.[10]

Now the women of the island city went for another purpose. To the windward of Coyohuacan they built little fires and broiled the fish that they could no longer take to market.[11]

The fragrance drifted deliciously over the hungry town. They broiled water fowl and frogs' legs, and the wind took the good odors into the streets where they could not go. Old men and women spoke querulously, longing for the food they did not have. Women with child grew ill with desire for the delicious meals they could smell. Children wept until their eyes were swollen. A joke, the men described it—but a reminder of the trade that Maxtla had stopped. The bitter laughter of the women of Tenochtitlan was their revenge. Day after day they built their little fires to the windward of Coyohuacan, baking in beds of coals, broiling on hot rock griddles.

"Our young women lose their unborn children. Our old people die," cried the Coyohuaque in despair.

Once more the fiesta of the Old God with the wrinkled face, god of fire, was upon them. Maxtla took the next step.

"Let us invite the Tenochca and talk with them, for clearly now they intend war since their women come no more to our markets."

"Let us invite them and kill them when they least expect it," suggested Cuecuex.

"That would dishonor us. Let all proceed in its order until we decide the outcome in battle," commanded Maxtla.[12]

The invitation went to Tenochtitlan.

"Your humble burden bearers," said the envoys, with false and elaborate humility, "invite you to come to a feast. We await you."

The Tenochca accepted. But when the envoys were gone Tlacaelel and Itzcoatl consulted.

"What is this? What do they plan for us?" asked Itzcoatl.

"It is best that you stay here," replied Tlacaelel. "The rest of us will go and see what this thing is."

They came to Coyohuacan—the sons and nephews of Itzcoatl. Moteczuma was with them, the silent and angry one. Huehue Zacan, his brother, was there, full of songs and jokes. Now, coming to the feast they brought food—fish and birds, insects and mosses and eggs from the lake.

Maxtla and his followers received the gifts with gratitude. The day was bright for the end of the feast. The sacrifices had been completed after midnight, and the slaves thrown upon hot coals before their hearts were torn out. Now the time of rejoicing had come.[13]

The Tenochca ate in the house of Maxtla, and in honor of the god the dancers turned to the drumbeat of the carved wooden teponaztli and the huehuetl. The pole with the dough image at its top stood in the square waiting the climbers.

When the feasting was done, Cuecuex and other leaders among the Coyohuaque came to give the Tenochca gifts. They came not with the roses of the festival but with armloads of kindling wood and hoes such as a tribute town might use; and they laid before them women's blouses and skirts of maguey fiber, the coarse cloth of the common people.

"Maxtla bids you put them on and wear them," they said to their guests.

The feast was over. The declaration of war was made. Silently the Tenochca permitted themselves to be clothed in the garbs of slaves and of women, each man of them in turn, Tlacaelel first and then Moteczuma, and then one brother after another, even the flippant Huehue Zacan accepting the formal insult.

The men of Coyohuacan looked at them in contentment, as out from the house of Maxtla the Tenochca danced with slow dignity, turning to the beat of teponaztli and huehuetl, dancing in the great square of Coyohuacan on the feast day of Xiuhteotl, god of fire, dancing in the garb of women and slaves. The other dancing groups on the plaza, and the men and women who stood watching them, knew that the declaration of war had been accepted.

Back and forth they went in the rhythmic pace of the dance until with one turning they danced away from the plaza, and without saying farewells, silently took their way back to Itzcoatl waiting for them in their island city.

Like a pause in the dance came more days of preparation.

Out from Coyohuacan again went Cuecuex to see whether the Mexicans were advancing. This time he found guards stationed. As Tlacaelel had once done to the guards of Azcapotzalco, he shouted defiance, leaping and whistling, and, with beating on lip, sending across the distance the pulsating war cry. Then he and the Mexica returned to their own cities to report the encounter.[14]

So that they could see far out over level reed and water, sentinels on both sides built platforms on high poles. From one Tlacaelel sighted the misted distances and saw smoke rising.

"I will go to see whether this fire is built by men of Culhuacan or Chalco, and whether they are minded to fight with us," he said.

When he came near he called to them.

"Who are you? Where are you from? What do you want?'

They answered him in terms of relationship.

"We are your brothers. We are your nephews. We are from Culhuacan, and have come to put out our nets to catch birds. What else can we do? Thus did we always, we of Culhuacan, your grandmothers and grandfathers and brothers."[15]

"Look at me and you will see that I do not believe this," replied Tlacaelel. "What are your names?"

They answered frankly.

"So be it then, and keep your nets," said Tlacaelel. " I am Tlacaelel and we are friends. I will come back. In the meantime, if you see others, ask where they come from, and if they say from Coyohuacan, kill them."

"It is well," said the three men.

Tlacaelel reported to Itzcoatl.

"Let us not trust these men too far," warned the Speaker-king. "They are at the edge of Tepanecan country. Watch them from time to time."

Tlacaelel continued to watch for the approach of the Tepaneca. Finally he saw Cuecuex stationed on his own high lookout, watcher and listener for Coyohuacan.

"The time has come to fight," Tlacaelel reported to Itzcoatl.

Hurrying out to the nets of the bird hunters he gave them shields and weapons and insignia.

"My brothers," he called.

Moteczuma too was distributing arms to the fighting men of Tenochtitlan.[16]

The first encounter was at Momaztitlan Tlachtonco, the frontier where Cuecuex had shouted defiance.

"At them," shouted Tlacaelel.

He struggled forward with his three bird-hunting companions from Colhuacan and two Mexicans—a group of six that held together during the coming days. They swept on to Tlenamacoyan.

"How do we do now?" shouted Tlacaelel proudly. "We whom the Coyohuaque called women! Let the six of us cut a right ear from each of our prisoners to keep the count and claim our own."

They remembered an earlier day when the Mexica, poor and struggling, had lived within the city of Colhuacan. Together then they had fought against Xochimilco and gathered ears in baskets to keep the count. By that memory they would affirm again an old alliance, and feel their audacious little group within the Mexican army one at heart.[17]

The nobles of Tenochtitlan were joined now by Nazahualcoyotl and his Texcocans. Moteczuma battled step by step, earning new honors. Itzcoatl, the Speaker-king, received the reports sent back to the island.

At last the victorious Tenochca swept on to the plaza of Coyohuacan itself. There before the Old God the Tepanecans were dancing again. Instead of plumes they were wearing women's clothes, carrying spindles in their hands.[18]

For a little while the victors watched them, savoring their humiliation. Then they began to seize prisoners and destroy the temple.

"Have mercy!" cried the people of Coyohuacan.

The victorious islanders did not accept their surrender, but pushed on now up the hills to the woods. On Ajusco they struggled, hurling their spears, wielding their obsidian-toothed clubs. There Moteczuma fought.

Suddenly in front of him he saw Maxtla's Otomi priest and soothsayer, who served Old God, God of Fire, God of the festival where Moteczuma himself had danced clad in women's clothes.

But Huitzilopochtli had once defeated the god of the Tepaneca, the god of the Otomi.

Moteczuma faced the Otomi priest and soothsayer in the woods and slew him there.

And Maxtla, his city and his god defeated again, wept and fled.[19]

Over the mountains the Tepaneca were fleeing to the towns that had refused them aid—to Atlapulco and Xalatlauhco and on toward Ocuilan. In the woods of Ajusco the Coyohuaque who were left cried out again for peace.

"Have mercy. We will make you bridges of wood. We will bring you rock for houses."

"You clothed us in skirts of women's shawls," the Tenochca reminded them.

"We will build you a conduit of fresh water. We will carry your clothing and arms and provisions on all the roads you may take. We will give you beans and corn and chilli."

"Have you finished?" asked Tlacaelel. "We do not want you to say that we have tricked you into a peace treaty, for we have won this victory in a just war."

"We will never say that you tricked us. We began the fight. We take our defeat and retreat in our own hands. We carry on our backs ropes and planting sticks to serve the Mexica. Our hot spears rest."

The report of victory went back to Itzcoatl. Word came that Maxtla had fled to Tlachco, the town of the ball court.[20] The dancing now was in the plaza of the island city and the prisoners were counted for the sacrifice to Huitzilipochtli. No man danced in skirts or carried spindles in that dance of victory.

The city of Mexico-Tenochtitlan began to shape itself anew. To the Speaker-king, who stayed home, guarded and remote, the petitions of his people came through an intermediary. It was Tlacaelel who spoke for him.

The first word was of gratitude.

"Rest now, after the work you have done for the peace and greatness of your city."

Then he spoke on the subject all longed to hear.

"It will be good now to give the lands of the Coyohuaque to those who have won them in good warfare."

"Here am I," agreed Tlacaelel. "And here are the principal men who won Azcapotzalco and Coyohuacan. It is fitting that you distribute to them what is right for each one, their sons, and heirs."

At the command of Itzcoatl he called together the nobles of Tenochtitlan and bade them be seated before the straw icpalli of the Speaker-king. But it was he who spoke.

"It is the will of Itzcoatl that we go to Coyohuacan and take our shares of the land, for ourselves and our descendants."

"The king is good. May Huitzilopochtli give him a long reign and more land," responded the nobles.

It was enough for that day. Now they knew that when they were counted they would be given land—the king himself would have his share to provide for the needs of his household to which envoys and traders from afar would come in increasing numbers; Tlacaelel would be given ten allotments in places around Coyohuacan in each of which he had fed the earth and gods with blood;[21] each man among them would have his two or three shares awarded to him in due time and drawn in color on the maps.

The next day they came together again. Prouder than gifts of land were the honors to be given now: titles that would be carried along with their names; clothes and jewels assigned to each title, that they alone could wear, and by which they would be known as valiant soldiers and conquerers, men who had killed the enemy—or even better, had brought home prisoners for the sacrifice.

The first four titles were given—rulers of the conquering city, from whom the Speaker-king could be elected. The two highest surprised no one. Tlacaelel, long called Atempanecatl, found that his recent title was to be given to another, and he was made Tlacochcalcatl, keeper of arms, in this time of war perhaps the most responsible office of all. Moteczuma Ilhuicamina was named Tlacatecatl, the post he had wished to hold ever since Itzcoatl had gone from that office to that of Speaker-king. Director of arrangements in Itzcoatl's own household, companion of those who came to it from afar, a noble in line for kingship.[22]

No one could foresee which of the four would be chosen as king in the future. But the two half brothers, twin-like in their achievement and their glory, were the likely ones—those who had heard the warsong of Huitzilipochtli in the sound of lake waters.

Prayers were said to the gods for them:

"Those who must rule, or have to be tlacatecatl or tlacochcalcatl, give them ability that they may be fathers and mothers of the men of war who go by field and by upland, by cliff and by canyon. It is in their hand to sentence the enemy and criminal to death; it is in their hand to give honors and ranks and arms in war, the right to wear rings and lip plugs, to wear precious chalchihuitl stones and turquoise, to wear rich plumes in the dances, and necklaces of gold."[23]

Parents described them to their children as "fathers and mothers of the sun, the tlacatecatl and tlacochcalcatl, who give food and drink to the sun and the earth with the blood and flesh of their enemies."[24]

They pointed them out carefully:

"They have for riches the shield and arms, and they merit the rich earrings, the lip plugs, the tassels on their head and the bracelets on their wrists and the yellow thongs on their ankles. They have them because they are valiant. They deserve the flowers and tubes of incense, the good food and drink and clothes and houses of nobles, and the corn of valiant men. They are fathers and mothers of their people, like the shadow of a tree.[25]

Moteczuma as tlacatecatl would wear the long hanging headdress of quezal plumes,[26] and jewels of chalchihuitls set in gold, and blue feathers set in crystal.

There in the house of Itzcoatl the other titles were announced—twenty-one in all—given to the sons and nephews of the king.[27] They would be leaders in war, in judgment, in execution of judgments. Sculptors would chisel them in rock with their name signs; painters of histories would tell of their exploits in bright color on paper made from the pounded bark of the amatl tree and on paper of maguey fiber.[28] When lesser men, graduates not of the calmecac, the house of long corridors where the sons of nobles studied, but of the telpochcalli, used the titles for duties of a temporary and lower nature such as executing the drunkards at the end of the Festival of Great Lords,[29] none would confuse them with these nobles whose deeds in making Tenochtitlan a city free of tribute and strong in its own right were honored now.

When the titles had been given there was a silence. The three bird hunters who had strung their nets above the reeds and water, came forward.

"Are we to be forgotten? We too, in spite of this disguise as hunters, are of a rank worthy to receive a title. Did not we of Culhuacan fight valiantly for Tenochtitlan?"

Tlacaelel had not forgotten those who fought at his side.

"These three men from Culhuacan and these two Tenochca—father and son—fought bravely."

He could produce the right ears to prove what havoc his companions had wrought. Itzcoatl assigned titles to all five. And all knew at last that the hunters from Culhuacan had foreseen the victory and had been seeking honors when Tlacaelel had sighted the smoke of their campfire in the marshes.

In their turn all those who had fought in the conquest of Coyohuacan brought their prisoners to be counted. One by one they were awarded the right to shave their hair in the proper manner and wear the insignia that indicated whether they had taken one or two or three prisoners for the sacrifice. Down to the simplest macehual who worked his plot of ground each soldier was given his reward.[30]

The ceremonies at last were ended.

"Let us rest," said Tlacaelel.

In Coyohuacan the vanquished were left to ponder on their defeat. They had accepted the outcome of battle and called it just. But now their bitterness turned on Azcapotzalco, the first of the Tepenecan towns to surrender. They made a quick march in the night to the town that was now only a slave market. They drew their victims out of their houses and once more fed the gods and the earth with blood. Then quickly in the night they were gone.[31]

The Tenochca rulers made a half-hearted search for the raiders. But a quarrel among the Tepaneca was not an issue for them. The city that had been called the Ant Hill settled again into quietness with only a memory of its greatness.

In Coyohuacan too there was only memory. The people watched their common land being worked by their conquerers. Drawn themselves into the center of their town, limited to their own garden plots, they found no hope. There was no place where they could breathe.[32]

VIII

The Flower Fields

THE FLOWER FIELDS of Xochimilco began now to feel the smothering pressure of the expanding power of Mexico-Tenochtitlan. Their leaders met in council.

"Better than face destruction, let us yield to them with good grace," said those who were for peace.

"I who am noble—should I sweep and do hand labor and irrigate fields for the Mexica?" replied another scornfully.

Fear haunted their days of waiting for what might come. But still the flat-bottomed chalupas went back and forth across the lake on market days, and the women of Xochimilco took their flowers and sharp chilli and green beans to the islanders, and the island women carried fish and game birds of the lake to the gardeners and goldsmiths and workers of precious stone in the chinampa.

The fear deepened. The people of the Flower Fields remembered the baskets of ears from an early and a later time.

The fish and birds sold in the market place by the women from Tenochtitlan were cleaned and washed and cooked. But though their food was so carefully prepared, the nobles could not eat. Like a nightmare they seemed to see in the curled white meat of the fish, and in the angle of a bird wing, a human ear.

"The Mexica will bring their terrible and perverted war

to us with club and shield and obsidian knife," they cried.

They had not long to wait. The messengers of Itzcoatl came over the lake waters.

"Your burden bearers,[2] the king and nobles and common people of the reeds and the water," they began with formal courtesy, "beg of you a little stone and some pine logs to work on the house of our god Huitzilopochtli."

The Xochimilca understood.

"Are we your slaves to serve you with tribute of stone and wood? Are you drunk with pulque?"

The reply went back to Mexico-Tenochtitlan. Itzcoatl and his four chief counsellors heard it solemnly—Tlacaelel and Moteczuma Ilhuicamina chief among them. It was a proud word from a proud people.

Again the order went out that was the preliminary of war.

"Let no one from here go to the markets of Xochimilco, and no one from there be permitted in the markets of Mexico-Tenochtitlan. Let all the ways of going and coming be closed."

The blockade shut down. In the Flower Fields the gardeners and farmers worked. In the houses along the canals the workers of precious stone cut and polished the black obsidian and green chalchihuitl, turquoise and rock crystal, and set them in gold.

At night they sang to the gods who had invented the working with precious stones and adorned their images with thin sheets of gold, and shields made like fine nets of gold, and masks of mosaic, until they shone in the temples on top of the pyramids, red and blue and gold.[3]

Though the road to Mexico-Tenochtitlan was closed to the people from the Flower Fields, they could still follow the trail over the wooded mountains to Cuauhnauac—the warm land of cotton and fruits. It was a trail that had been travelled also by Tenochca since the day when Ilhuicamina's father had thrown a reed and chalchihuitl stone into a hidden courtyard. The islanders had paused in the market in the Flower Fields, and had chatted with those they met in the resting places on the mountain trail. They would still be travelling that route through the high pines.

It was with no surprise that the Xochimilco traders found them there. They had set down their long staves and the loads of fruit and chilli and cotton they were carrying on their shoulders to rest awhile. It was a place of meeting between those who were on their way down to Cuauhnauac and those who were coming back, carrying the valley produce to the uplands. Here they could exchange news and gossip as they rested.[4] But now the meeting was tense with fear.

"Where are you from?" demanded the people from the Flower Fields.

The Tenochca were on guard.

"Why do you ask us? Are you hunting for slaves? Are you robbers? We come in our poverty, Mexica who have sought food in Cuauhnauac."

"And we are hunting you, our enemies!"

The Xochimilco fell upon them and seized their clothes and goods. And the Tenochca went naked down the trail to the lake and came naked into the presence of Itzcoatl and Moteczuma and Tlacaelel.

"You see us as the Xochimilca have left us," they said.

"This is mockery not to be endured," said Tlacaelel.

"We have not yet sent out our scouts, our eyes and ears," said Itzcoatl. "Rest and wait."

The slow and rhythmic steps toward war continued. On their little garden plots near Coapan the farmers from the Flower Fields were working. Warily they watched for guards on the frontier. Suddenly they saw in front of them five nobles and five young men of the common people, armed guards from Tenochtitlan.

"Who are you?"

"And you?—where do you come from?"

They did not need to ask each other. Even before the Mexica began to tear up their corn and beans the Xochimilca knew. They fled for help, and with arms and reinforcements pursued the Tenochca almost to the edge of their city.

The Mexican council went into session again.

"Let us send messengers to Cuitlahuac and to Mixquic to see whether they stand with Xochimilco or with us. And let us send messengers to Xochimilco to see whether they are determined to fight us—the old men and the young men—to see what they want to happen to their women and their children."

The threat in the words was clear. Two titled messengers carried it. The Xochimilca came out to meet them.

"You need not keep on to the Flower Fields," they said. "Say to Itzcoatl that the time has come."

Nezahualcoyotl hurried from Texcoco to talk with Itzcoatl and Moteczuma about what should be done. Once more, allied with each other, the troops marched into battle. The Texcocans defended their own frontier set toward Xochimilco, rejoicing that in their part of the line not a single Mexicatl was needed to fight on their side.[5]

On their own front the eagle and tiger warriors of Mexico-Tenochtitlan picked up great stones from a promontory of stone at Teyacac.[6] Not as weapons but as symbols of a moving frontier they carried them into battle. And against them fought the men of Xochimilco with jewelled spears like the sun.[7]

On to Ocolco, on past the garden lands and through the rock defenses encircling Xochimilco the Mexica struggled. The soldiers were forbidden to loot the city of jewels; in due order they would be given their spoils. Tlacaelel, keeper of arms and leader of the army stood at last on Xochitepec, Hill of Flowers, and shouted encouragement to his men.

"Today the Xochimilca die!"

At Atotoc the Mexica laid down their stones. This would be the new boundary of Tenochtitlan.

The Xochimilca came to them there.

"There is nothing left," they said.

The land hungry Mexica took their share of the Flower

Fields. Land was assigned to Itzcoatl, to Tlacaelel, and to the other leaders of the expanding city.[8]

"The great mountain is for you—with wood and stone," said the Xochimilca humbly.

Materials for the temple of Huitzilopochtli, clear road for traders all the way to Cuauhnauac.

To Texcoco, the city of the arts, the goldsmiths and jewel workers went,[9] and were given their own section of the city to work in, bringing their best work to the council of arts each eighty days for praise or for blame, for reward or for punishment.

And to Tenochtitlan, the city of builders, the strong laborers and farmers went to bend their backs at the order of the conquerers. With them the Tenochca called together the men of Azcapotzalco and Coyohuacan.

"Together you will build a road and causeway fifteen arms in width," they commanded.

The work went swiftly. The workmen dug up earth and marsh grass from the lake bottom as they did for building the gardens in the chinampas. They brought rock from hill and quarry.

The Tenochca waited until the causeway was finished to have the ceremonies of conquest. But the day came quickly when the road stretched wide from Tenochtitlan, past Coyohuacan and on to Xochimilco, built strongly with bridged openings to let the water flow through.[10]

Then over the lake the Tenochca went to claim their land with due ceremony. They went with quetzal plumes, green and gleaming, and leather thongs adorned with green stones on their wrists and ankles.

Now Huitzilopochtli had conquered the people who adored Chantico, goddess of the fire that burned on the hearths of simple gardeners, and in the crucibles of goldsmiths.

The people of the Flower Fields came out to meet the conquerors. They put before them food and blankets and jewels. Then they brought out roses and wooden drums, and all danced together to give authority to the dance and the conquest.[11]

With roses and drumbeats the Tenochca claimed the land in shares four hundred armlengths square. And the people of Xochimilco with roses and music said to the people of Mexico-Tenochtitlan.

"Here is your house. Here we wait you whenever you wish to come and rest."[12]

Then the music was done. And the people of the Flower Fields wept.

IX

The Boys' War

IN THE VALLEY of Mexico the remaining actions against the Tepanecan towns went on. Nezahualcoyotl led campaigns against the rebellious towns of the Texcoco area. Now it was the turn of Chiconauhtla, where once old Tezozomoc had his hunting lodge; of Tepechpan, where the friendly Quauquauhtzin was living; of Acolman, the dog market, where many Tepanecans had taken refuge and now fought in a last desperate stand; of Tecoyucan; of Teotihuacan near the grass covered pyramids of a forgotten people, where the gods must have been; of Otumpan far at the northeast end of the lake country.[1]

Remotely, in the background, the Speaker-king Itzcoatl watched the achievements of his council and armies, and the building of the pyramid to Huitzilopochtli. In every section of the city the telpochcalli stood, the house of young men. And their parents brought their boys to the teachers there to train for war. The teachers accepted them without promises:

"It is certain we do not know the gifts this child has been given—we bring our fortune with us when we are born. We pray that he may be given the riches of our god. We will do our duty in bringing him up like his parents. Certainly we cannot enter into him and give him our heart. You could not do that yourselves, though you are his parents. Commend him to our god with prayers and tears, that our god may show us his will."[2]

The boys swept the houses of Tezcatlipoca, the Smoking Mirror, god of night and darkness and war. They carried wood from the mountains for the fires which burned on the pyramids and in the school and in the house of the dance. They carried shields and weapons into battle for more seasoned soldiers. And sometimes they themselves took a prisoner for the sacrifice and won titles in the school, like the titles of the men who governed the city.

When the day's work was done in the House of Young Men, they put on a garb of loosely woven maguey fiber adorned with small shells that tinkled as they moved—netlike over their brown skin. And they went into the house of the dance, where the girls awaited them, the house of Xochiquetzal, Flower Plume, goddess of flowers and of song and of love.

"From the land of mist and rain I came,"[3] they sang of her, and remembered her in the land of the flowering tree to be plucked by happy lovers, and above the ninth heaven in the clear cold airs where Tezcatlipoca had taken her when he had stolen her from the rain god.[4]

Xochiquetzal, the Flower Plume, taken by the god of war, the god of the House of Young Men.

They looked forward to the month of Quecholli when Mixcoatl, the Cloud Serpent, and Xochiquetzal, the Flower Plume, One Deer, would both be adored; when arrows would be shot into the maguey and victims be carried like deer up the steps to be sacrificed to the god.[5]

Then these girls could taunt the honest women, these girls from the house of song who danced for the naked goddess,[6] these girls who would not fear to go into battle at the side of their lovers.[7]

"They lift roses to her in the land of flowers,
The land of the beginning,"[8]

sang the young warriors.

Itzcoatl spoke with his council and sent two titled messengers through the reeds and the lake to Cuitlahuac, the city in the silver mists near Chalco, where Mixcoatl, the hunting god, was worshipped as their defense, where he fell as a deer from the heavens.[9]

The demand was different this time—not for stone or wood to glorify the house of a war god, but a tribute of youth and beauty.

"Itzcoatl sends for your sisters and your daughters," said the messengers, "that they may sing and dance in the house of song; and he sends for you that you may bring roses for our gardens."

"Does he mock us? Shall we send our daughters and our sisters to the house of song? Return and tell the Mexica that we wait for what they will do."

The messengers went back to Itzcoatl.

"The Cuitlahuaca will not give the bodies of their sisters and their daughters," they reported.

"The men of Cuitlahuac are warlike," said Moteczuma and the rest of the council.

"Take them honeyed gruel and go again," said Itzcoatl smoothly.

"Itzcoatl sends for your sisters and your daughters to dance in the House of Song by day and by night," repeated the messengers, "and twenty rose bushes for our gardens."

"We wait for him," repeated the men of Cuitlahuac grimly.[10]

The council met again in Mexico-Tenochtitlan. They considered the strategy of an attack on Cuitlahuac, so near to the powerful Chalco whose decisions were always shifting and calculating. But there Coateotl still governed, the friend and relative of Moteczuma.

"Send messengers," commanded Itzcoatl, "and see what the Chalca will do."

The messengers spoke in smooth words to the Chalca.

"In planning this war we need to know whether you will

side with those proud and warlike men of Cuitlahuac, because in that case we must plan quite differently. We do not need much equipment for the Cuitlahuaca. But we would need a great deal to fight the Chalca, our equals in arms and valor."[11]

Coateotl had seen the vision of the rising power of Tenochtitlan. Not only friendship but political acumen dictated the answer from Chalco.

"We have seen the Cuitlahuaca building defenses—but we ourselves know nothing of this war."

Relieved, the messengers returned to Mexico.

Once more the council made its plans and Tlacaelel and Moteczuma proceeded to fulfill their function as leaders in the preparations, distributing obsidian-toothed clubs and spears, insignia and masks, shields and cotton armor, drums and wind instruments.

But for this war to bring girls to the house of dance and song, roses to Xochiquetzal, they did not go to the macehuales who worked the land in time of peace and fought in time of war. They went instead to the house of young men where the warriors were trained.

And the boys knew that this was not to be a mock war for their training, with a flint-tipped lance shorter than a real one.[12] This would be a war in which they could fight for prisoners and for honor—and for the girls who would live in the house of song, and come to their arms after midnight when the dancing was ended. In the school in each calpulli they took the weapons eagerly. Those ready and old enough to give their twenty blankets to their teachers and leave the school, those who were waiting impatiently for the command of the king that would release them, went gladly to this war.[13]

They went with their drums and their shrilling whistles along the shore, until across the lake waters they could see the island town of Cuitlahuac opposite them. As they filled the waiting canoes they shouted exultantly, and shouting and singing pushed off from shore, bright with plumes and insignia, young and excited, because their warfare for prisoners and for women was a lifting of roses to the Flower Plume, a dance for a goddess.

The Cuitlahuaca met them in their carved canoes, hidden behind sheltering shields and plumes, white and red and yellow and blue and green and black, a waving barricade of color.

The islanders met each other and they cried out to the water animals, the shrimp and the beetles and the snails and the water snakes. They wove spells and recited prayers as they fought in their canoes, the men of the lake calling on the animals of the lake to help them. Oars and throwing sticks and arrows floated on the churning water. There the wounded swam desperately and were seized as prisoners for the sacrifices. There the dead floated.

It was a boys' war and it was a boys' victory. Whatever might still be necessary to bring the gods of Cuitlahuac to Tenochtitlan,[14] this was the battle to be told in story and song, this day when the plume-decked canoes beat wooden and hollow against each other, and with the atlatl, flint-pointed, and the obsidian knives set in clubs, and the arrows flying, the islanders met each other, and the shouting, singing boys from school won their insignia of war, and the girls to whom they would come in the house of song.

For the prayers to the living things that moved in the lake were ended at last. And in their canoes the defeated Cuitlahuaca came with gifts of white fish and ducks and frogs. But their surrender gave more than these tokens.

"We will bring our sisters and daughters to the public place of dance and song of our young conquerers," they said. "We will plant our roses in Tenochtitlan."

The time of the falling of leaves came and the time of the hunters. The birds came down from the north and the late fall roses bloomed. It was the month of lovers. The songs of the young men sounded in the clear air,

"Thou art my beloved, a gift to me, my rich plume."[15]

Some sacrificed to Mixcoatl, god of hunters and of the

arrow and some to Xochiquetzal, Flower Plume, goddess of the house of song and the public women.

The women of the house of song pulled the women of good repute through the streets mocking them.

Up the steps of the pyramid young girls went to be sacrificed. Some went singing, and some went weeping.

And of the sacrifices of this month the people of Mexico-Tenochtitlan said,

"They are in memory of love."

X

The Balanced Dance of Power

THE DAYS WERE LONG SINCE GONE when the ruler of Tenochtitlan had barely enough to eat, when a newly elected Speaker-king was warned that he was offered not rest but work.[1] Now in remote magnificence Itzcoatl, the Obsidian Serpent, announced his favors through the council. The gracious word went forth to the defeated ruler of the Flower Fields.

"He may henceforth eat in my presence," said Itzcoatl.[2]

Beyond Xochimilco stretched the road to Cuauhnauac, clear now for cotton and fruit to come to the high country without interruption. The ties which had been close since a Cuauhnauac girl had been chosen by the tlatoani of Tenochtitlan became still closer. But the islanders remembered that Cuauhnauac was a far outpost of the old Tepanecan kingdom, once tied to Azcapotzalco by marriage and by tribute. Itzcoatl and his council waited their opportunity.

Finally messengers came over the mountain from Xiuhtepec. They spoke, seated on the ground, with eyes downcast before the king. The ruler of Cuauhnauac, they told him, had promised his daughter to the lord of Xiuhtepec. Gifts and festivals had celebrated the agreement. Then she had been given to another.

"You are strong. Your god Huitzilopochtli favors you.

Come and avenge us," begged the men from Xiuhtepec.

It was sufficient excuse. Gladly the allies from the high country marched down to the warm land of fruit. They closed in on Cuauhnauac from three directions, the men of Texcoco, Tlacopan, Cuauhtitlan, Tlatelolco and Mexico-Tenochtitlan working in a closely planned strategy. When the battle was over and the prisoners taken there was no question that the last of the Tepanecan tribute area was firmly under control.

The council met in Mexico-Tenochtitlan and discussed the cotton armor and blankets and blouses, the packets of paper, the fruit and the chilli that would come in tribute. They came to a decision. From the green valley where Moteczuma Ilhuicamina's mother and wife had lived the Mexica would take tribute for only two years. Whatever came afterwards to the lake country would come to Texcoco. There a special room would be set aside for envoys and tribute from Cuauhnauac.[3]

Even in Tlachco the final defeat was recognized. Hidden there in the town of the Ball Court with his priests and forecasters, the beaten Maxtla gave up hope at last. Word came to the lake country that he had died. On the ball court the evening star had set and gone down into the land of the dead.[4] The discord brought by Old Coyote, the Mischief Maker, the god who had set the Tepaneca against their neighbors and started wars in the world, was for the moment quieted.[5] Now Mexico-Tenochtitlan could turn to the works of peace.

Across the newly built causeway from Xochimilco and Coyohuacan traders and messengers came and went. Men from far cities were received with honor and in the outer rooms of the tlatoani's house were given food and rest. Cuauhnauac seemed near now, and even Moteczuma's sons began to be known—Citlalcohuatzin, Iquehuacatzin and Axicyotzin—and their names spoken with the respectful suffix, three sons of the same mother whose town had once seemed alien.[6]

Across the old causeway laborers came from Azcapotzalco, and slaves trudged to the island with halters across their necks. For thirteen days out of the two hundred and sixty

in the Count of Suns, they could remove their yoke. They looked forward to that day One Death. The rest of the time they labored without respite.[7] They carried heavy rocks and timbers for the construction of the pyramid platforms for the temples to the gods. Work went forward on the temple of Huitzilopochtli, god of war and warriors, who when they died would escort him in blazing splendor from the east to the zenith each day, who as hummingbirds would sip the honey of the sun. And work went forward on the temple of Cihuacoatl, Snake Woman, Our Mother, goddess of the women who died in childbirth—those women warriors who had taken a prisoner from the universe and had died in that battle, and who would lead the great Huitzilopochtli each day from the zenith to the west.[8] For death and life were war, and birth was death.

The Songs rose to the goddess:

"Our mother the warrior, our mother the warrior.
The sun has risen, the cry of war has sounded,
Let the captives be dragged away."[9]

With the end of the Tepanecan power at last assured, the final ceremonies to re-establish Nezahualcoyotl in his city of Texcoco could take place. No longer there by permission of a tyrant in Azcapotzalco, no longer fearful of rebellion in the towns subject to him, he could at last be tecuhtli and ruler according to the ancient Toltec ceremonies which his father had adopted.[10]

The nobles of the allied cities gathered for the festival. In splendor of plume and insignia they escorted him across the lake from Mexico.[11] Cuauhtlatoa, Talking Eagle, from Tlatelolco was among them.[12] The ruler of Tlacopan, heir to the Tepanecan tradition, but only briefly its defender, would share in the ceremonies. And Itzcoatl of Mexico-Tenochtitlan was chief among those who would install him in sure authority, seating him on the icpalli of his father.

The nobles of Texcoco met them at the edge of the lake. In due order they placed the blue robe on the Hungry Coyote and blue sandals upon his feet. And when the time came it was Itzcoatl who placed upon his head the band of lined and stiffened blue cotton like a crown.[13]

"Now Nezahualcoyotl has sat down in Texcoco," it was announced in the Aztec cities.[14] "And he has thrown down his woven mat and his seat everywhere."

The allies turned to the problem of dividing the tribute which had begun to pour in — the wooden baskets of corn and beans, the honey and the pottery bowls.

Once Coateotl, the singer of Chalco, had warned the Tepanecan towns about the impossibility of solving that problem peacefully. Now ruling in the one remaining valley town independent of the rising Tenochca power, he could see the city of his friend Ilhuicamina facing the inescapable necessity.

The allied rulers met and pondered the division of tribute and of land.

They ran a line across the lake, sighting by the mountains. The line ran north and south with a little zigzagging to avoid towns. It started near Xochimilco and touched the hill of Cuexomatl, and went on to the river of Acolhuacan. Then it went on to the hill of Xoloc and to another named Techimali and on to the country around Tototepec. East of the line would be territory belonging to Texcoco; west of it would be territory belonging to Tenochtitlan.[15]

But the kings of the two main cities knew that this was not enough to solve the problems that would arise. The Tepanecan realm had been widespread and strong. Conquered now, it would be sending troops to its conquerors' wars.

"It would be a pity to do away with a tradition from which so many heroes have arisen," said Nezahualcoyotl. "We could make Tlacopan our ally."

"We might start a fire greater than the first," warned Itzcoatl.[16]

But the threefold pattern of alliance that had gone on so long in the Valley of Mexico asserted itself again.[17] Tlacopan was recognized as an ally, not equal to the other two, but given the tribute of the towns in its area—from Mazahuacan, the deer country, and the country of the Otomis.

The division of tribute from the cities the alliance might yet conquer together had yet to be decided upon. All recognized that the inclusion of Tlacopan was a matter of political expediency and that she had no real power. It was agreed that she should receive only one fifth of the tribute. The rest should be divided equally between Texcoco and Tenochtitlan.[18]

Titles of honor would be given the rulers of the three cities—titles that would emphasize the backgrounds they were proud to claim. Nezahualcoyotl became Aculhua tecuhtli, Lord of the Aculhuaque, and the Great Chichimecatl Tecuhtli in accord with his investiture as a boy as heir to his father's titles and powers. Itzcoatl became the Culhua Tecuhtli, Lord of the Culhuaque, remembering the ancestors of the Mexica who took their wives from Culhuacan, heir of Tula. The ruler of Tlacopan took the title of Tepanecatl Tecuhtli, that the glory of the Tepanecan realm might not be lost to memory.[19]

The conference settled on a further thing—that Tenochtitlan should hold the military command. Already the teponaztlis and pipes of the people of Mexico-Tenochtitlan had sounded the song of Huitzilopochtli under the sun.

Tlatelolco did not appear as a member of the alliance. Close to the people of Mexico-Tenochtitlan, it had marched with them in the campaigns against the Tepaneca. But Talking Eagle and Obsidian Snake made no treaty until the year Eight Reed. Then the Tlatelolca went to Nezahualcoyotl to state their problem and have him help them solve it.

"Our fathers came to Tlatelolco—and it was populated only with grasses. No one was to be seen, not even signs that anyone had built a fire. We cast our nets here to fish, and we gathered small animals and water flies, and there were birds here. We took this place for our own, for our nets, to fish and to hunt.

"But now, these people that come around the lake, entering our dry land little by little, hunting—they say—something to eat—can it be that they do not eat the water birds and the tender greens? Are they eating other things?"

Nezahualcoyotl listened to the plea of those whose land was being eaten away. Only in the judgment of battle could an agreement be reached that both sides would declare just, that they would let stand unquestioned forever. In the marshes the Mexica from Tenochtitlan and the Mexica from Tlatelolco fought each other. At the end the men from Tlatelolco could sing with laughter,

"They came against us once with hard reeds and weapons of flint. They came forth to fight against those who were simple men of the lake and fishermen, but who had as chiefs the lords of Texcoco. The Tlatelolca took the Tenochca prisoners and carried them away with plumes to the sacrifice."

Nezahualcoyotl arbitrated the conference on the treaty. Once again the lines were sighted between the rocky hills that rose in the middle of the lake and the hill of Tepeyacac. Dry land and fishing rights were assigned to Tlatelolco, won in fair fight from Tenochtitlan. But it was to be a treaty of compromise.

"You must bend the head," said the Tenochca.

And Tlatelolco divided the marsh that there might be a channel and harbor for both to share.

When the conference was ended, each had yielded some rights on water and on land. Each had bent the head. They gave their word before the nobles of Texcoco and made a map to be guarded by three old men.[20]

Texcoco's turn was next to seek a balancing of the dignity and power of the lake cities. The Texcocans remembered that Nezahualcoyotl had been supported by the military skill of Moteczuma in the reconquest of their own city; and when at last he had come back to Texcoco to live, it was at the hands of Itzcoatl and Mexico-Tenochtitlan that he had been invested with authority. Were they then tributaries to Mexico-Tenochtitlan—they whose white-clad troops had closed in from Tepeyacac on the great city of the Ant Hill, and without whom Mexico-Tenochtitlan itself would not be free? The decision of blood must give the answer.

Itzcoatl understood and made the next step easy. Across the lake he sent twenty-five girls, daughters of those who had been given titles, girls of noble birth, bearing gifts of rich mantles and plumed insignia.

"Give them welcome. Let them rest," said Nezahualcoyotl.

Women instead of women's clothes had been sent by the Obsidian Serpent to his ally. Like a pattern of a dance once more the steps toward war were taken in their order. When the girls had rested Nezahualcoyotl called them into his presence.

"Return to Itzcoatl," he told them, "and tell him that he and I speak to each other not with women but with arms."

He gave them a gift to take back to Itzcoatl—a little gold snake, shaped with the cunning of the craftsmen who had come from Xochimilco to Texcoco. And the snake was coiled and biting itself.

"We understand each other well," he said.

The white-clad troops of Texcoco stood once more on the hill of Tepeyacac. Once more the drum signaled the start of battle.[21]

For six days they fought on the causeway and in canoes. They surged ever closer to the entrance to Mexico-Tenochtitlan. The Tlatelolca stood aloof, understanding that members of the alliance could feed the gods with blood and yet be one.

The names of the brave were known. The Texcocans knew the name of the Mexicatl who defended the entrance to the city and knew when he fell at the hands of a boy who was only a ration bearer. But the name of Moteczuma was not mentioned among them. He who had fought with them, did not fight against them now.[22]

At last the white-clad troops swept into the city and burned a temple in sign of victory.

Itzcoatl sent out old men to meet them.

"Look only at the white hair of your uncles," they said.

The dignity of the two cities had been put in equilibrium. All things were in order. Knit together by treaty and conquest the valley rested.

Itzcoatl took measures to shut out the memories and ideas from a time that had been different.

"Let the books be burned," he commanded. "Not all men are capable of interpreting them or appreciating them. Better that they be destroyed than that they fall into the hands of the ignorant. There is sorcery in them."[23]

And so the memory grew fainter of the things the ancient and newer books had contained, painted by the book makers with care, showing the way the calendar and the count of days were made and changed, the way the governing was done anciently in Tula and later in the days of Azcapotzalco's glory, and among the Chichimeca when they came into the valley, and among the Mexica when they came out from the slavery of Culhuacan and settled on the lake island. These things became a faint memory and a song:

> "The Mexica who escaped from the hands of the enemy,
> The ancient ones who went to the middle place of the water,
> Carried the books with them.
> Here where the reeds and grasses move whispering
> Timidly they settled under their own law."[24]

To safeguard the new order, the rulers of the alliance listened carefully for rumors of rebellion and proceeded diplomatically to cultivate the nobles of the conquered cities and the one city of the valley which was still independent.

Nezahualcoyotl in the year Eleven Rabbit went to Chalco, surrounded by Tepanecan nobles related to him. He sought out those who were his friends, the shining and courtly ones, close as the hairs on his breast. He talked with Coateotl about the purchase of equipment for war—the arrows and wooden drums that the carvers of wood could provide for him. And from all the divisions of Chalco from the lake shore to the lumber land on the uplands, the nobles gathered to transact business with the Tecuhtli of Texcoco.

In the year Thirteen Stone Moteczuma Ilhuicamina too went to Chalco and stayed with his friend Coateotl, directing the work on the arrows and carved drums which had been ordered there as equipment for war. They spoke of the danger of Tepanecan revolt against Tenochtitlan. And guardedly Moteczuma spoke to his friend about his desire to be out of the city in these days. If he said more about the murmur that was rising anew against him in Tenochtitlan now that Itzcoatl was reaching the end of his days, the words were kept between the two friends.[25]

In Tenochtitlan Itzcoatl, the Obsidian Serpent, called Nezahualcoyotl to him. A last time he tried to cement the alliance forever.

"Let there never be war between us," he said.

He called the nobles of his own city.

"Let the temple to Huitzilopochtli be built more sumptuously," he said. "And let sculptured rock hold the memory of my rule forever."[26]

They were his last orders. It was the year Thirteen Stone. And Mexico-Tenochtitlan mourned his death.[27]

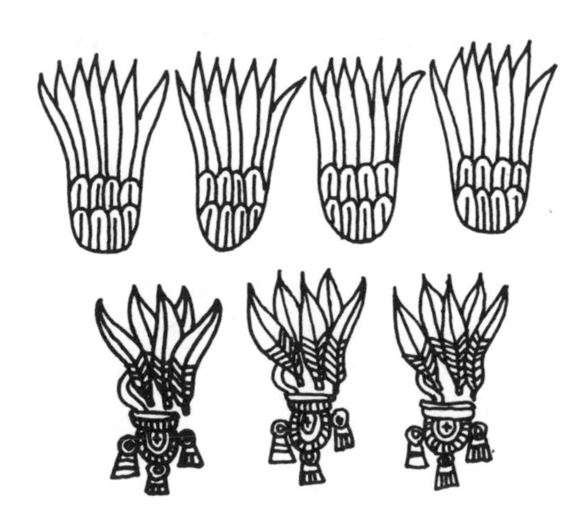

XI

The Band of Turquoise

WHEN THE EIGHTY DAYS of mourning were over, with their feasting and their gift-giving, Mexico-Tenochtitlan turned to the election of its new Speaker-king.[1]

"Moteczuma is not with the council," it was whispered in the city. "He has gone to Huexotzinco."[2]

The electors met without him. Tlacaelel called them to order and spoke the traditional words:

"Now the light that illumined us has gone out; the mirror in which we saw ourselves is darkened. But we must not remain in this darkness. Let another sun give brightness to our city. Who will follow in the footsteps of Itzcoatl? Who will defend what he has gained? Who will be the help of the orphan, of the widow, of the poor, of the little ones? Say what has impressed you and what you have seen in those who are leaders among us."[3]

The members of the council were there—three out of the four from whom the king must be chosen; the larger group of titled ones whose names were held in honor for bravery in the battles of Azcapotzalco and Coyohuacan; the old men distinguished in war and priestly service; the Speaker-kings of Texcoco and Tlacopan who must approve the choice.[4]

They sat gravely. Their words were careful and measured.

There could be no hurry, for all must agree at last.

They could choose from four, but they talked of two.

There was Tlacaelel, who had called them to order, long the spokesman for the king and council. They remembered his embassy to Azcapotzalco and his military leadership. Itzcoatl had seen him as the one to put in charge of arms in this city of war. He was one whom the people knew.

But Tlacaelel's own decision was firm.

"Better to be councillor than to be king," he said. "I can serve the city better so."[5]

Then there was Moteczuma Ilhuicamina, the grim Archer of the Skies.

He had refused the election once.

"I will provide the people their water and their food," he had said.

And in the years since then the city had become rich in tribute of corn and chilli and fruit, of cotton for clothing and for armor. He had been messenger to Texcoco, to Chalco—even in exile, to Tlaxcala and Huexotzinco—and help in the war of independence had come from other cities through him. He looked beyond the lake, and was known afar.

Some might think that this tlacatecatl, in line to be tlatoani, was too little known at home. His closest ties were in Cuauhnauac, the city of his mother and his wife. The old oppositions to him arose again.

"He is the brother of Tlacaelel," said some, and hardly knew him for himself.[6]

"Where is he now? Why is he not here?" said others.

His friends spoke for him.

"Perhaps he hides himself to escape so great a burden."[7]

They pointed out the qualities that would fit him for rule.

"He is brave and has fought in the wars. He can speak when it is necessary. Though he is severe, he is kind. All men know his sobriety and that he is never in danger of condemnation to death for drunkenness. Neither has he sought after many women and given himself to vice."[8]

The austere character of the Angry One, the Archer of the Skies, strong in the background if not in the foreground of so many recent events, tied to so many distant cities, loomed strong among them. When their own choice was clear to them they called on Nezahualcoyotl to speak his mind. His pleasure was apparent to them as he approved the choice of his friend.

"I know his valor and his skill in arms," he said.[9]

The council of those who were skilled in speech and in war found themselves at last of one mind. They listened to the final speech with approval, as a friend spoke for the absent tlacatecatl.

"Your words have been precious. They are like green chalchihuitl stones and rich jewels. Unless he should die soon and go into the shadows of death, Moteczuma will not forget you. If by good fortune he can stay in command of his city for some years—years that will go like a dream—he will reward you. And if by chance, since rule is slippery, and the harsh words and arrows of the envious and ambitious may make him forget, I will remind him. He has taken his place in the ball game, and you have put on him the leather gloves and the belt, that he may hurl back the ball that is thrown to him, for the business of rule is like a ball game."

The long speech continued, smooth in its phrases, sharp in its understanding of the dangers of the future. And sharply at last,

"And now, this man whom we have elected, will he turn back from his election? Will he hide himself? Will he fail to fulfill the word of our god and of the people? Is he wise enough? Does he know himself? Will he fulfill all that he must say and promise? I think not. Perhaps as time passes he will sometimes fall. That we do not know. That we cannot see. It is for us to pray. Go now and rest. You have done well."[10]

Over the mountains, down from the pines to the valley beyond the volcanoes, went the messengers to Huexotzinco. They came to Moteczuma.[11]

"You are worthy of being cherished more than all precious

stones, more than all rich plumes," they told him. "Our god has put you over us as our king. Itzcoatl has left you the burden which he carried on his shoulders like those who travel the roads. He cannot return. No one will see him here among those that are living or those that will be born. He did not hide his hands nor his feet beneath his mantle with indolence, but he has worked for his people.

"Now you possess the icpalli of your city. Yours is the burden of those who have gone before you. On your shoulders is the burden of a people, fickle and changing though they may be.

"Can you hide from this sentence? Can you escape? In what consideration do you hold the nobles who elected you? Take heart then, and shoulder the burden which you have been given."[12]

Moteczuma listened with eyes fixed upon the speaker. He turned his head neither to the right nor the left. His face was grave as the messenger went on:

"No one knows what our god may send that may make your rule brief as a dream. Perhaps wars will bring you defeat; perhaps the gods may send hunger and need to your people."

Back of the moment was the song of Huitzilopochtli, and the hunger of earth and sun for blood. The voice of the messenger went on:

"You are the image of our god and represent him. He rests in you and uses you like a flute. He speaks and sees in you."

And now the admonitions were given to him who would have the life and death of men in his hand:

"Do not use words jokingly, for jokes do not become your dignity. Do not be moved by the jokes and wit of others though they be your relatives and friends. As king you are as a god. Let your words be few and grave, for already you have a different being—you have majesty."

Quietly the new tecuhtli listened to the long oration:

"You walk a mountain road with a precipice on both sides. Do not give yourself to women for they are death to men. Better, as you turn on your mat sleepless, to think of your work; and sleeping, to dream of your burden. Men will envy you your bread, but it is the bread of sadness."

The king now was looking at the second speaker, who stood before him with his sandals removed and his mantle knotted on his shoulder in sign of humility.

"Oh king, more precious than precious stones, you are a tree in whose shade we rest. Take up your burden."

It was Moteczuma's turn at last. After this an orator would always be by his side. Now his words were brief.

"I am unworthy. What have they seen in me? It is certain that I do not even know myself nor understand myself. I do not know how to speak two words straight. But I know you have done me kindness in saying these things. They are like the words of a mother and father, not often spoken, and to be remembered always. Go and rest. You have done well."

The new tlatoani turned his steps toward Mexico-Tenochtitlan, ready for the ceremony on the pyramid before the temple of Huitzilopochtli.

The day was chosen carefully that the omens might be right. The priests studied the lord of the thirteen-day period to which it belonged, the lords of the day hours and of the night hours, the day sign and the bird. They settled on the day One Crocodile.[13]

"This carries good fortune and honor and food," they said.[14]

They thought of the lord of the thirteen-day period which One Crocodile began—Tonacatecuhtli, Lord of our Food, Lord of our Year, Lord of the hot country and the corn that grew there, Lord of fertility, with two ears of corn above his head and pleated paper and quetzal plumes. They remembered him as Cipactonal and Oxomoco, male and female, the ancient man and woman who dwelt in a cave near Cuauhnauac and who first began the count of two hundred and sixty days which still held the meanings of man's life.[15] Strange and appropriate that this day chosen to begin the rule of the Archer of the Skies should recall his promise of food for his people and the place where the count of his own days had begun, the green valley which was for him the beginning of time.

They considered the directional relationships of One Crocodile and saw that it was the day of the east, from which the sun came with flaming fire.[16]

They looked at the lord of the Day Hours and the lord of the Night Hours. Over both presided the ancient one, the Old God of the wrinkled face, Xiuhtecuhtli, god of fire.[17] He too was a god of time—of the turquoise year of three hundred and sixty days. He was patron of merchants who went to far lands down in the country of cotton and bright birds. And strange in its contradictions, the signs showed One Rabbit as his date name—One Rabbit, which as year bearer brought hunger, and as beginning of its thirteen-day week brought abundance.[18]

The priests balanced the good and bad implications of the count of days. The answer seemed clear.

"The signs are good," they decided.

And on the day One Crocodile Moteczuma Ilhuicamina and his new council took part in the ritual together. His two sons were chosen as tlacochcalcatl and tlacatecatl——Citlalcohuatzin and Iquehuacatzin.[19] A new title had been given to Tlacaelel. He would be Cihuacoatl, priest of the Snake Woman, powerful in ceremonial and political affairs, higher than the council itself.[20]

Over the plaza of Mexico-Tenochtitlan the procession moved. Stripped of the rich mantles of their rank the king and council went, humble and naked men, for a god to exalt. And they moved in a great silence.[21]

At the foot of the pyramid to Huitzilopochtli the procession halted. And there before the god they were robed in garments of those who would offer incense and pray and fast.

Over the king's shoulders they hung the cotton cloak of dark green, painted with the bones and skulls of dead men, for he too in time, like the silent throng on the plaza, must die. Over one shoulder they hung a gourd full of sweet-smelling herbs and in his right hand put an incense burner full of live coals with paper ornaments hanging from its handles like bright tassels. Before his face hung a mantle painted with a skull so that the god and the throng were alike invisible to him and death cloaked the living day. Guided by priests who took his arms on the right and left he climbed the great steps and stood before the wooden temple and the image.

Now with his robe drawn aside he sprinkled the sweet-smelling herbs on the live coals of the incense burner. With sharp points of tiger and deer bone he drew the blood of sacrifice from his ear lobes. And his prayers were to Huitzilopochtli, Hummingbird on the left, and to Tezcatlipoca, the Smoking Mirror:

"Do not hide from me the light and the mirror that must guide me."[22]

And to Xiuhtecuhtli, the Old God:

"I am a man of little reason and judgment to be placed among those who speak with thy voice and rule thy people that they may follow the will of the Old God, the father of all gods, the god of fire, who is in the battlemented water-pool circled with stones like roses."

From below the people watched silently as he moved the incense burner before the image of Huitzilopochtli. High above them the priests put upon him the insignia of a Speaker-king.

And now upon his head was placed the turquoise diadem of Tonacatecuhtli—lord of abundance, twofold lord of creation, who had once lived in a cave in Cuahnahuac, lord of fertility of men and earth, and measurer of time.

"No other king has worn the turquoise band of Tonacatecuhtli," marveled the watching crowd.[23]

They saw with wonder that it was Nezahualcoyotl who placed it on the head of their king.[24]

"Do we receive the crown from Texcoco?"

But some saw the significance of the action, remembering

that Nezahualcoyotl had received his own kingly insignia from Itzcoatl. Once more the firmness of the alliance, and the equality of the cities, was asserted, each giving authority to the other. The two friends stood together during the prayers to the gods of their own and the conquered cities.

And now the music of rejoicing crashed with wooden and windy splendor over the silent plaza as from the pyramid platform the wooden drums and the conch shells and the pipes sounded. Down the steep steps, guided by priests to right and left, came Moteczuma Ilhuicamina, wearing the turquoise diadem. Behind him came his council, but he walked in a great loneliness, for the people dared not lift their eyes to look at him as he passed.[25]

And he went from the crowded plaza to the house of penitence and fasting.

XII

Friends at War

THE FOUR DAYS of fasting were finished. The day set by the priests for the inaugural festival had come.[1] Moteczuma Ilhuicamina watched the rejoicing in the streets and canals of the island city, and the dancing groups from afar that with rhythmic dignity celebrated before the temple of Huitzilopochtli the election of the new Tlatoani, the new Colhau Tecuhtli. He gave rich gifts of plumes and mantles and jewels to each group. The principal lords, invited from both friendly and unfriendly towns, were seated before him in their order on low chairs and mats made by the weavers of reeds who adored the gods of netmaking. And they drank rich cocoa from pottery jugs.

Day and night the solemn dance and song went on. Then it too ended and over the lake by canoe and causeway the weary visitors went away. The new Speaker-king faced the days to come alone.

Alone except for the half-brother who now stood as his counsellor and support, speaking with military authority and with the authority of the Warrior Mother Cihuacoatl, fighter priest and spokesman for the silent, austere king who wore the turquoise diadem.

They faced together the problem of bringing the alliance again into balance. Moteczuma had taken his turquoise diadem from the hand of Nezahualcoyotl. Was Mexico-Tenochtitlan a tribute city to Texcoco? There was again one way to make the answer clear for the people and for the record. Yet the last request of Itzcoatl had been, "Let no war come between our cities." And Nezahualcoyotl had spoken to his own people:

"Take care that no occasion for war arises. Treat with courtesy all whom you meet on the roads. Flee from their enmity, for you know their fame in war. Be in peace—especially let the travellers and traders take care, for they are the ones who walk the roads to far places to seek their living. We who stay at home have no cause to trouble anyone. We who are the principal ones will not bring war. Do not let it come through the shortsightedness of the poor and ignorant."[2]

He went across the lake to pay a formal visit to Moteczuma, and was seated in honor at his side. Within the hearing of the Mexican nobles he spoke the words that might balance his action in bestowing the turquoise diadem on the ruler of their city.

"We come under your shadow. You are a great ahuehuetl tree beneath whose shade we find the freshness of your love. Let there never be war between us. Receive us without war."

No longer could the two friends speak together in quiet solitude. Tlacaelel and Moteczuma together now must decide the path of their city. Moteczuma listened to the stern reminder of his brother.

"You are under obligation to bear the burden of a king, to widen the borders of your house, to extend your domain."[3]

To the people of Tenochtitlan it was not clear which man led in making the final decision, for the two were ever as one.

"We will go with the power of the Mexica, the dwellers in the lake in the midst of the reeds and the grasses. We will burn a house of their god," said Moteczuma.[4]

"Let peace be only on one condition—that we do not yield our authority," said Tlacaelel.[5]

Nezahualcoyotl agreed. He too had been in this position

after his coronation by Itzcoatl, and knew the necessity of the formal action. Friendship between two men was not enough to avert it. But friendship could temper it.

"We will make a smoke signal in the marshes; we will go to the border between our cities. And when we arrive there we will burn the temple and all the Mexica will see this," announced Moteczuma.

With double meaning Nezahualcoyotl replied,

"At the border of our land I will fulfill the wish of Moteczuma the king and Tlacaelel the priest of the Snake Woman. I, who receive young fruit trees and magueys from Cuauhnauac, am content."

They met at Ixtapalapa at the foot of the hill of the new fire. They fought the feigned war from town to town. And with his own hand Nezahualcoyotl set fire to a temple, in token of surrender.

The shouts rose among the Mexicans;

"Let the battle cease. It is finished."

And Nezahualcoyotl repeated,

"Let the battle cease. You have your desire."

The word went back to Moteczuma in the city of Mexico Tenochtitlan.

"Everything is well ordered," he said.[6]

Ordered now so that the Mexica could help Nezahualcoyotl build his houses in Texcoco without shame, knowing that once they had fought their way to the entrance of his city.[7] Ordered so that the Texcocans could come without shame to help in the great public works of Tenochtitlan remembering that once they had gone there as victors. And in each city they spoke only of their own victory.[8]

Only the Chalca spoke sardonically.

"Nezahualcoyotl arranged his own defeat. The war lasted half a day, and the Texcocans went home for lunch."

Moteczuma turned his attention to his obligations to carry on the building of the temple of Huitzilopochtli—to see that the gods were fed with blood and the fifth sun did not fail.

"Let us send messengers to Azcapotzalco, Coyohuacan, Xochimilco, Cuitlahuac, Mixquic, Culhuacan, and Texcoco, asking them to send light stone and heavy stone, and to send workmen to build a great pyramid to lift higher the temple of the god."

"It is fitting that the temple be built," agreed Tlacaelel. "But let us invite the lords of those cities to come here. Then we can be sure that the invitation to work will be given in terms that we wish and not confused by weary messengers. Then we can better assign the work to each city."

Moteczuma Ilhuicamina spoke humbly.

"It is true that I am king, but I cannot command in all things. We both have to rule the city.[9]

According to the plan of Tlacaelel, priest of the Warrior Mother, the word went forth. The rulers of the conquered cities and of Texcoco assembled. Tlacaelel spoke for the silent soldier king.

"You are the adopted children of Huitzilopochtli," he said.[10]

The men from the cities of the burned temples listened respectfully as he spoke of the need for a greater temple in Tenochtitlan.

"We should build it high, with room enough for the sacrifices," he concluded.

Nezahualcoyotl took the lead in replying, the ally and friend who could meet the request without loss of dignity.

"Tlacaelel and the great king Moteczuma," he responded, "this command gives us happiness. It is right and good that we are beneath the favor and help of Huitzilopochtli, happy in his shadow as in the shade of an ahuehuetl tree. It is right that we do this thing."

The lords of the lake towns went home to give orders for light stone and heavy stone for the temple of the god of warriors, for the sun that must not go out.

Moteczuma's thought went out to Coateotl in Chalco. He spoke again to Tlacaelel.

"Let us send messengers to Chalco—not with fiery words, but with compliments, not commanding them but begging them with humility to send rock for sculptures to adorn the temple of Huitzilopochtli. If they listen to us, they are friends."

Tlacaelel raised no objection.

"Let the messengers go. If the Chalca accept, it would be gratifying to us. If not, it does not matter."

The word that came back was brief. Coateotl, friend of Moteczuma though he was, now spoke for the dignity of Chalco.

"Who will command the macehuales to carry rock for the Tenochca?"

"You have done well. Rest awhile," replied Moteczuma automatically to the messengers.

He consulted with Tlacaelel.

"Let us not send the messengers again," he suggested.

"Is this a new generation of Tenochca?" Tlacaelel asked.

The silent warrior king yielded.

"Since this is what you wish, let the same messengers go again. You know what is best, my brother."[11]

The ordered steps toward war repeated themselves. A second time, according to custom, the messengers went to Chalco.

"Are we slaves?" asked Coateotl.

"What shall we do?" asked Moteczuma of his brother. "I am king, but you are guide."[12]

The scouts brought back word that the Chalca were armed and waiting. Through the city of Tenochtitlan again sounded the call to war. Moteczuma's sons, tlacatecatl and tlacochcalcatl in the new government, went to the different calpulli, distributing arms and recruiting men. The boys training in the schools were called to fight by the side of older men, to take their prisoners, and to win their honors.[13] The encouraging voice of Tlacaelel spoke for the king to the warriors:

"The Chalca are not lions and tigers. They are men with the same arms that we carry. This is the hour!"

Day broke on the camp of the Mexica pitched at Ixtapalapa. The Chalca and the Mexica met on the plain between Colhuacan and Cuitlahuac. When night came the Chalca called for a truce.

"This is not a battle of one day. We will fight for many days here. Let us return now to our houses and our rest. Tomorrow, with daylight, we can meet again. Here we will await you."

That night in Tenochtitlan the soldier king gave his orders and mapped his strategy.

"Let our watchers and listeners go now to all the conquered cities," he said, now in clear command. "See that no call goes out to them from Chalco. Set guards everywhere."

The scouts went to the conquered Tepanecan towns, and even to Texcoco. But their streets were silent. No fighters were gathering.

"Let the scouts go out again every five days," commanded Moteczuma.

The news spread that Moteczuma himself had gone into the field to inaugurate his reign with the blood of sacrifice.[14] Not since Tlacaelel had urged Itzcoatl to keep the perspective and dignity of distant command had this happened.

Day after day the Chalca and the Mexica fed the gods with blood. This was no mock war between the two powerful cities of the lake.

At last the feast day came again when the Chalca would honor Camaxtli Mixcoatl, god of the hunt.

"Let us take a five day truce," said the Chalca.

"It is well," said the Mexica. "By this our god Huitzilopochtli will also be served.[15] We too will sacrifice our prisoners and lay them on the fire."

Thus to the old God of Fire the Mexica sacrificed the Chalca.

When the truce was finished even young boys of twelve were recruited in Tenochtitlan.

"They can carry supplies and arms; they can bring rope to tie the prisoners," said Tlacaelel.

At midnight at the end of the fourth day of the truce, the Tenochca marched swiftly again to await daybreak and battle with the Chalca.

"Our festival lasts for twenty days," they shouted. "We need more prisoners."

The shouting armies met again. Again earth and sky, hungry for blood were fed, and prisoners were taken to be offered before the temples. The blood ran on the steps of the pyramids. On hot coals in Tenochtitlan the flesh of the prisoners was roasted, by command of Tlacaelel. Solemnly the roasted flesh was eaten in the common feast of god and man, and the sacrifice of Moteczuma's coronation finished.[16]

They went back into battle strong in faith and courage. Once more the armies clashed. In the high, cold air of the hills the battle raged anew. The snow of the Smoking Mountain was above them, gleaming white where the clouds parted. In the lake-bordered city of Chalco itself there was fighting too. And some of the people from Cuitlahuac fought there for their friends, with division of allegiance in their own conquered city.[17]

At last the people of the Tlalmanalco section of the realm of Chalco accepted their defeat.

"We will bring you timbers for your buildings, and stone, and carved canoes."

"We take no more vengeance," agreed the Mexica.

The city of Chalco itself still stood in its freedom and ancient dignity. But in Tenochtitlan the war was counted a victory, for Tlalmanalco had been taken, and from Cuitlahuac the conquered god would come at last to the city where Cuitlahuac girls were already dancing in the House of Song.

Only in Cuitlahuac it was said,

"How quickly would our sons be conquered completely if Mixcoatl were far from us! It is another image we have sent to Tenochtitlan of another god, alike in mask and attributes. But Mixcoatl is still here."[18]

And in Chalco, though they mourned the loss of the hill town, they waited for another time.

The sun shone on the streets and canals of Tenochtitlan and upon a people content with the ending of a war. Land was given to the brave and to their sons. A man who burned incense came to tell of a comrade who had died in battle seeking honors and lands for his children.

"Let his son be founder of the noble line of Tepotzotlan," said Moteczuma Ilhuicamina.[19]

No one but the king noticed—or thought worth painting into the books of the Mexica—the news that came in the year Four Stone that Coateotl was dead.

"They set fire to his house and made him come out. They tied his hands and feet. They beat him to death. They killed him brutally, cruelly, ferociously."

Moteczuma, to whom his subjects could not lift their eyes, heard the messenger through. The words from Chalco were careful, even kind.

"One does not know for sure why they have done this. Perhaps it was because he was a friend of Moteczuma. One does not know."[20]

XIII

Roads of Hunger

MOTECZUMA ILHUICAMINA, the stern tlatoani of Tenochtitlan, walked with the other two kings in a festival procession.[1] There was rejoicing from Tepechpan to Texcoco and on the hill of Tezcotzinco where already the water was running sun-warmed over rock channels to the pools where Nezahualcoyotl bathed, and where the gardeners had planted trees and flowers.[2]

With them walked a girl with honest eyes[3] going to her husband. The blessing of the allied cities was on her marriage to the king of Texcoco, and their rulers had come to put the stamp of their authority on the marriage that would provide the heir to the icpalli of Texcoco.

If there were murmurs of suspicion that she had been widowed so soon after Nezahualcoyotl had seen her, and even before she was of an age to be claimed as wife by the husband in whose house she was growing up, the suspicions were not spoken in this hour. No one suggested that Nezahualcoyotl had given the order for her husband's death.[4]

Innocent and young, with honest eyes, the girl walked to her wedding. Not one of the many concubines who had already borne sons to the king, but the chosen one who should bear the son who would inherit. The wife approved by three kings, and loved by one.

And the friend who had walked with Nezahualcoyotl at the funeral of Tezozomoc, walked now in the freedom of Texcoco, up the hill, through the gardens overlooking the shining waters of the lake.

Sprinkled with yellow powder like pollen because she was very young, the girl heard the words addressed to her:

"Now you are numbered among the old. Now you have left your youth behind. Put away the customs of your childhood. Greet those whom you wish."

And the girl with the honest eyes replied,

"You have done me a kindness, all you who have come. You have made your heart kind for my sake."[5]

After the marriage knot was tied in their garments the festival of rejoicing continued for four months.

The soldier king from Tenochtitlan watched the grace of the Texcocans, walked in the gardens on the hill of Tezcotzinco, and attended the gatherings in the great house of Cillan, the royal house in Texcoco itself. There he watched the conquered goldsmiths from Xochimilco bring their finest golden animals for approval, and the featherworkers their shields, and the singers their songs of great deeds. He heard Nezahualcoyotl himself sing with a dark sense of time and change and death behind the rejoicing,

"The flowers will die among the ahuehuetl trees."[6]

The stern one went back to Tenochtitlan. There the great pyramid platform for the temple of Huitzilopochtli rose higher. The conquered cities of the lake shore sent stone and workmen. It was a time of rest from war. Only the struggle with earth and weather for food went on. In that struggle no calling of the calpulli to arms could help.

In the year Six Rabbit grasshoppers ate the crops in the valley. In the year Seven Acatl they came again. The beans and corn of the chinampa gardens and the high shoreland were destroyed.[7]

In that year, when winter came, the snow that was always high on the circling mountains fell even in the valley. A second year the snow fell. The early crops were gone. And with the melting snow on the mountains the summer rains came to add to the already swollen waters.

Men worked in the lands of each calpulli with fear and doubt of the future. In Tenochtitlan they watched the lake rise higher and higher and come at last into the very houses of the island city.[8] From canoes and rafts the fleeing people surveyed the damage in despair.

"We will send to Nezahualcoyotl, who is wise," said Moteczuma.

The friends consulted.

"We will build a dike," decided Nezahualcoyotl.

It would cut the lake in two so that the rising waters of of the salt portion would not pour into the fresh water around the island city. Already the fallen houses and flooded land between the canals pointed to the desperate necessity. The shore cities joined in the fight against the rising water, bringing heavy logs from the mountains and rocks to build the dike.

Far out from shore nobles and macehuales worked side by side. Moteczuma and Nezahualcoyotl put their own hands to the task, remote no longer, but men small against the far surface of lake water, struggling for the lives of their people, and one with them.

Over the lake water sounded the beat of a drum and a merry voice singing. Along the dike, dark with straining men, a startled question ran.

"Who sings?"

And with it another question—

"Who is drunk at such a time?"

Moteczuma stood on the structure of timber and stone and listened to the singing. The beat of the drum and song floated across the water—a man singing and singing, playing and playing, while others worked and sweated. Was it a voice he had heard before?

"Who sings?" demanded the Speaker-king.

The answer came with reluctance, with truth.

"It is your brother—Zacan."

Zacan who had danced the slow dance of acceptance of war in Coyohuacan with him, who had served him already for a period as tlacatecatl, the high-spirited companion of his household who worried only about his little sick son.

But now he went singing, perhaps drunk, while other men worked. And the penalty for drunkenness was death.

Moteczuma breathed heavily in his anger.

"What will men say when they hear as far away as coast country that men have come here to work and seen us put to shame by this lazy one?"

His words came from his anger, and from his obligation as Speaker of the law.

"Let him die. Let his house be burned."

And he who had gone singing and singing, died in his burning house.

"This order was from the lips of his older brother. It was he who gave the order," marveled the men working on the dike.

With stern desperation the work went on, with no song and no laughter.[9]

Men worked for safety against the rising water, against the mixing of the salt water and the fresh. For the lake that gave food now gave only hunger and death. The fish and the frogs and the water flies floated dead on the surface of the water.[10]

At last the dike was finished, more than nine miles long and eleven arm-spreads wide.[11] Made with two parallel walls of logs, with the space between filled with rock and sand, it was built to stand through many fifty-two year cycles, if indeed at the end of one of the cycles the gods did not die and the stars come to earth and the works of man in this fifth sun end in destruction. Now when the gray summer rains wrapped the high country, the streets and houses of Tenochtitlan would not be flooded.

But even Moteczuma, calling on his friend Nezahualcoyotl for plans and ideas, and on the towns of the lake shore and beyond for builders and materials, did not have the power to assure his people food.

The snow fell again for five days and lay knee deep where snow had never fallen before.[12] Houses in the island city collapsed beneath its weight and old people died with cold and sickness.[13] The young corn was frozen for three years.[14]

"The gods are angry," said the priests.[15]

In the year Twelve Stone the sun itself was darkened. During the eclipse people cried out with fear and drew blood from their tongues that the sun might live again. In the temples the blood of white-haired men and albinos was offered to the gods.

"For now is this sun ended, and the darkness will last forever," they cried.[16]

Work was pushed forward on the temple of Huitzilopochtli. But when the call went out for workmen, Moteczuma could promise only one meal a day to be given when the day's work was done.[17]

An occasional battle with the Chalca provided blood for the god himself, who in these sparse days must hunger like men.[18]

The Feast of the Lords came in the year Thirteen House. Out from Tenochtitlan to the other towns went the appeal for food. What could be spared was sent. The rich opened their storehouses to the poor, and Moteczuma himself gave of what he had. At dawn the people drank corn atole. But it was cold that day and as they sat on the ground picnicking they wrapped their blankets about themselves and shivered. The talk that should have been happy like the twittering of birds was sad.

They reached out eagerly for tamales made of the ground dried corn. Hungry ones pushed into the line. But when the tamales were finished the hungry people still waiting cried out,

"What shall we do? The feast is ill fated this year. Our children are hungry."

For it was the feast of the young corn and the young ears

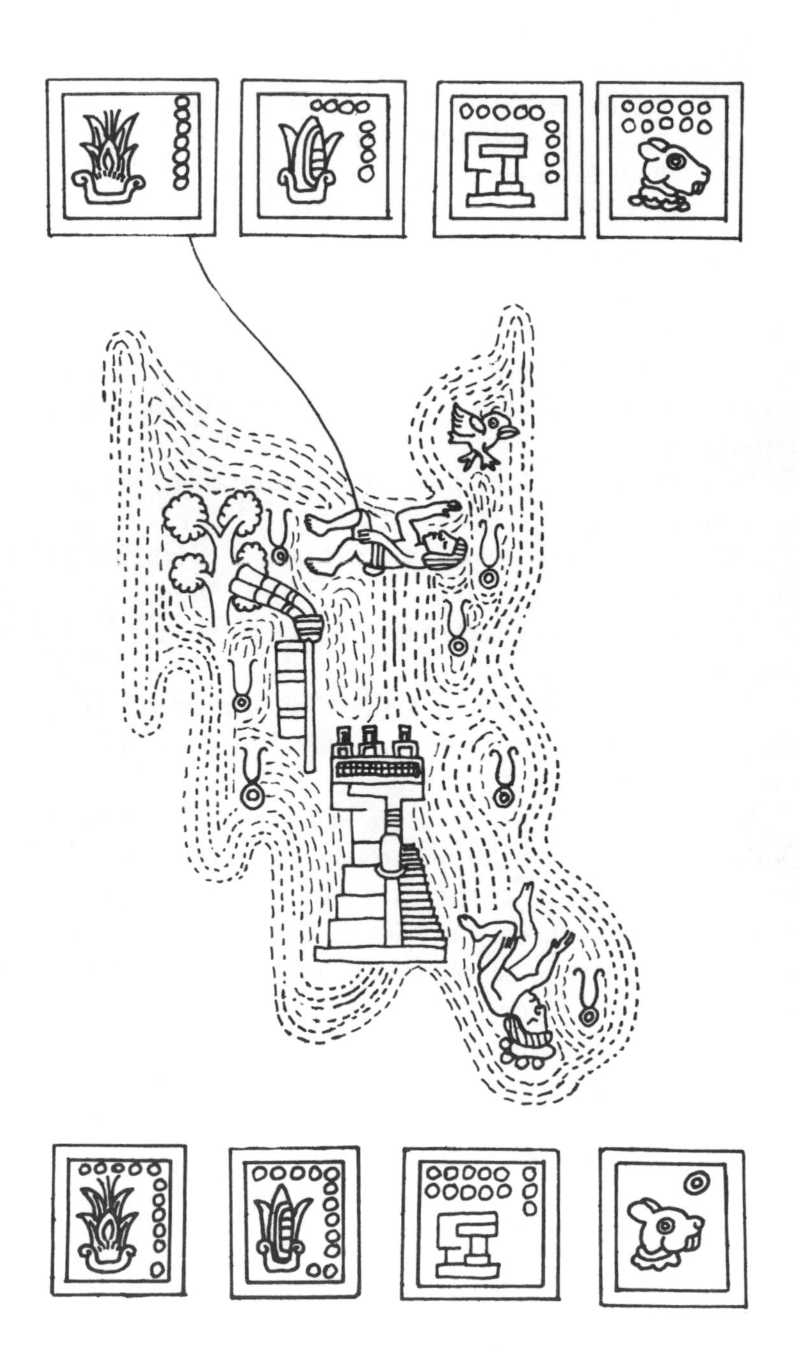

were already frozen. There was ice in the lake. The heat of the sun seemed gone forever.[19]

At night Moteczuma danced in firelight while the young men sang and the earth-drum beat—an austere dance of prayer, a dance for fertility, with the women from the house of song. As once Chimalpopoca had danced in this festival thinking of his death, the king danced now, and death was on the land, and the young corn was freezing while he danced.[20]

Day and night the feast went on. Now a girl ran to the four parts of the city. Tassels of precious quetzal feathers hung from her head like the precious tasseled corn. Her sandals were scarlet like chilli. The woman sang to her and the warriors danced to her in a twisting course like a snake. And her name was Seven Snakes and Precious Chalchihuitl Stone. Her name was Xilonen for she was like the young ear of corn—she walked delicately and tenderly like the young corn.[21]

"Oh Seven Ears of Corn, rise up, awake!
You leave us now, you go to the house of Tlaloc.
Rise up, awake,
You leave us now."[22]

She walked in the daybreak, dark and lovely with scarlet sandals, up to the temple of the corn god. To the god of corn and the god of rain her heart was offered in a blue bowl.[23]

And the young corn froze in the fields.

In that year Thirteen House, earthquake shook the high country and the hills danced.[24] Cracks opened in the fields. The sequence of crops that knit the loose earth of the chinampa gardens did not hold them now, and the gardeners stood helpless to see the made-land break up, and earth once flooded crumble dry into the water, back to the floor of lake and canal from which it had laboriously been dredged. The crops were gone and the land itself was being taken away.[25]

"The hills are full of water," said Nezahualcoyotl, and near his houses at Tezcotzinco men worked to bring it in. They built aqueducts skirting the hill, and they brought it to the king's gardens and to the farms where simple people lived.

"It is yours, for you have brought it in. It is brought with the strength of young men, so that even women may work with it, and children may drink it. No one may take it from you—but Huexotla may ask for a little.[26]

In Tenochtitlan the aqueduct which had brought water to the city since old Tezozomoc had granted it to his grandson Chimalpopoca now brought barely enough to drink.

Moteczuma called his friend again from Texcoco.

"In Chapultepec there is water," he said.

From the caves where the little Tlalocs stood ready to pour it from their jars, it might be brought to parched fields. There indeed legend said that a Toltec had found corn under the water.[27] They agreed on another great public work and Nezahualcoyotl, speaking for Moteczuma, summoned workmen to bring sweet water through a larger channel to the growing city.[28]

"But the water will not come this year," said the despairing Mexica. "Another Rabbit year comes, with famine."

And then it was the year One Rabbit, and there was no seed corn. The Mexica no longer went to the fields.[29] On the skirts of the hills Chalca and Mexica had no strength, and the fighting stopped.[30]

From Moteczuma's store houses in tribute towns from around the lake came twenty canoes of tamales each day and ten of corn gruel already made and ready for the weakened people. But the canoes did not carry enough. Men went out with nets to get the lake foods, but even then the people went hungry.

Moteczuma consulted with Tlacaelel.

"Let us send out messengers beyond the mountains and see where there is food."

They went out for many miles and came back with word of dried fields and trees. Even the prickly pear cactus drooped yellowing in the hot and rainless land and did not give its fruit to men.[31]

From the rich land of Chalco where corn had been stored

in earlier days, people went into the woods on the hills hunting for roots. And there they died and the buzzards circled slowly and came down.[32]

The scouts who had gone out seeking a green land came back to say that by the sea of the great sun the Totonaca had food and to spare. And from the hot country Totonac traders came with corn. Nevertheless, the amount they could bring was small, and Moteczuma watched the young men and the young girls become wrinkled as if with age.

Carefully he rationed what corn there was. He issued orders:

"He who takes an ear of corn even from his own field, if one grows there, will be put to death."[33]

The Feast of the Lords came again. Moteczuma stood among his people grouped for their ration of corn and beans and atole. The poor waited for what could come to them from the stored grain of the rich, knowing that even this was gone.

"Eat once more," said the king.

Tamales, each one big enough to satisfy a man's hunger, were passed out to the waiting people. From the canoes the atole was ladled, the corn gruel for the women and the children. They were given rich cocoa, brought by traders from the country of the great sun. When all had eaten the king spoke again.

"You know that there is nothing left of the stored food, and that the land cracks in the drought. For this we cannot blame enemies we can conquer. This comes to us from the sky and earth, from the woods and the caves of the winds."

The people wept, knowing that what he said was true.

"Now go where you will to distant country where food still grows. Let your children go there, knowing that if you sell them into slavery you will have food in exchange and they will be cared for, and can eat and drink."

The poor and the starving sold themselves to the rich—some even to the people of Chalco and the shore towns, others over the mountains to the people of Tlaxcala and Huexotzinco, or to the people of Tolucan or to the Couixca, who paid tribute to Cuauhnauac.[34] They sold themselves for a measure of grain —some more, some less.

The Totonaca, up from the hot country, drove hard bargains.

"A basket of corn for this baby—and when you buy him back you will pay for all that he has eaten and drunk."

Moteczuma issued new orders.

"Let the prices be fixed and no man sell himself for too little."

Then a young girl sold for four hundred ears of corn and a young man for five hundred.[35] Families wept as they were separated, and in a long line the Mexica, wearing the wooden yoke of the slave upon their necks, started the weary march down to the country of the Totonaca in the land of the great sun.[36] Some went not as slaves but as free men, to settle in that green coastal land.[37] But slaves and free men fell for very weakness under the blaze of the sun. The earth itself in that heat seemed to rain fire.[38]

In the woods for heat and hunger and thirst people crawled into a hole to die—it did not matter where. And there was none to bury them. Coyotes gnawed on the dead in the very streets of Chalco, and the buzzards gorged themselves.[39]

Moteczuma called the other two kings of the alliance for a conference. They agreed on a plan of colonization to the south in the land of the Mixteca.[40] Speaking for Moteczuma, Tlacaelel laid out the procedure.

"Let seventy families go from Texcoco and seventy from Tlacopan. Let the Chalco towns and Xochimilco, builders and craftsmen and farmers, supply as many as they can. Here in Tenochtitlan we will try to get six hundred families together."

When they had gathered in Mexico-Tenochtitlan Moteczuma himself spoke to them.

"Do not weep for leaving home. You go to a rich land, and you will be free from all obligations of tribute. We will have your neighbors there bring you jars and plates and grinding stones and help you build your houses. Be comforted."

The people spoke humbly—

"To die here or there is still to die."

"You will settle with your friends around you—the people from each town together. You will not be among strangers. I will send a governor with you, and the order in your towns will be the same as here in Mexico-Tenochtitlan. If you are attacked we will send you defense."

They went across the causeways and over the mountains. Ahead of them messengers went each day so that at the end of the day there would be shelter and food waiting for the women and children. And the people of the lake country in the high valley waited for word from them.

Word was coming back from all the roads of hunger.

Those who had gone over the mountains through the valley of Cuauhnauac to the country of the Couixca had been sacrificed.

"Twenty in one place, ten in another," came the report.[41]

"And they were slaves who had been bought, not prisoners won in a good war," mourned the Mexica.

Those who had gone to the Totonac country also would not come again. Stricken with disease in that land of heat and slow green rivers they died there. And some who had served the time for which they had sold themselves, and some who had gone as free men to find corn in those fertile fields, struggled homeward to their parched high country carrying corn and beans to their families, and fell, shivering with fever and sick, on the way, and died still tied to the loads of food which they carried on their backs and would never bring home. Over the trails of heat and sorrow the buzzards circled.[42]

The Mexica spoke with new words. When they wished to say *to starve* they said now *to rabbit*; when they said *to die of disease*, the word that all understood was *to totonac*.[43]

Those in the hot country who had not started home again heard of the fearful road.

"Better to stay here, for who knows whether we could reach home, and who knows how often such hunger as this might strike there again in a Rabbit year?"

Those who had gone down past the Tlaxcala country to beg fields near the market town of Tepeacac had been met with suspicion. Word came back of fighting to be calmed before they could sow beans and chilli.[44]

But those who had accompanied the colonists to the country of the Mixteca came back with good news for Moteczuma. The movement of families together had not been feared like the movement of an army. They had met with welcome and friends. People had come from the towns around Coaixtlahuaca on the Plain of Serpents[45] to help them build their houses, and had brought them gifts. The colonists had danced in festivals there in the south where they had placed their cooking stones and their grinding stones.

In the lake towns the hot dust still blew under the angry sun and the buzzards walked in the streets.

"The gods hunger for blood," said the priests.

Again the war in Chalco flared and prisoners were brought back to Tenochtitlan.[46]

But now men remembered the Wars of Flowers when the fighting was a game and the joy was of sacrifice. Even the war with the Chalca had once been carried on for nine years, as a game near Colhuacan. And once there had been a war of flowers between the Tlacochcalca and the Chalca.[47] Wars not for conquest then but for food to give the gods. They remembered too the Rabbit years in Tula when the children of Huemac the king were sacrificed, and the blood of men had replaced the old offerings of snakes and birds and butterflies.[48]

The kings of the lake cities met. With Moteczuma was Tlacaelel, wearing the turquoise diadem like his brother, for now his commands were those of authority, and when he walked he too wore the king's insignia.[49]

"There must be another war of flowers," they decided, "so that we may have food for the gods, and food again for men.

Let us have enemies within the house—enemies who are friends."

Nezahualcoyotl put in a quiet warning.

"Let them not be of our own families. I have heard that in Tenochtitlan one man has given five children to be sacrificed."[50]

A young man from Tlaxcala who often visited Nezahualcoyotl and who in his own city was rising to prominence solved the problem.

"It can be a formal war between Tlaxcala and the towns of your alliance. We can be the enemies within the house," suggested Xicotencatl.

It was agreed.

"This war can be a market where the gods may find food," concluded Tlacaelel.

Monthly the warriors met, and the captives were offered on the pyramids.[51]

In Tenochtitlan Moteczuma watched for clouds to gather on the mountain ridge of Tlaloc, for rain to come to the cracked and barren land. Prayers rose to Tlaloc, god of water and of rain, in whose green land corn and beans grew:

"Now is a time for tears.
With the rattle of mist, water is drawn from the land of Tlaloc."[52]

Small dough images of the mountains stood on trays in every house—Smoking Mountain in the center and the others around it. Faces were drawn on each one, for, like the stars and the skies, the mountains were living and holy.[53] Seeded dough was placed on crooked snake-shaped planting sticks, cut from mountain trees.

In that festival to Tlaloc those were remembered who had drowned in the lake during the building of the dike in time of flood, and while seining for the little food that of late in time of drought the lake had given, shrunk as it was between foul-smelling mud-flats. The god of water knew them in the land of the unknown, the land of the how, the land that was forever a question. And in Tenochtitlan their images of dough and seed stood beside those of the mountains.

"Send me to the unknown land.

I shall go, for now is a time for tears."[54]

The dough images of the mountains and of the dead were offered in the temple and dismembered there with an obsidian knife as though they were sacrificial victims. And each man took the pieces home and dried them on the rooftops and ate them. Food had been given to the gods, and divine food to men.

"It is not enough," said the priests.

Four women died that day for Tlaloc the rain god—four women who represented the divinity of the four mountains. And two sisters died who were Hunger and Plenty. In each calpulli a little of their flesh was eaten in solemn rite.

From the sacrificial stone on top of the pyramid platform four priests flung corn to the four directions and to the Year Bearers: Reed to the east, House to the west, Stone to the north, and Rabbit to the south—black, white, yellow, and many-colored corn. Black corn fell to the wild and open country, and white toward the sown fields that in this time men had not had the heart to sow again, yellow toward the lake, and red to the irrigated land of the south. As the people danced the mist rattles called the rain.

Moteczuma watched the clouds form and fail on the mountain peaks in the distance. Gods and men had eaten, and death would be life.[55]

"It is not enough. We must go to the mountains themselves," he said at last.

Into the canyon beyond Coatlichan, up through the dry timber of the mountains the trails led—up to the shadowing pines on the mountain of Tlaloc. The shrunken waters of the lake were far below, the silver and green of it a memory of the Jade Skirt of Chalchihuitlicue. And to Tlaloc of the water and rain and thunder and lightning, and to Chalchihuitlicue of the river and springs, male and female divinities of growth, the prayers ascended on the hills.

A place of prayer was built of wood cut on the mountains, and the image of Tlaloc was placed in it. In brush shelters each in his place apart, the people waited, hearing the wind in the pines.

Then the three kings came. There on the mountain a child was slain, small like the dwarfs of Tlaloc that poured out the rains, small like the child an ancient Toltec had sacrificed in an earlier drought in an earlier Two Reed. He was slain in such a way that the people could not see. To the music of trumpets and conch shells and clay flutes he was offered so that no one could hear his cries.

When it was done, Moteczuma with his nobles entered the courtyard of the god and placed a crown of rich plumes on the image. In the slow movement of a dance he withdrew and Nezahualcoyotl of Texcoco entered and hung around the neck of the god another crown. The stately sequence continued. The king of Tlacopan entered and laid a crown at his feet. The cities of the lake alliance had crowned the god of rain.

Now the blood of the dead child was put on roasted birds, and the birds and rich cocoa were placed before the god. A guard was set so that no hungry enemy might steal the food—not even the Tlaxcalteca, the enemies within the house. The pilgrims went down the mountain so that the god, like kings, might eat alone. And they made offerings of turquoise and jade to the lake.

On every mountain and hill the people prayed. On mountain and plain they made the running water of springs and streams glad with precious chalchihuitl stones, with jade and turquoise and the plumes of quetzal birds. And when they went away the wind sounded in the branches of the ahuehuetl trees whose roots were in cool water; the drum of water sounded.[56] On the slopes of Popocatepetal and Iztaccihuatl, the Smoking Mountain and White Woman, the divine singer thundered with deep rumbling.[57]

The end of the cycle was at hand. Fifty-two of the turquoise years had passed, and now the sense of death and of ending was upon the land. This time the stars would descend as ravening beasts like the coyotes seeking the dead in the streets. This time would be the end of another sun, even as four suns had ended anciently.

In every house the people made an ending, breaking their pottery and throwing away the goods that had accumulated through the years. They drew blood from themselves in penance—"Because from our evil came hunger and sickness and slavery," they said. They looked with fear on pregnant women who this night when the darkness might be everlasting might turn into raging beasts and consume them. They put out their fires, since on this night the sun itself might go out forever with the dying of the years.

Through the darkness over the causeway the fire priests came, walking slowly to Huixachtlan, the hill above Ixtapalapa. Here where Tlaloc had been called upon for rain, they looked to the east, the direction of the year bearer and the new fire. For this year was Two Reed, and even more than for rain they reached out for the light of the sun, and for the new fire.

The obsidian knife cut into the heart of the slave who must die on the hilltop. The fire sticks whirled. The spark came. The firestick was hurled toward the sky.[58] A blazing torch was sped across the lake to the temple in Tenochtitlan. And now swift runners and boatmen carried the fire like stars that had fallen to earth, not with terror but with life, to the temples around the lake.

From the east the sun would climb, ready to labor again—the sun strong with the blood of war and sacrifice, at his side the warriors who had died in battle, the hummingbirds of Huitzilopochtli.

"Now the pestilence and hunger is ended," men cried rejoicing.[59]

Yet without seed no man planted. Only from the top of

the pyramids had corn been thrown to the hot winds of the four directions.

Moteczuma, from whom men turned their eyes away in reverence, waited in the island city. Now clouds hung over the dark heights of Tlaloc's mountain range. Cloud-dark rain swept across the valley. Day after day the earth drank.

Out of the houses came the people, wrinkled and yellowed with hunger, and reached their hands to a land that was rain-wet and green.

Even on their thatched roofs seed was sprouting. And word came at last of corn and beans and chilli growing together in fields where no man had sown, in open country toward the mountains, in the roads where the hungry had walked.[60]

Now Moteczuma looked beyond the mountains at the end of far roads, to the markets for gods and men.

In those distant places as at home the hymn of Huitzilopochtli sounded:

"They dance with me in the place of song.
I sing my song."[61]

The Couixca, who had sacrificed the Mexica who had come to them in their great need, now sent extra tribute through Cuauhnauac to the island city in hard payment—chalchihuitl stones and quetzal plumes.[62] Near Tepeacac water now stood in abundance on the fertile fields tilled by Mexica settlers.[63] Those who had gone weeping to a far land to die now danced in the festivals on the Plain of Serpents. Traders came regularly from the Totonac country. There near the sea of the sky were people of Nahuatl speech who had chosen to stay in the hot country, remembering the names of the towns from which they had come as belonging to another time, giving the old names to the sections of the towns where they had settled.

"For the food of the Mexica must come from a distance," they said.[64]

Two years and a half passed by. Moteczuma called his brother to him.

"Give me your opinion. I think of having my likeness carved on the rock of Chapultepec."

"It seems good to me," said Tlacaelel.

"Give orders to the sculptors," said Moteczuma.

Tlacaelel called the stone workers and artists and gave them the king's command. When the cliff was carved, they came again.

"It is done as the king ordered," they reported.

"Let us go and see," said Moteczuma.

Early in the morning they went together to the Grasshopper Hill and stood before the carved cliff.

In Tenochtitlan as in Tula the memory of a king would be preserved. They looked at the carved features in silence.

"It is like me," remarked Tlacaelel.

Had the sculptors shaped the portrait of both men—these two who were like one?

They looked at the date sign carved in stone. It was not the date of their birth. It was, as Moteczuma Ilhuicamina had commanded, the year One Rabbit, when the Mexica had taken the roads of hunger out of the valley.[65]

XIV

Masks of Trade and War on the Plain of Serpents

IN FRONT OF MOTECZUMA the traders sat. They had been called to meet him face to face. The blunt king, usually leaving words to his brother, spoke now directly and permitted them to speak in turn.

These were men who knew the hard trails over the mountains down into the hot country: the trail down through Tollantzinco that the Texcocans already held in tribute; the road through Cuauhnauac which shared with the Tenochca the tribute which came to it from beyond; through Tlachco, where Maxtla had died on a ball court and left the far outpost of Tepanecan power to the young strength of Mexico-Tenochtitlan; to Tlaxcala and Huexotzinco, friends and enemies within the house; to Cholula where hymns had been sung from the times of the Tolteca to Quetzalcoatl and Xochiquetzal—hymns which the traders now sang as their own; to Quauhtinchan, which now was sending tribute to Tlatelolco. They spoke with intimate knowledge of the coastal country near the sea of the sky, bringing rubber and paper and corn to Tenochtitlan.[1]

The king spoke to them as an elder—

"You have known hunger and thirst and weariness. You know what it is to cross swollen rivers, or to wait in danger until the rivers go down. You know what it is to suffer unbearable exhaustion as you go from town to town, spent with heat and cold, wiping sweat from your brow, sore from the tug on your forehead of the strap that holds the weight of your load on your back. You know what it is to sleep in caves and on mountainsides. You know what it is not to sell what you carry."[2]

These were men whom the blunt king could talk to and understand. They understood already why he had called them; they spoke to him in terms of relationship.

"Your uncles, the merchants who are here, have risked our necks and our lives—not acting as merchants only, but as captains and soldiers. Disguised, we march to conquer."

The king accepted and repeated their word of relationship.

"My uncles, it is the will of Huitzilopochtli, god of war."

To the merchants who knew the far trails and were his eyes and ears, he gave his directions carefully. They would go to the great market of Coaixtlahuaca, the Plain of Snakes—a market rich in gold and plumes and cacao, in pottery and clothing and thread of many colors made from rabbit fur.[3] Atonal, Water Day, the ruler of that town, was making many conquests, it was said.[4]

He laid before them sixteen hundred blankets.

"These you can use in trade," he said. "Before you go you can buy rich clothing and jewels, things for men and women, for rich and poor, to use in trade when you reach the great markets."

They talked together in detail of the open and the masked business of the trip. Tlacaelel, priest of the Snake Woman, recognized the skill of his brother in this planning, his kinship with those who went out from the mountain valley on hard journeys, and with those who worked with skilled hands on the goods they would take with them.

"These are the men who make the splendor of our city,"

Tlacaelel said. "The silversmiths, the stone cutters, the builders, the fishermen, the makers of mats, the polishers of precious stones—and especially the traders, and the men who go with them to carry their goods on their backs. These are the men my brother Moteczuma Ilhuicamina likes best. He is the one who first sent them to spy out the towns and temper and strength of peoples, to trade—and to see to the king's business."[5]

The shrewd men who were used to the hard trails went from the king's presence. He heard in the next weeks of the organization of their expedition—the division of the blankets between the Mexicans of Tenochtitlan and of Tlatelolco, the careful bargaining for jewels with the workers in precious stones at Xochimilco and Texcoco and for reed mats with the weavers in Chimalhuacan.

They consulted with the priests who understood the count of days, and chose One Snake to bring good fortune in riches and in war.[6] They thought of the fire snake of Xiuhtecuhtli, God of Fire, Turquoise Lord, God of the Middle and the Center.[7] They thought of the Lord of the Red House of Dawn, and of the sacred war when the rising sun put to flight the first and last of the stars.[8]

As the day drew near they made the paper offerings and decorated them with thick, slow drops of melted rubber to make the face of Sun-Fire, and the face of the Earth god, and the snakes of the day One Snake. They cut the paper in intricate design and made light-flying butterflies for the gods of the road, of the grassy and the sandy and the rocky trails.[9]

And as they stood in front of their hearth drawing the blood of sacrifice, burning paper offerings to Xiuhtecuhtli, God of Fire, they thought of Chantico, goddess of the hearth and of fire and of goldsmiths; of the painted butterflies that changed and took new forms, disguised as workers of magic might disguise themselves, and as merchants might take the clothing of the country to go unnoticed in the market place where they were eyes and ears of a king.[10] They stood, ready for the journey, with shaven heads to which the black obsidian razor would not be set again until their return. They made their offerings of rubber and paper to the fire gods of the hearth and the house, watching to see whether the flame burned clear.

"If there is smoke we will sicken and die in a far country," they said. "We will be placed in our carrying crates and lifted to the sun on a high hill, and like the men who die in battle we will suck flowers with the hummingbirds of Huitzilopochtli."[11]

And when the flame burned clear their hearts lifted—

"You have had mercy, Lord of Fire," they said.

They went into the patio and made their offerings to the god of earth. From their fingernail they snapped drops of their own blood to the sky and to the four directions—to the east and west; to the north which was the Right of the Sun and the Left of the Earth; to the south which was the Left of the Sun and the Right of the Earth. And they thought of the hummingbird of this day and of Huitzilopochtli, Hummingbird on the Left, god of the south, to which they would go.[12]

To a long black staff of cut reed they fastened more paper in honor of Yacatecuhtli, the god of the reeds, guide of the road. This staff, tall and without knots, would go with them and stand in their night camps. They would walk and camp with prayer.[13]

When the night prayers were finished and day was come, they sent out invitations to all their relatives and business associates for a final banquet, in which the words they spoke were like final words. The principal merchants of greatest wealth and honor sat on the right around the walls on their woven mats and low chairs. Those of less importance sat on the left. The first one on the right spoke gravely:

"We beg of you that you do not turn back. Better to die and leave your goods spread by the road if honor and renown come of it, than to turn back and bring dishonor on yourselves and on us. Endure food without chilli and salt. Wherever you go walk humbly, performing the services the gods require, shaking out the reed mats, bringing the gods flowers, careful in all humble tasks."

The old spoke to the young who were going on their first journey:

"You will know all the work and weariness of this long road. You will go wiping the sweat from your face, chafed and sore with the straps that hold your load, and worried for fear you cannot sell what you carry. But do not be dismayed; do not turn back from what you have begun; do not think of home."

The old merchants spoke to those already used to the trail:

"You are not children. You know what you must meet on the road you have already walked. Take care of those who go with you for the first time. Treat them like your younger brothers. Do not separate, but stay together. Go in peace, do your work, be strong."

In another and simpler house, a trader of less wealth gathered together the men who would accompany him. There too the old spoke to the young, friends to friends, parents to the men who would have their sons in charge.

"We will guard your words in our hearts," the traders promised.

The last day was filled with work. In the house of the leader of the expedition the goods were laid out. Merchants, both men and women, who were shipping merchandise south, stayed to watch until they knew who would carry it.

"Take good care of these things. When you return we will divide the profits," they said.

The captain gave his orders.

"A little more in this crate—a little less here—so that the burden may be equal."

To a young boy he said,

"You will carry light things—a few cups and tortoise-shell whippers for cocoa."

The carrying crates were filled for traders and hired

burden bearers. The leather straps and rope of maguey fiber were checked for the last time. The canoes which would carry men and cargo across the lake to the beginning of the mountain trail were drawn up, bumping against each other in the choppy water.

And now it was night and it was One Snake, the chosen time. In the light of a bonfire figures moved back and forth loading the crated goods into the canoes for the first leg of the trip to the Plain of Serpents—the wide plain where men could look far off—and to the market where they would be eyes and ears for Moteczuma Ilhuicamina.

At the end there seemed to be much to say. Once more, "Take care"—

"Take care of the goods, of the boys who go with you."

"Take care of the families we leave at home."

"Do not think of home. Do not turn back."

Now though words crowded for speech, the time of speaking was ended. The traders picked up their staves, fluttering with paper prayers to Yacatecuhtli, and to the gods of the road. From a green jar they picked the pine incense and threw it on the bonfire.

They did not turn again to those who watched them go. They did not look again toward the women they were leaving. No man turned back for the thing he had forgotten, or the words he would hear, or the words he had failed to speak.

Silently the figures, dark against the firelight, moved to the canoes. Those on shore heard only the sound of wooden oar against wooden canoe, and the sucking sound as the oars dug into the water.

Ilhuicamina, busy with public works and the order of sacrifice, waited for word from the men with staves who as the count of days and the turquoise year moved on would be marching now over pine-cold mountains, now down into hot country, now mingling with the market crowds who brought goods and gossip from far off. Sometimes he inspected the temple to Huitzilopochtli as the steps of the pyramid platform mounted higher and higher for the god-victim to walk. Sometimes he watched a sculptor carve a stone basin into which the blood of the victims would fall. These were measurable things—not like the lightness of song in the gardens of Texcoco—not like singing over the water.

He welcomed Nezahualcoyotl when he came to see how the enlarged aqueduct from Chapultepec was coming in its slow construction across marsh and lake. This man who judged a song and the craft of a goldsmith in his Texcoco convocations could judge the line of a dike and a ditch and know how to build them. But he spoke a language strange to his blunt, hard friend in Tenochtitlan. He spoke of the temple he was building in his garden at Tezcotzinco where there would be no sacrifices—a temple to the God of the With and the By, the God of the Near Vicinity. Did he mean all the gods to whom that name was given—Xiuhtecuhtli, god of the center, god of the hearth? or perhaps Tonacatecuhtli—lord of corn and food, who needed no human flesh? or perhaps a god different from all the others?[14] The hard-driving tlatoani of the Tenochca wasted no time considering these problems. It was best to see that the gods were fed, that famine did not come again for gods and men.

Then across the lake a message came from his friend.

"I need you to help me judge a matter."

Moteczuma went to Texcoco. He went through the great courtyard, past the rooms where poets and historians held their classes and the painted books were kept; past the room where those who studied the stars and the animals and the flowers gave their reports to the king. There he had sat at the right of Nezahualcoyotl and listened to the musicians play the huehuetl drum in the center of the room and the singers sing the history that had been made by warriors and wanderers.

But Nezahualcoyotl was not listening to song today.

"It is my son Tetzauhpiltzintli," he said. "It is for you to judge him, as I cannot. Your judgment will be without prejudice. Let the law be fulfilled—without thought of me."

What had the boy done, the one son that had come of that marriage to the girl with the honest eyes?

"There is evidence that he is planning to rebel against me," Nezahualcoyotl explained.

Moteczuma knew that the law was death.

"I will not be present," Nezahualcoyotl went on. "It is in your hands. I will go to Tezcotzinco and wait there in the gardens I have planted. Remember, he is only a boy. It is because of his youth and lack of understanding that he has lost his senses."

Moteczuma understood. The friendship had been long between them since that day when he had poled through the marshes before daylight to help in the escape of a boy who had just watched his father killed. They had been exiles together, and comrades in arms. He himself had called on Nezahualcoyotl when he needed a man of thought. Now his friend called on him for strength.

He watched the poet king go out toward the gardens where water fell over the stones to the bathing pools.

And now with the tlatoani of Tlacopan at his side he sat in the hall of judgment, one hand on the skull, and one holding a golden arrow. The decision should be that of the alliance.

A woman testified, one to stir a man more given to women than was the austere Tenochcatl.

"I first suspected this when my son, a worker in precious stones, took a jewel bird to this misguided youth, and was reproved for not sharing in his conspiracy against his father," she said.

"She was the king's favorite before his marriage," people whispered.

"Let me talk to the boy who found this thing out," said Moteczuma, the Angry One, who could talk comfortably to craftsmen. And the boy told him how his father had directed him to take the bird, worked from precious stone, to his half-brother as a gift.

"He thanked me but said I should take an interest in war —and he showed me his collection of arms—of obsidian-toothed clubs and bows, all stored in his house."

The warrior king of Tenochtitlan was puzzled. What songs there were in Tenochtitlan were songs of war—and war was good.

The woman urged her son on.

"Tell the Speaker Judges from the other two cities what he said he would do with the weapons."

The boy went on obediently.

"He said he wanted to conquer the world, and be greater than his father."

The king whose wars were markets for starving gods and men pondered what the concubine and her son had said.

"The meaning of this is not clear," he stated cautiously. "Has no one else gone as a listener and a watcher?"

A man testified.

"I was sent to see whether what this boy said was true. I saw rooms full of weapons."

"We ourselves will go to see," decided Moteczuma.

The two kings went quietly with a few attendants to the house built around the ahuehuetl tree. The young man greeted them. Proudly he showed the house that had already won him fame as a builder like his father. They saw the room filled with obsidian-toothed clubs and arrows and bows.

He was young. What had his father said?—for lack of understanding he must have done this. But his father had said to do justice. His father was the thinker and had thought this through. He was depending on the strength of his friend, on the man who did not draw back from action to ponder or to sing.

Moteczuma gave a signal to the men who accompanied him. They went forward to give the smiling boy flowers, to put a wreath around his neck. They drew the strand tighter and tighter.

Then quietly they went away.

"Tell the king that we have done justice according to the law and his command," Moteczuma said.

He was back in his own city, remote again from all but Tlacaelel his brother, when he heard that Nezahualcoyotl was mourning still in the gardens at Tezcotzinco.

"Why did I give away the burden of judgment?" Nezahualcoyotl had cried out to his friends. "I loved the boy, my son, the child of my wife."

He stayed alone at Tezcotzinco and wept.

Moteczuma, the Angry One, understood now.

His friends had counted on him not for strength but for tenderness. He had not known.[15]

In Tenochtitlan the families of the traders waited for their return. When they bathed they did not wash their hair, but waited for eighty days before that symbol of ending and of new beginning.[16] The Speaker-king waited too for the return of the men who were his eyes and ears, for the night when they would come quietly into the city and leave their loads at the house of a friend, and come, even before they sought out their own house, to make their report to him. Probably on the day One House they would come again with fans from the south, and with their staves decorated no longer with paper but with parrot plumes,[17] to feel the security of their own house around them again, shutting out the dangers of the trail. Before their own fire they would offer the heads of turkeys to Xiuhtecuhtli, god of fire of their hearth, and to Yacatecuhtli, who had gone before them on the road. Night and the house would be around them with comfort and safety.[18]

The day One House came, and the men that entered by night into Tenochtitlan and came to the king's house to report were few in number. The hair on their shaved heads had grown long.

The first formal phrases were without haste.

"Know that I have come with health and life," said their spokesman.

But a hundred and sixty traders had not come back to the lake towns.[19]

"We had traded in the market of Coaixtlahuaca—full of foreign traders and goods both from here in the country of the Mexica and from the coastlands. We had bought colored thread, and pottery and feathers full of powdered gold. We had heard people of strange tongues and had understood them through interpreters, for there are Mexica nearby in Tlachquiauhco, and we have friends there.[20] But Atonal must have conspired against us to attack us when we left the market and took the road for home. A hundred and sixty men from our towns were already on the road."

"Which towns were they from?" asked Moteczuma.

"They came from this city, and from Texcoco and Xochimilco, from Azcapotzalco and Coyohuacan and the other old Tepanecan towns—some even from Chalco."

They told how the attackers too had asked where they were from, and then had said,

"Do we send our goods to the Mexica? Are we vassals of Moteczuma?"

And in that narrow place they had hurled the Mexica over the cliff and robbed the bodies of all they carried and fled.

While the messengers sat on their haunches before him in attitude of humility, Moteczuma turned over in his mind what they had said. There was a silence.

"But you escaped," he said at last. "Where are you from?"

"From Tollan and Toltitlan," they replied. "We were not with the others. We left the market later and came upon them dead and dying there by the road. We came swiftly then, travelling by night."

"You have done well. Go now to your own towns and your own houses."

They went out to seek their own houses whose shelter they would feel around them, and the feasts of their return.

In Tenochtitlan and Texcoco and all the towns to which the traders would not return, the word went of men and boys killed in battle, their bodies raised now on tall stakes to the sun.

"They are not dead. They have gone like warriors to lead Huitzilopochtli across the sky. They are sucking honey with the hummingbirds of the south."

And in their houses their families made images of the dead of pitch pine ready to burn like torches in the middle of the night in the courtyard of the temple of their calpulli.

In Tenochtitlan the king talked with his brother. His spies had not failed.

"Now we know the pride and intention of Atonal," he said. "This attack is upon us."

But vengeance waited on due order. The messengers of Moteczuma went south over the trail which to the merchants had been a trail of death. They took the word to Atonal.

"If your order was responsible for what happened to the Mexicans, if you wish us ill, then we bring you word from our king that you must arm for war and wait for us. Without delay we will be here."

Water Day heard them quietly. He gave an order to his attendants and they brought jewels and laid them before the messengers. But these were not truly gifts of courtesy to Moteczuma.

"These are samples of what I receive in tribute from my vassals," said the lord of the Plain of Serpents. "Take them to Moteczuma and show him how much I am esteemed by my people. Let him tell me what he receives as tribute from his conquests. If I conquer him in this war he must give me the tribute he receives. If he conquers me I will give him my riches. Go in safety with the jewels, and tell him what I have said."[21]

The messengers returned to Tenochtitlan.

"It is not necessary to wait longer," said Tlacaelel.

The word went out to the cities of the lake country, each of which mourned its dead and knew that it was war. War far away this time, along roads that only the far-travelling traders knew. War among strange peoples of a strange tongue.

"This war belongs to you as well as to us," said the messengers from Tenochtitlan firmly.

They sent out a call to arms to places controlled by tribute or by trade; to Tollantzinco, to Huexotzinco; to Cholula; to Itzocan and Acatzinco and Quauhtinchan; even to Tepeacac, the market town to which the whole world went; and to Toluca in its aloof independence.[22] They gathered from their storehouses the clubs with sharp obsidian blades. They cleaned up their conch shell trumpets and made ready their masks of tigers and eagles and serpents and lions, made of well tanned leather hides and snake skins, fit to strike terror to the heart of the enemy when they went singing and dancing into battle. They made ready their cotton armor, their shields of wood with spokes of reed, decorated with bright plumes. They gathered food for the journey, rations for the long trail. And in all the towns of the central alliance they waited the command of Moteczuma to start.

He was organizing the plan of march from Tenochtitlan. His first order concerned his brother Tlacaelel, veteran of many battles.

"He is getting old—too old for this long march. Better that a young man be put in command, and he stay here with me in our city among the reeds."

He called on the merchants to name men from their own number who would be given military rank and would give directions on the trails and among the strange peoples whom they already knew.[23]

Finally he gave the marching order.

"Leave tomorrow—at the quarter moon. March in the cool of the day."

Then Moteczuma and Tlacaelel watched them go. The women stood weeping, and began their night watches. In the middle of the night the women rose to sweep and to bathe, longing for the men that might never come again. They went in the night to the temples to offer sacrifices of tortillas and fried maguey worms. They carried with them a twisted rope as a sign that their husbands would come again, victorious with prisoners, and they carried a weaver's shuttle like the lances their men would carry into battle. In the night they remembered and waited and feared.[24]

The king waited fasting. When he went out he did not wear rich jewels, but his clothing was simple, befitting a time of war. Even the ball games stopped and the ball courts were empty. Only when the festivals to the gods came around did the city listen to the sound of music and the rhythm of feet dancing a prayer that gods and men might live. Word came to Tenochtitlan that in the gay city of Texcoco the command had gone out that all songs cease.[25]

To the silent cities the ragged broken troops of Moteczuma came back. They came without prisoners for sacrifice. And to the waiting families they named the dead and the captured, far away in the south to the left of the sun.[26]

Now the dancing was to the measure of sorrow, and smoke hung over the city from burning pine effigies of the dead.

It was Tenochtitlan's first defeat since the war of independence. Through the months that followed, messengers came from the south bringing news of the aftermath. Atonal's people were boasting that the Mexican troops had been pursued to their own frontier. Already a legend was growing up:

"Dzahuindanda, Rain Day," they said in their own language, "climbed the dark mesa near Achiutla—a mesa so dark with trees that the sun never enters. He carried a bag and among some low hills on the mesa top he prayed for soldiers and he shook the bag and they came forth with arms and shields. He trained them and then marched in great silence until he met the Mexica. And he pursued them to their own country."[27]

The king heard the reports of the boasting of the people on the Plain of Serpents. But he found more disturbing the news of the shifting alliances in the wake of the Mexican retreat. Tlaxcala and Huexotzinco—the enemies within the house—had united against the Mexica. Now they were enemies indeed. Xicotencatl, in spite of being a frequent visitor in the gardens of Tezcotzinco, now looked with doubt on the expanding alliance and had found an ally in Atonal. The little Mexican garrison and settlement in Tlachquiauhco near Coaixtlahuaca had been wiped out by the combined forces. Malinaltzin, their ruler, had sent the bitter news north.[28]

Now Moteczuma knew that he must proceed without haste. This time when the assembled troops set forth from the highlands they must be equipped with all types of supplies and their numbers must be great enough to meet all those that Atonal might train on the dark mountain, and those that Xicotencatl might recruit from those trained in the War of Flowers. Men would tell some day of a Mexican army that was in numbers like grasshoppers that darkened the sun.[29]

They marched this time as if they were going to found a city, swearing that they would not return until they had defeated Atonal. They carried grinding stones and griddle stones, jars and bowls and plates. They knew that they must dress lightly for hot country and they made thin clothing of maguey fiber. They carried poles for stockades and shelters. They went laden with hard dry biscuit for the road.

From all the cities beside the lake they marched and came together on the plain near Itzocan. Together they marched south. The canyon walls shut in around them and the canyon water roared by. And they came out into open country and set up their camp with stockades and shelter against the sun, and sent out their scouts to see the defenses on mountainside and plain which Atonal's army had built.

Speakers, trained in words, addressed the troops:

"Here we are—let us show our valor. Let us remember we have conquered the Chalca."

They tried not to remember that the center of Chalco remained to be conquered, and thought only of Tlalmanalco, and the few Chalca camped with them now as allies. They tried not to remember the wild tribes that they had heard of that fought like savages in this southern land.[30]

They put on their stuffed cotton tunics, strong enough to withstand the arrows of the enemy and to soften the blow of an obsidian-toothed club. Over the cotton of the nobles was the gleam of jewels and featherwork—for those of the north could display their riches as well as their courage against Rain Day.

Not dancing, but silently, they made their attack. In distant Tenochtitlan, Moteczuma Ilhuicamina and his brother Tlacaelel knew that the army of Huitzilopochtli struggled now for empire. The fishermen reached out from the island in the lake reeds for the corn and the precious green stones.

"We will give you blankets and chilli and cotton and salt from the sea. We will give you dyes and paint. We will deliver it all the way to Mexico," cried the people of the Plain of Serpents at last.

It was not enough. The Mexica fought on.

"We will give you green and blue and gray precious stone, and rock crystal fit to adorn kings. We will serve in your temples."

The fighting stopped, and the Mexicans feasted in the house of Atonal, Water Day, lord of this town where people spoke with a strange and foreign tongue.

The grace of long tradition lay on the house from the time when another Atonal had brought the Toltec tradition to the Plain of Serpents.[31] These people cherished the old screen-folded books telling in their printed pages of an ancient time already being forgotten by the Tenochca since Itzcoatl had burned the books of the lake islanders.

As they feasted, the Tenochca were given new gifts of plumes and gold disks. And they watched the wife of the conquered king, Wreath of Cacao Flowers, as she moved among the women, tall and stately. She was wearing a fine woven mantle and anklets of gold. Around her neck hung a necklace made of coral beads from the sea, and copper and rock crystal and shell, all combined with agate tiger claws and an agate eagle head with eyes of mother-of-pearl. She moved softly in her rubber sandals as if she were barefooted, and the eyes of the Mexica followed her.[32]

Outside the houses of the feasting lords the people murmured against Atonal who had led them to defeat.

"He invited the armies of Huexotzinco and Tlaxcala down to our country, and then turned them against our city of Tlachquiauhco. He weakened us against the Mexica. Small wonder that Coaixtlahuaca fell with all the cities around."[33]

"Let him fall too now that the Mexica have conquered us."

And on the Plain of Serpents they killed Atonal, Water Day. The triumph of the Mexica was complete.

"His own people killed him," said some.

"The Mexica killed him in their hour of victory," said others."[34]

The Mexica harried the surrounding towns. The lord of Yanhuitlan joined Atonal in death.

"He died by treachery—which Moteczuma arranged," said his people bitterly.[35]

North at last from the Plain of Serpents came the Mexica. They were laden with a third of the tribute in advance. Eventually Coaixtlahuaca and its subject towns would send to their conquerers a semi-annual tribute of eight hundred bunches of quetzal plumes and twenty bowls of gold dust; two strings of chalchihuitl stones, and forty bags of scarlet cochineal for dye; insignia for the king; four hundred bundles of mantles of the finest weave and four hundred in embroidered colors; four hundred bundles of black mantles and four hundred bundles of loin cloths. They would send clothing for soldiers, because henceforth armies would be on the march to the country of the great sun.[36]

Slaves, most precious tribute, came up from the hot country, riches for Huitzilopochtli, Hummingbird of the South. In the towns where they passed, people came out to see the victorious Mexica laden with riches and accompanied by their slaves. And when they came across the causeway to Mexico-Tenochtitlan, the prisoners came dancing, holding on to the rope that tied them together, singing a sad song to the god whom they would feed. The old men came out to meet them and incensed them as dedicated ones, giving them pulque, the divine drink fermented from the honey water of the maguey.

They were led first to the temple of Huitzilopochtli and then into the presence of Moteczuma, Archer of the Skies. He watched them come, prisoners from the south. He spoke to them as befitted those who were an offering to the gods.

"You are welcome, you who will be an offering to him who passes over our head and embraces the world with his power each day, lord of earth and of all things."

They bent and touched the earth and put earth to their lips in token of humility.

"We are not worthy to be in your presence. We praise you who have let us see your face."

They were led out then, and away, weary and sick with the long march, to be fed with rich food, and fattened for the day of sacrifice. Though men of strange speech and foreigners, they must be fit in body for the feast of the gods.[37]

Among them was a tall woman who came with her own slaves, walking with dignity and apart. She was not led away. The king had noticed her.

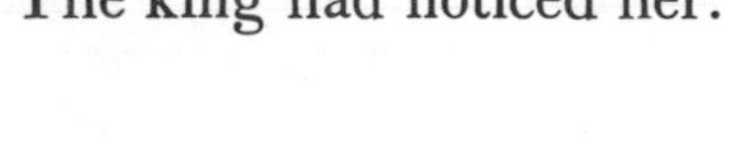

XV

The Skin of Gold and a Broken Chalchihuitl Stone

IN THE WIDE SQUARE in front of the pyramid the people were gathered for the sacrifice of the prisoners from the south, the festival that would bring to the sun food from the market of war.[1]

The Tall Woman watched as the children of the sun climbed the pyramid, the eagle men whose blood would fall into the eagle vase of sacrifice, men from her own city where Water Day had died.

The eagle vase was ready, with the deeds of valor of the Mexica and with symbols of the sun carved with stone on stone, as a goldsmith might work delicately.[2] The god's image was above them; a bonnet was perched on his head,[3] and from his shoulder a wide strip of golden leather hung over his right arm.[4] He wore sandals of tiger skin and carried a tiny vase worked from precious stone and filled with seed.

Near the god stood Moteczuma, the Warrior King, Archer of the Sky, and beside him his brother Tlacaelel. Painted black, they wore gold bracelets to the elbow rather than the golden skin. Priests as well as warriors,[5] they were otherwise dressed like the god. And they waited with their flint knives in their hands.[6]

Now the first prisoner from the Plain of Serpents stood at the foot of the pyramid, straight and certain, praising his own city.

"You will speak of me there in my homeland."[7]

"Go now for us," said the Tenochca, "and salute the sun that he may remember us."

Their voices went out over the waiting plaza.

They gave him the staff of a traveller and the shield of an eagle warrior to travel to the sun. Painted red, he stood in the morning light. And above him five red killer-priests waited beside the blackened Ilhuicamina and his brother Tlacaelel.[8]

"I have reached Coaixtlahuaca, the Plain of Serpents; I
carry its shield of turquoise;
I shake in the breeze the red flower of our flesh.
He descended, he descended there above the ahuehuetl
trees,
Moteczuma went down where they cut flowers,
Went down to battle, and with him Nezahualcoyotl.
Let my captive go forth."[9]

The kings of Texcoco and Tlacopan looked on as the red figure mounted the first step. They and the lords of all the lake cities and of the country around Cuauhnauac watched him pause.[10] For a long time he waited there. And his captor watched him, sending him as his representative until he too should die in battle or by sacrifice, a warrior of the sun.

He mounted another step, slowly, as the sun climbs the sky.

And the Tall Woman watched her red-stained countryman go step by step up toward the Archer of the Sky, standing with golden bracelets on his arms and a flint knife in his hand.

High on the pyramid at last the captive warrior stood at the Stone of the Sun, now at the zenith, at noon. He stood facing the stone of the sun, and turned to face the sun itself whose light poured down on the square. He shouted to the sun as a messenger with the shield of a warrior and the staff of a traveller—a staff such as the image of Xipe carried—the

Flayed One.[11] He was an eagle man, before the eagle vase of the sun. They bent him over the stone, mouth to the sky, and the blackened Moteczuma, priest as well as warrior now, plunged the flint knife into the breast and threw the hot blood east of the sun. And the red sacrificers tore out the heart and offered it to Huitzilopochtli, like cactus fruit to nourish him, the Turquoise Prince, the Soaring Eagle. Into the eagle vase of the sun the heart of the eagle man was placed, and his body, like the setting sun, hurtled down from step to step.

Slowly, slowly, the next victim began his climb.

They sent a thigh to the king and the rest of the meat to the family of the captor. But the captor himself would not eat it, however reverently, for the victim was his representative until his own time should come to make the journey to the sky.

"My son," he had said to him on the battlefield.

"My father," his prisoner had replied.

And the Tall Woman remembered his name.

The next day the visitors to Mexico-Tenochtitlan watched a prisoner fight on the stone of combat. Armed with a pine club he struggled for one half hour more of life. The length of rope with which the Wolf Man had tied him to the middle of the flat stone let him only reach the circumference. Naked he struggled against the eagle warriors and the tiger warriors, pitting his untoothed pine club against their obsidian blades.[12] Around him sat the representatives of the gods—Huitzilopochtli, Hummingbird on the Left; Opochtli, the Left, who invented nets; Quetzalcoatl, the Plumed Serpent; Yopi and Totec who were Xipe; the Obsidian Butterfly; Toci, our Grandmother with her dress of roses, Mother of the gods, whose victim was flayed in her sacrifice; rank on rank and from all the calpulli of the city, they sat watching the fighter who knew defeat and death lay half an hour ahead.[13]

Conquered by Huitzilopochtli,[14] all the gods were one as they watched.[15] And beside them the prisoner's captor danced, studying him, watching him fight.

"My son, who goes before me."

And now the two tiger warriors and the two eagle warriors wearied and the Four Dawns fought against the prisoner, white and green, yellow and red.[16] They fought left-handed, but the obsidian blades found their mark. And each time the seashell trumpets sounded.

At last the captive fell, bleeding and exhausted, wishing indeed to die, to cast off forever the burden of death, and go to the sun.[17] The killer priest who was Xipe Totec dragged him to the vase of the sun and raised his heart high. And to every temple the blood was taken in a green bowl and touched to the lips of the gods.

One by one through the morning hours the captives fought and fell and were dragged to the sacrifice. The king gave orders about how the skin should be removed and the victims flayed, and he watched the priests don the golden skin of Xipe.

"Thou drinker of night.
Put on your mask,
Put on the garb of gold,
Put on the garb of dawn.
May it rain, may the water come."[18]

Now from the temple of Huitzilopochtli in top of the pyramid came the burning paper fire snake, twisted around a pole and adorned with plumes like flames. It writhed slowly down the pyramid. In the eagle vase of the sun they burned it, and the blood of the prisoners from the Plain of Serpents was consumed with it.

"My God, your rain of precious chalchihuitl stones has come down,
Has turned the tall trees into quetzal plumes.
The Fire Serpent has turned into the Serpent of Plumes.
Oh my God, a gift of precious stones is your water.
Falling over the places where the water runs
You adorn the tall trees with quetzal plumes;
The Fire Serpent has left me."[19]

The king and his brother came down from the pyramid.

Anointed and clothed they sat with the kings of Texcoco and Tacuba. In front of the pyramid Mexica and guests from the other cities, rich and poor, moved in solemn dance. They sowed their rattles like seed in the market place.[20] And while men clothed in drying skins collected alms through the city, hymns rose in the House of Song.

Out across the causeways and through the channels of the marshes into the open lake the spectators from the lake towns went home at last. Around the shores, and over the mountains in Cuauhnauac, the tale was told with horror of the new rite introduced in Mexico-Tenochtitlan by Moteczuma Ilhuicamina—the Angry Archer of the Skies.[21] Some remembered the red priests of Xipe in the south and west from which the troops had so recently returned, and beyond them among the shore people.[22] And they shuddered for fear of what might happen to them.

"Our own people taken captive by the Tenochca might be

sacrificed to the god of the golden skin," they said.

"Better to stay with the alliance than to rebel," decided the recently conquered Tepanecan towns of the high country.[23]

Secure from attack at the rear the troops marched down to the hot country, garrisoning the conquered towns. The fear of them went on ahead.

Ilhuicamina and his brother laid out the tribute collection.

"We will send our own man Cuauxochitl to Coaixtlahuaca to collect the tribute promised in the treaty."

The collection headquarters were set up in Coaixtlahuaca. Every eighty days Cuauxochitl traveled the long road home to report to the king. Before him came the loads of blankets and plumes, of corn and chilli, the necklace of green chalchihuitl stones, the little bowls of gold dust panned in southern rivers. When he arrived Moteczuma called him into his own presence and greeted him warmly, giving him rich gifts as the king's representative in a far country.[24]

He, and those who like him dared to come in to the presence of the king, saw that he wore his hair shaved these days according to the fashion of Coaixtlahuaca[25]—like the warriors who had gone to the sun as messengers of their conquerers and in their name now spoke the prayer for corn and precious chalchihuitl stones, like men whom the Tall Woman remembered.

The Tall Woman, whom her own people had called Wreath of Cacao Flowers, moved with remote dignity among the nobles of Mexico-Tenochtitlan. Even the king saw her timidly and from afar, afraid to speak what he would say.

His remoteness was known to the city, and they remembered how little he had to do with women, and how austere his habits were.[26] Only the wife from his mother's town of Cuauhnauac was known to them. They called her the Chichimeca Woman, but her name and the names of her children were seldom spoken.

"He has only a daughter," said some.

"He has two sons," said others.

"He has many sons—do you forget those on the council? But he says they cannot all rule and he is having them taught to work with their hands—to cut precious stones, and paint books, and carve wood. He is having them trained in skills and trades and keeps them away from the public eye."[27]

But in spite of the king's remoteness it was known that he sought the Tall Woman. She watched him directing the work of the city as the pyramid of Huitzilopochtli grew and was embellished, as new stones were carved to recall the famine, the new fire and the tying of the years, the gods of the Mexica and the conquered. Side by side he and his brother walked forth with the insignia of kings. The sea shell trumpets sounded the day hours.

Work went forward on the aqueduct from Chapultepec—two-channeled and built with stone and sod across the lake and marsh. In each calpulli the macehuales farmed corn and beans. The goods from distant places filled more space in the market place.

The Tall Woman watched as the merchants reported to the king and received more mantles from him for trading. She heard the names of far places—of her own city of Coaixtlahuaca where now they went safely to the market place. And she watched them go out from the king's presence to go to other cities—to Cuetlaxtlan and Tochpan and the neighbors of the sea.

Always behind the building and the increasingly intricate web of trade and tribute was the strong Tlatoani, a man younger than his sixty years, strong and on-driving as her husband had been; blunt and direct with those who worked with their hands to build a city, to shape its possessions and its exports with craft and beauty; sure in his direction to those who carried its power outward.

But between him and the Tall Woman lay silence, in hard beauty, untouched, like a precious chalchihuitl stone brought over the mountain barriers from the hot south.

(The ancient ones knew what they meant when they spoke

of these things—things that belong to us, to the Tenochca, not to Tlatelolco nor to any other town.)[28]

One night he came to her. He lay in her arms that night and life was strong between them.

But now that he was here, though she reached for him, her own name for Water Day trembled on her lips. The Pity Woman of Water Day reached out for the living man but in that moment fled. The life that had flowed strong between them was broken now—the chalchihuitl stone was broken. From their aloneness their hearts cried out to each other and failed. And in her arms the strong king fainted.

They lay side by side afterward—a gentleness and a despair between them. From the twofold gods of creation could come no footprints, no descending chalchihuitl stone of life. The shield of Our Mother with its chalchihuitl stone could not be pierced by any arrow.

In the dark the king lay beside her, he who had stood strong and terrible on the pyramid with his flint knife.

"My heart is a chalchihuitl stone.
My heart will grow cold."[29]

XVI

Neighbors of the Sea

LIKE A DANCE the march of conquest moved across the lands of the sun. And the black staff of the merchants went on before.

Tribute began to come to Mexico-Tenochtitlan from Cozamaloapan. And far ahead the town of Quauhtochco feared and took council about the men from the high country in their market place. In the year Eight House news came to Moteczuma Ilhuicamina that his traders had been killed. In sure sequence the companies marched out in plumed cotton armor, red and blue and yellow and white; and afterward the prisoners from Quauhtocho were sacrificed at the dedication of the temple of Yopico,[1] an offering to the skinned god.

To the north by way of Tollantzinco the power of the alliance was also creeping toward the sea. From that city, already long tributary to Texcoco, Moteczuma Ilhuicamina heard that his traders had been hurled over cliffs and killed by the people of Tzicoac and Tochpan, on the road beyond.

"And now they have built around them reinforced barriers, five deep, one inside the other," the report went on.

The Archer of the Sky gave gifts to the messengers. In slow pace he and his brother Tlacaelel talked over what they would do. A few days later word went out to Texcoco and Tlacopan and the cities of the lake.

"This is not a thing to be endured. Our traders have been killed. Fortifications have been built by our enemies. Let war be declared and supplies gathered by our command."[2]

The men in charge of recruiting sent out the summons. Equipment for the hot country was gathered and doubled in case the towns on the route should not supply what was needed. And Nezahualcoyotl rejoiced that he was to be put in command.[3]

Tlacaelel laid out the plan for the assembling of the troops.

"Each town must carry its own banner with its own sign," he directed. "Then you will know each other. You can cry out, 'Mexico! Texcoco! Xochimilco!' "[4]

In Tenochtitlan each company, two hundred strong, was put under the command of its own captain. They all went a last time to the temple of Huitzilopochtli, and then, along the narrow ways between the canals, took march in their companies of color, their banner flying from a pole fastened firmly to the shoulder of the color bearer.[5] The women watched them go, and began their weary waiting, fasting with ashes on their heads that their men might know someone at home fasted for them. The men marched rejoicing, knowing that honor and rewards awaited both slave and noble,[6] and even the young warrior fresh from the Calmecac proving his courage for the first time in battle.[7] In the hope of honor these young recruits too would be strong to fight, with older men on their right and left, against the people of the hot country.

The people of Tollantzinco came out to meet them with roses. They had prepared them turkey, rabbits and doves, and tamales of different colors, and steaming cocoa. And their men were ready to join the march to the land of the sun.

They went down to the wide land, heavy with the sweet hot breath of fruit and fields, soft with slow green rivers whose flowing made strong and quiet music under birdsong. They marched in thin clothing of maguey fiber under the great sun. They could see the blue hills of Tamapachco and smell the salt Sea of the Sky beyond Tochpan.

They pitched their camps by their towns and companies. And some, covered with straw, circled behind the town, dug themselves in, and made ready to attack from the rear. The speakers rallied their men.

"Forget your women, your children, your mothers and your brothers. You are here at the edge of the sea to gain fame and honor, to get riches and slaves—or else to die."

They spoke a warning to the boys in battle for the first time.

"You are here to use the weapons for which you were born. But do not let your youth blind you. Follow those who are old and experienced. Do not advance and retreat suddenly, but wait and watch. Let him who has strength and ability try his luck, and let him who is not sure wait and see what will be necessary later. For this is not your last war. This is your task forever."

Day came and on the plain the armies met. The eagle warriors and the tiger warriors with their gaping masks charged forward behind their banners, each flagbearer with his flag fastened so firmly to him that he could fight freely and it could not be wrenched from him. They went shouting the names of their towns, and the names were like the call of the conch shell trumpet as they went into battle.

"Mexico! Texcoco!"

The Huaxteca advanced shouting threats.

"We have herbs whose very touch will finish you," they boasted.

They came with their earrings and noseplugs of gold and quartz, with headdress of yellow parrot plumes, with shields and armor and small round mirrors of obsidian shining in the sun. They came singing, and shaking their rattle belts like rattlesnakes, dry and harsh in the blazing sun.

They fought there in their companies. The straw-covered Mexica crawled up from the rear; the tiger and eagle warriors attacked head on. Together they forced the neighbors of the sea back from one earthwork defense to the next until they passed the fifth embankment and burned the temple in sign of victory.

The Huaxteca called their interpreters and shouted their surrender.

"We will give you our tribute."

And they brought blouses woven and embroidered in bright colors, and mantles and parrot plumes. They brought ointments to cream the hands and feet. They offered chilli and spices.

"These we will give you every year," they promised.

"You must deliver the tribute yourselves, and when we call, you must come swiftly and humbly," replied the victorious soldiers of the alliance.

The Huaxteca took them into their houses and fed them fish and shrimp and sea turtle and fruit from the lands of the sun, and gave them paper. And when they marched out of the towns which they had conquered, the prisoners marched before them with sad song.

On the road to the high country the earth trembled before them. They sent messengers two days ahead to tell their needs, and people came out to meet them bringing turkey and rabbit and fruit. When instead they hid in fear, the conquering highlanders sought them out and stripped them of their clothing and destroyed their fields.

"You are tributaries of Texcoco," they told them.

The annual tribute from Tzicoac and Tochpan was determined: thousands of bundles of mantles and blankets, some plain, some striped, some to be used to carpet the house of the king; deerskins, and a hundred live deer; a hundred parrots; crates of white feathers to make featherwork blankets and garments; workers to serve in the palace of Texcoco; four hundred paintings of tiger heads and sea snails in movement. Carefully Nezahualcoyotl worked out the division with the other members of the alliance, and appointed Huehutli to serve as his tax collector in Tochpan.

Those from Mexico-Tenochtitlan who had marched under

the leadership of Texcoco came home at last. The old men who were the speakers went out to meet them at the hill of Tepeacac, incensing them and welcoming them. The victors going on into the city, climbed the temple of Huitzilopochtli, and drew blood from their ears in sacrifice. Then they came into the presence of Moteczuma Ilhuicamina.

"Rest," he said, "and dance."

And they danced to the wooden beat of the teponaztli drum, and the king gave them clothing and sandals like those which a Speaker-king wore.[8]

"These are yours—these are shadows of the king," he said.

For two years the prisoners were guarded—the vassals and children of the sun, waiting to be sacrificed. The stone cutters worked on the carved sacrificial stone on which the captives should fight for one more hour of life. And the priestly killers, paid well in mantles and jewels for their hard task, looked ahead fearfully and with revulsion to the day when they would do their work.

"You must get drunk—and rehearse," said Moteczuma grimly.

They took dummies and cut out their hearts and pretended to throw blood into the air and put the hearts into the god's hands. Then on the painted stone the neighbors of the sea fought their last hour, and were killed for Huitzilopochtli and the gods he had conquered. On the market square before the pyramid the people of Mexico-Tenochtitlan danced with the heads of the victims raised high on poles. And those who wore the drying skin of Xipe went through the streets begging alms, each with a boy walking before him to help him see.

Moteczuma addressed the returned warriors and said to them,

"Now you have seen each other's courage. Be ready and prepared each day to go to fight, to subjugate, to win honors and fame. Now you know that this will never end."

"Now you know that this will never end," people repeated in distant Tlaxcala. The enemies within the house pondered.

Xicotencatl, who had been the friend of Ilhuicamina and of Nezahualcoyotl, saw their armies circling him—the Texcocan around by the north, the Mexican around by the south. The highland alliance was converging, shutting him off from the sea of the sky, shutting him off from salt, and the rich coastal lands.

Now Moteczuma was sending messengers to Cuetlaxtlan—parrots they were called, who had learned to speak for the king.[9] They carried the king's words to other cities as they went.

"We go through your town only once," they assured the people of Ahuizalapan. "We are on our way to Zempoala and to Cuetlaxlan to ask for turtles, and sea shells, and fish and oysters."

"Send us shell trumpets and pearls and turtles—and see that the turtles arrive still alive. We would see the richness of your towns," they said to the people of Zempoala where the avenues of pyramids stood under the great sun.

Over the level distances they came to the low hills and the ridge where Cuetlaxtlan stood.[10] They saw the white and colored shells and the turtles that came from the river; the wide shade of the acaxtli trees with fern-like leaves over the green water; the dug-out canoes, made from the tallest acaxtli trunks, drawn up by the banks.

They talked to the ruler One Water, Ce Atonal Tecuhtli, whose day-name was like a forecast of conquest as they remembered the name of the dead king on the Plain of Serpents.

But there were others in that place—enemies within the house, messengers from Xicotencatl waiting for this moment.

"Are you slaves?" they said to One Water Day. "Are you defeated by the Mexica in war that you must pay them tribute? Kill the messengers and merchants. If war comes, we are your allies."

There in Cuetlaxtlan, even on the outskirts of Tlaxcala, the traders died that no message might be taken back to the high country.

But some from Ixtapalapa came back. They sat once more before Moteczuma. Like a refrain came his formal words—"Rest." And they took their reward as messengers.

Moteczuma consulted with his brother.

"We might wait. Perhaps the Cuetlaxtlan people will take the blame and we can win the town without battle."

"It is not necessary to wait," declared Tlacaelel. "The riches we demanded were for Huitzilopochtli. This is not to be endured."

The call went out to the towns of the high country. Nezahualcoyotl of Texcoco, strong in his victory of Tollantzinco and Tochpan, Totoquihuaztli of Tlacopan, Moquiuixtzin of Mexico-Tlatelolco all gathered for the council.

"Your brothers, your merchants, have been killed. This war touches you. We of the alliance were not created to wear women's skirts."[11]

"It is our war—ours!" replied the Tlatelolca grimly.[12]

Moteczuma gave the allied kings bracelets of gold and gilded sandals and rich mantles. They went back to their own towns to gather the provisions—double rations for the march and light clothing for the country of the great sun.

And once again on the road of the merchants the soldiers of the alliance marched down toward the sea of the sky. A day's journey ahead of them the messengers went to announce their coming and prepare quarters in the towns and to pitch tents of straw matting. Again the earth trembled before them. The lords of the towns came out with roses to meet them. The people hid in fear and the roads were deserted. At the end of each day's march the camp was ready for the soldiers of the alliance when they arrived. They had only to be assigned, each town to its own space.

As they marched they took the corn from deserted cornfields; they rounded up turkeys and fat little dogs, bred for roasting. Seldom as they raided for provisions did a man have to fall back on the handful of toasted corn he carried as an emergency ration.

Down through the green pass cutting through blue folds of mountain they marched to the wide hot plain, and out over the level distances to Cuetlaxtlan. It lay before them apparently ready for the taking. Nezahualcoyotl had secured the route from the north. The Mexica working up from Coaixtlahuaca had secured the route from the south. Moteczuma in strategic command from Tenochtitlan saw Tlaxcala and Huexotzinco being encircled—the towns that had sheltered him and Nezahualcoyotl in their youth, that had supported their war of independence, that they could not attack directly.

But now word came to the high country that, as they had on the Plain of Serpents, the Tlaxcalteca intended to fight the expanding power of the alliance that was cutting them off from the sea. Down into the hot country the fighters were marching from Tlaxcala and Huexotzinco, and from Cholula, their neighboring city, where fires burned on the many pyramids of Quetzalcoatl. Allied with Cuetlaxtlan and Zempoala they would present opposition trained in the War of Flowers and would fulfill their pledge to support Cuetlaxtlan.

Moteczuma Ilhuicamina, directing the strategy from afar, estimated his strength. He dispatched a messenger with new orders.[13]

"Retreat," he commanded. "This is not the time to bring the battle to an issue."

The forces in the field held council.

"We are not cowards," said some.

"We must obey orders," said others.

Among the Mexica were three young men, grandsons of Moteczuma Ilhuicamina who had sent the order—Axayacatl, Tizoc and Ahuizotl.[14] While they debated, Moquiuix of Tlatelolco rallied his men.

"We are not cowards when we see how many have joined against us. Let the Mexica-Tenochca go home. We, the Mexica-Tlatelolca will conquer alone."[15]

The masked eagle and tiger warriors of the alliance took heart and surged forward. News of unexpected reinforcements swept their ranks with added hope. They shouted welcome to the new forces:

"Texcoco! Texcoco!"

The name of his city and his house was shouted before him, and his banners went ahead, as Acapioltzin, the son of Nezahualcoyotl, joined his allies.[16]

"I knew a short cut," he boasted in delight. "My brother Xochiquetzal left six days before me. He will be here yet—in command of our Texcocan forces."

He went into battle with youthful zest, and at his end of the front forced the Cuetlaxtecas back toward the river. The slow green water was turbulent with struggling men, falling and drowning in their heavy quilted cotton armor, dying under the flailing obsidian-knived clubs of the Texcocans. Xochiquetzal arrived to command, angry that his brother had taken the lead and the glory. But he brought new men to pour into the mass of warriors struggling among the low hills beside the river.

When it was over, and they came back victors to the high country, each city danced before the gods and sang its heroes, young men who had taken command when it was not theirs to command, who had gone forward against orders.

In Texcoco they sang the glory of two brothers, and each had his partisans claiming for him the great victory in the hot country. The two danced in the public square and the rivalry of the dancers was like another battle.[17]

Long afterward they would be named in songs of those who had drunk the intoxicating flower-water of war, and joined the warriors of the sun.[18]

In Mexico-Tenochtitlan, Moteczuma Ilhuicamina was not angry that a high-hearted youth from Tlatelolco had countermanded his orders. Rejoicing, he gave to Moquiuix, hero of the day, his granddaughter for a wife.[19] They danced with skulls in the market place at the dedication of the skull frame.[20] They sang their song of victory.

"We celebrate a festival for you.
You, Moquiuix, spread out a sky of song,
A frame and canopy masked with skulls
For the god of dark omen.
We fought for Huitzilopochtli.
The men of Huexotzinco, Tlaxcala, Cholula, and
Cuetlaxtlan are destroyed.
See how they are turned back.
Where now is Water Day? Where is Atonal?"[21]

Now after four years it was noted that Moteczuma no longer wore his Coaixtlahuaca haircut. He had ceased to identify himself with those who after that campaign had gone as his messengers to the sun. Others had come to climb the pyramid to their death.[22]

He named his governor and tax collector—Pinotl, who moved with his family to Cuetlaxtlan, and every eighty days would send the bearers of tribute from all the towns of that province to Tenochtitlan. They would carry green chalchihuitl stones and powdered gold, ground turquoise of the gods, mantles and earrings, cacao for foaming hot drinks, amber and dried fish from the sea, and exotic fruits never before seen in the high country.[23]

In Mexico-Tenochtitlan the business of the inpouring tribute grew increasingly involved. Houses were set up for the headquarters of each tribute town. The accounting was kept exactly, both of the goods taken in and the division according to the treaties of the alliance.[24]

The Speaker-king announced a new appointment. In charge of the varied tribute coming in from all the conquered towns he put a woman, trained like others of her countrywomen of the south in administration and command—the Tall Woman from Coaixtlahuaca.[25]

XVII

Music of Bones

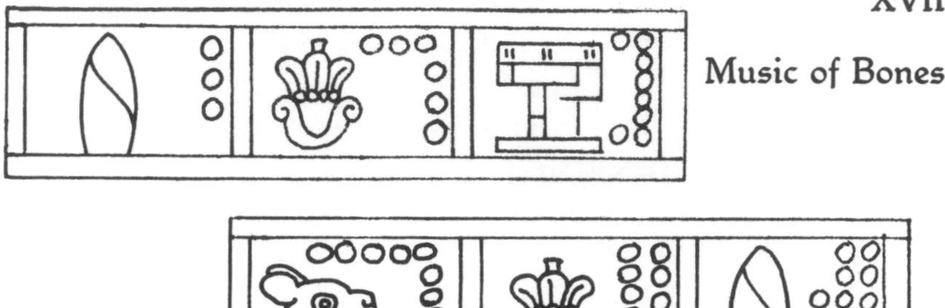

MEXICO-TENOCHTITLAN looked at the wide arc of its conquests where the song of Huitzilopochtli had sounded in the country of the great sun, among the neighbors of the sea. But the arc enclosed nearer cities which still bore arms against the Mexica, and refused to send tribute and declare their gods conquered by the Hummingbird on the Left. Chalco, which had had to yield Tlalmanalco after the coronation campaign of Moteczuma, still stood unconquered itself. The war of arrows had broken out at intervals[1] and in the year Three Stone the Mexica had reached the very entrance of the town of Amecameca before turning back. In the year Six Reed, Moteczuma, guarding the rear during his march to the lands of the sun, would not prepare the tortillas of war.[2] But in Eight House and Nine Rabbit and Ten Reed, there was fighting again on the lake.

Then came the year Eleven Stone when the hot winds blew and trees fell and again the earth rained fire. Tenochtitlan gathered its strength to bring the long struggle to a close. The men of the island city camped on the hills toward Chalco and toward the hill town of Amecameca.[3]

In this time of drought, under a sun like the blaze of the low lands along the sea, Mexica and Chalca fed blood to the gods there on the lake and in the dying corn. The Mexica sent back a report that three of Moteczuma's own brothers were killed. He wept for the captives and the dead.

Tlacaelel reproved him.

"It is true that our brothers are dead, your brothers and mine. Rejoice that they died in battle."

Moteczuma turned to the task of command.

"To arms!" he ordered. "We will pitch camp this time against the armies of Chalco without returning again to Mexico-Tenochtitlan for rest or sleep. Let the tlacatecatl and tlacochcalcatl give out the insignia, the tiger skins, the masks of tigers and eagles and lions. Let us paint our bodies as for death."

Supplies were brought from the city to the army in the thatched huts, and the king himself gave the charge to the men in the field.

"Let us not remember those who wait for us in Mexico-Tenochtitlan—our fathers and mothers, our wives and our children. Let us keep before us the memory of the dead. Let our hearts mourn for them."

They remembered the king's brothers. Then suddenly a new report came back to temper sorrow with solemn pride.

"It was not in battle that your brother Tlacahuepan died," Moteczuma was told.

He had been recognized in Chalco—a prize indeed, a man who had been given the title of Ezuauacatl after the war with Azcapotzalco, a man whom the Mexica had placed on the council from which the king must be chosen, a man who had taken part in wars and embassies, the brother of the Tlatoani of Tenochtitlan.[4]

"Let us save this man from death. Let us make him a tecuhtli among us, a leader of our city."

They called him out from the prisoners waiting to be sacrificed and offered him life.

"I laugh," he said, "because for us who went forth to battle there was no other course. We risked our lives to kill you or to rule you. Now we are in your power—yet I may

rejoice. Let me sing and dance with my companions. Bring me a great tree trunk, twenty arm-spreads high. Set it up with a platform on top."

It did not seem strange to them that their new tecuhtli should take authority and give the orders for the festival of this month of Xocotluetzi.

They brought the trunk of the tree, heavy and tall; they dug a deep hole to insert it, and they set oars into the ground to peg and brace it. Then bit by bit, tightening the ropes, they raised it, lifting it with the strength of many men united. It slid deep into the hole at last and stood high against the sky.

"Now bring drums, that to the beat of the teponaztli and huehuetl we may rejoice."

The captive Mexica waiting to be sacrificed were brought to the plaza. To the music of drums they began a song, low and sorrowful.

"Now I go, my brothers. Die with valor," said the man whom the Chalca had chosen to be a tecuhtli.

It did not seem strange that he should climb to the place where the dough image of the god should be.

"Thus he shows that he accepts the honor we have offered him," decided the Chalca.

Dancing around the base of the pole, the Mexica watched him climb to the little platform at the top and dance there against the sky to their music. They could hear his own song, and then his voice speaking.

"Men of Chalco, know that I buy your lives now, to serve the Mexica. I buy your blood for mine. Sing on, Mexica."

And while his comrades sang and danced in sad measure, he hurled himself from the high platform to the ground.

The confused cries of the Chalca rose over the song.

"What is this? He put us to sleep. He has made us slaves of the Mexican."

And now the plaza of Chalco became the place of sacrifice with arrows. And the Mexican captives were carried like the deer.

Moteczuma, in the field as he had been in the early days of his reign, heard the report of the death of his brother. From camp he sent his order back to the city.

"Let the families of those who died in Chalco go into the plaza before the temple of Huitzilopochtli," he commanded. "Let there be music and sad dance."

In the camp in the hills the owls of ill omen came close that night.

"Chalco, Chalco," they seemed to say. "Tecolo coco tetec yolo yolo"—"Owls . . . cut, cut . . . hearts, hearts. . . ."

Under the thatched shelters the men lay awake listening.

Tlacaelel, warrior priest of the Snake Woman, camped in the hills with them like his brother, moved quietly among them.

"What do the owls say?" he asked.

"They talk of Chalco, and of this place where we are in

Cocotitlan. They talk of cutting out hearts in the sacrifice."

"That is what we will do to the Chalca," said Tlacaelel. "The owls speak not to them but to us of victory."[5]

With the first light of morning three men came to the camp of the Mexicans and asked to see Moteczuma himself.

"I am the son of Coateotl," one said.

The name of the man who had died because he was a friend of Moteczuma was sufficient for a password. The young visitor was taken to the king.

"We have come to serve you, fearful of the ruin of our own city," he said.

So had his father spoken long ago.

"We can lead you by an unguarded way to Amecameca."

Moteczuma and Tlacaelel consulted.

"It is a trick," decided Tlacaelel. "If it is false, we would be betrayed into the hands of the Chalca. If it is true, we would lose the glory of victory and these men would claim it. We have begun the war. In the end we will win it. Let them go if they wish, or stay if they wish, but we do not follow where they lead."

Moteczuma listened to his brother's counsel. Once more the destiny of an old friend's son was in his hands. All his life he had walked with death, he had walked with harshness.

He sought out the young man.

"You are in your house," he said gently. "Rest here. You need not go into battle today."

The words spoke neither confidence nor doubt. But they spoke life, and not death.[6]

In the same cold daybreak in the Texcocan camp facing Chalco, two sons of Nezahualcoyotl were eating their breakfast on a shield. They laughed to see their young brother Axoquentzin coming toward them. Acapioltzin, who knew what it was to be young and seeking honor on a battlefield for the first time, called out his greeting.

"It is good to see you," he said. "How did you come over the battlefield without fear?"

"I wanted so much to see you, I did not think of fear," the boy replied.

An older brother spoke sharply.

"This is a place for men. Get back and away from here."

"He has shown his courage. Let him breakfast on the shield," said Acapioltzin kindly.

"Better let him cling to the skirts of women and breakfast like a child," replied the other.

The boy cringed at the taunt and ran away from them into the hut where the arms of his brothers had been left. They did not see him when the call to battle came with the rising sun.

Again men struggled for victory. Warriors masked with eagle beaks and tiger heads marched singing into battle.

"It is already late. We have waited for you," taunted the Chalca.

Ahead of them their old ruler was carried on a chair into battle, nearly blind but still directing the fighting of his people.

Suddenly from among the Texcocans a boy sped forward. He seized the old man by the hair.

"You are my prisoner. I avenge now the death of two of my brothers who were captured and killed by you when they played in the fields outside Texcoco."

"Stop!" cried the Chalca. "Give him the respect due to his age, the respect due a noble prisoner."

"I will take him to my father, treating him with nobility as I am noble," replied the boy proudly.

Acapioltzin arrived with support for the young brother who had dared to enter the battle. The news sped across the distance that the old tecuhtli had been captured by a boy.[7]

The Mexica in their singing companies swept on. Fleeing to the hills the old men and women of Chalco could see the fighters of the allied cities pushing on to victory. Even Tlalmanalco, conquered twenty years before, was being overrun again. In Amecameca the people huddled on the hill by the temple looked down as the fighting in the streets gave way, and the struggle up the hill began, and arrows were shot into the temple.[8]

The last day's fighting was swift and certain.

"The Mexicans attacked at sunrise. By noon we were friends. By sunset they controlled the four parts of Chalco—Amecameca, Tlalmanalco, Tenanco, and Xochimilco-Chimalhuacan."

So spoke the weary Chalca, conquered now, accepting defeat.[9]

The lines of refugees headed over the pass to Huexotzinco and Tlaxcala. In alarm Moteczuma and Tlacaelel and Nezahualcoyotl held council. Even with the swelling tribute from the hot country, the storehouses of grain and the vegetables of Chalco were necessary for the island city. The skilled builders of Chalco were needed on the public works. Even more important, the defeated Chalca must not be permitted to join the Tlaxcalteca who had conspired with both Coaixtlahuaca and Cuetlaxtlan against the expanding Mexican power.

Before the victorious rulers stood two Chalca, making the promises of surrender.

"We will come into Mexico-Tenochtitlan," they said.

"Are you nobles?" asked Moteczuma.

"He is noble, but I am not," one replied.

Moteczuma turned to the one of the noble class and gave him authority.

"You take the message that the Chalca should not flee to Tlaxcala and Huexotzinco," he said.

"Now that the war is over, give us land as your heart pleases," suggested the Chalca, asking proof.

Moteczuma named their boundaries.

"Where otherwise will you put down roots?" he asked.

He and Nezahualcoyotl gave them plumes and gold, golden tanned skin for collars and for clothing, blankets and firewood. They left with their message of clemency.[10]

Months later the Chalca came back humbly from the roads

beyond the volcano and from the woods where they had hidden in fear.

"We will bring you rock and wood and workmen for your buildings. We were defeated fairly and without fraud. We could not fight longer against you."[11]

The Mexica received them with honor.

"We have never met such valiant warriors—equal to us in courage!" said Tlacaelel, the warrior priest.

And the defeated Chalca were given the noseplugs and the insignia of the valiant and noble.[12]

Where the axes and fires had been laid on the hills in declaration of war, now at last the shield and arrows were buried.[13] And now the dead were remembered in sorrowful dance.[14]

The old men moved to the music of their drums, and the wives of the dead came wearing their hair loose before their faces, each one alone in the privacy of her grief. They came bearing in their hands the clothing and jewels of the dead. Here a woman carried her baby in her arms; and the children who were old enough danced and sang, lifting the bewilderment of loss to the ordering of the ritual.

When the old men tired, they seated themselves before the dancers and comforted them as they passed.

"Behold and speak to the god of the sun, of the wind and the times."

At the end of the day a line of men came to the plaza bearing gifts to the families of the dead—to the men blankets and loincloths, plumes and jewels; to the women skirts, and embroidered blouses. They brought corn and beans and chilli and firewood. And they brought slaves who would be sacrificed and go with the dead to serve them.

Then each family began to make an image of the dead warrior whom they mourned. They took a stick of pitch pine, and wrapped it as the dead were wrapped, painting a face upon it and covering it with a shield and plumes and insignia of rank, and they took it to the house of arms.

There they danced again for four days—the old men and the young, the women and the children. And this time they danced to the rhythm of notched deer bones rasped against each other, and to bone horns. To the music of bones they danced in memory of the dead.

They came again to the open plaza before the pyramid of Huitzilopochtli. There, on great bonfires, they burned the pitch pine effigies. A little ash from each one was taken still warm and brushed over their heads with twigs of living green. All men knew them as they passed during the eighty days of mourning, for they were marked by the ash caked with sweat and tears.

At the end of the eighty days the ashes of the burned effigies were buried for a time in their own island earth in the midst of the lake and the whispering grasses. From their faces the mourning families scraped ash and dust and wrapped it in little twists of paper. These too they buried.

"These are the relics of tears," they said.

The days slipped into their pattern again. For another eighty days grief grew quiet. The gardeners worked in each calpulli. In the ordered ceremonies of the temples the fires burned and the conch shell sounded the times of day and night.

The next task was for the old who knew death and how to leave it behind. They took the buried ashes away from the island over the lake waters to a hill at the Chalco frontier. And there on the top of the hill they left them under the sky.

On the fifth day after they returned to Tenochtitlan they burned the clothing of the dead in the place where the effigies had been burned. They had a feast in their name, and made offerings of tortillas. And they poured on the new ashes pulque, fermented from the honey water of the maguey.

Those who mourned knew that on this day they would not be stoned for drinking pulque. They drank it, cool and fresh and sour. And they wore new clothes that the king had given them.

The old men spoke for the living to the dead:

"Now, my children, you have come to the gods, and are near the Fire Youth, the Eagle that Soars, the joy of the Sun."

And they spoke again, releasing the tight bonds of sorrow:

"From the caves, from the plains, from the towns and the mountains we call you forth, that you may not be in mist and in cloud, but that the sun may shine for you, that you may do your work in the fields of the sun in dawnlight and splendor. With this we leave you; we let you go, to joy."

XVIII

The Law Is That They Sing

IT WAS A TIME OF JOY in the lake cities, with war forgotten. Song rose to the conquered gods:

"In the house of Mixcoatl they are raising songs,
They sing in the house of Amapan.
Already Tlacahuepan and Ixtlilcuechahuac come shouting.
The law is that they sing: the law of brotherhood, the law of the noble."[1]

The Chalca, skilled in masonry, labored now on the public works of Mexico-Tenochtitlan and Texcoco.[2] They built a temple in Texcoco nine stages high and on the ninth level as from the ninth heaven of the Twofold God of Abundance music sounded in praise of the God of the With and the By. They worked on the never-ending constructions in the center of Tenochtitlan—the temple of Huitzilopochtli and Tlaloc and the lesser shrines of the conquered gods. They built houses of many rooms and courtyards for the three kings of the alliance.

The years of war had brought death to so many of the Chalca that there were not men enough for the work, and women too labored on the heavy construction.[3]

The sun beat down, raining fire of another year. Nezahualcoyotl looked with pity on the conquered workers.

"Let us build them big shelters with straw roofs," he said.

And they had shade to rest in during the intervals of work in that year Thirteen Rabbit.

Hunger came to Chalco in the Rabbit year. But though hot winds blew and the land was dry, and though because of war and death the fields around Chalco had gone unplanted, the highland towns knew no hardship like that of the year One Rabbit. Over the roads of hunger that had led out from the valley only twelve years before, food now poured into the lake towns, carried on the backs of the conquered neighbors of the sea.

This time when the kings opened their granaries to feed the hungry Chalca there was food that could be replenished day by day—chilli and beans and corn, more precious than the gold and chalchihuitl stones in the market place. No longer did the workers have to be reduced to a meal a day. The roads of hunger had turned to roads of supply for two million people in the Valley of Mexico.[4] In the market place cotton and grain and breads, sweetmeats, turkeys and eggs, rabbits and deer and doves and ducks, fresh fish from the lake and dried fish from the sea, were on display for the thousands who came to buy on market day.[5]

Water too could be brought to dried fields. "The hills are full of water," Nezahualcoyotl had said in the famine of One Rabbit. And now irrigation ditches ran to the gardens of Tezcotzinco and even to Texcoco, where a big square of ahuehuetl trees had been planted to celebrate the victory over Chalco.[6] In Mexico-Tenochtitlan work progressed on the channel which would bring fresh water from Chapultepec. Still Nezahualcoyotl directed it, and now the Chalca labored on its rock and sod.[7]

Life was bright in the land where death had been. Word came to Moteczuma from Texcoco that the girl with the honest eyes had borne Nezahualcoyotl another son,[8] and he knew that the sorrow of his friend's heart for the boy condemned to death could now be partly healed. Coateotl's son had been given a wife in Tenochtitlan. No one now would ever know whether, when he came to Moteczuma's camp, his intention had been to betray the Chalca or the Tenochca. What was done was done. And for a little while the friendships of the Archer of the Sky did not turn in his hands from tenderness to death.

His heart looked now to his mother's green country.

"I am told there is a beautiful place there called Huaxtepec—a place of rocks and springs and flowers," he said wistfully to Tlacaelel.

His brother needed no more than the suggestion.

"Let us send for Pinotl, the tribute collector we have placed in Cuetlaxtlan. Let us have him arrange to bring the plants and trees of the hot country to Huaxtepec, with gardeners who will know how to set them out. Let us make pools and dams and irrigation canals. Let us carve our ancestors on rock."

The messengers went to Cuetlaxtlan on the hot coastal plain beside the slow green river. And to Huaxtepec, half way up to the high country but still low enough so that the sun warmed the earth, the gardeners came, carrying young seedlings wrapped in straw mats, roots hanging. They brought flowers and medicinal plants. Forty families came to do the transplanting and irrigating, their hands gentle, knowing the ways of growth in the country of the great sun, working now in the king's gardens and orchards.

The king who never went out from his own houses and courtyards except for the most needful things, came from Mexico-Tenochtitlan to watch.

From that high place he could look out over hills misted with blue. At his feet the water ran in the new irrigation canals from the mountain stream. The trees stood in their rows.

The gardeners from the hot country finished their transplanting.

"The trees should bear fruit in seven years," they said.

"Bring us now paper of the amatl tree, and pine incense, and rubber."

There in the newly set out orchard they prayed to Xochipilli, god of flowers. They drew blood with sharp obsidian points from the lobes of their ears and touched it to the plants in sacrifice. They burned incense and sacrificed small doves. They prayed to the god of flowers and of pleasure that these plants and trees should not die, but live and bear fruit in this mountain place of sweet air where the river ran gently.

And the king watched the workers in stone carve the living rock. Year signs told of events long past, of men and gods. A small pyramid rose, step by step. A coiled stone snake below the clear running water seemed to move in the shifting light and shade.[9]

Here the king was content, talking to simple men who knew the ways of earth and tools, content with peace.

Then again war moved in the land to the old measure.

Messengers appeared before Moteczuma.

"Merchants from the lake towns have been killed in the market of Tepeacac," they reported.[10]

Fear was again moving in the land. The market place of Tepeacac, meeting place of traders from the hot country and from the highlands, had watched the power of the alliance circle them; had seen it come close at Quauhtinchan; had watched it now conquer the rich town of Chalco.

As in the rhythm of a dance the gestures of defiance had been made and were returned. The feathers and war paint, the shields and weapons were carried from Tenochtitlan to Tepeacac.

"With these gifts, wait for us."

"Tell Moteczuma we are grateful. We will be ready for him when he comes."

The lake towns again made ready for war. Men of noble rank went from Mexico-Tenochtitlan to their allies asking for grain and beans, for chilli and salt, for thin clothes for the journey to the country of the great sun. Axayacatl, grandson

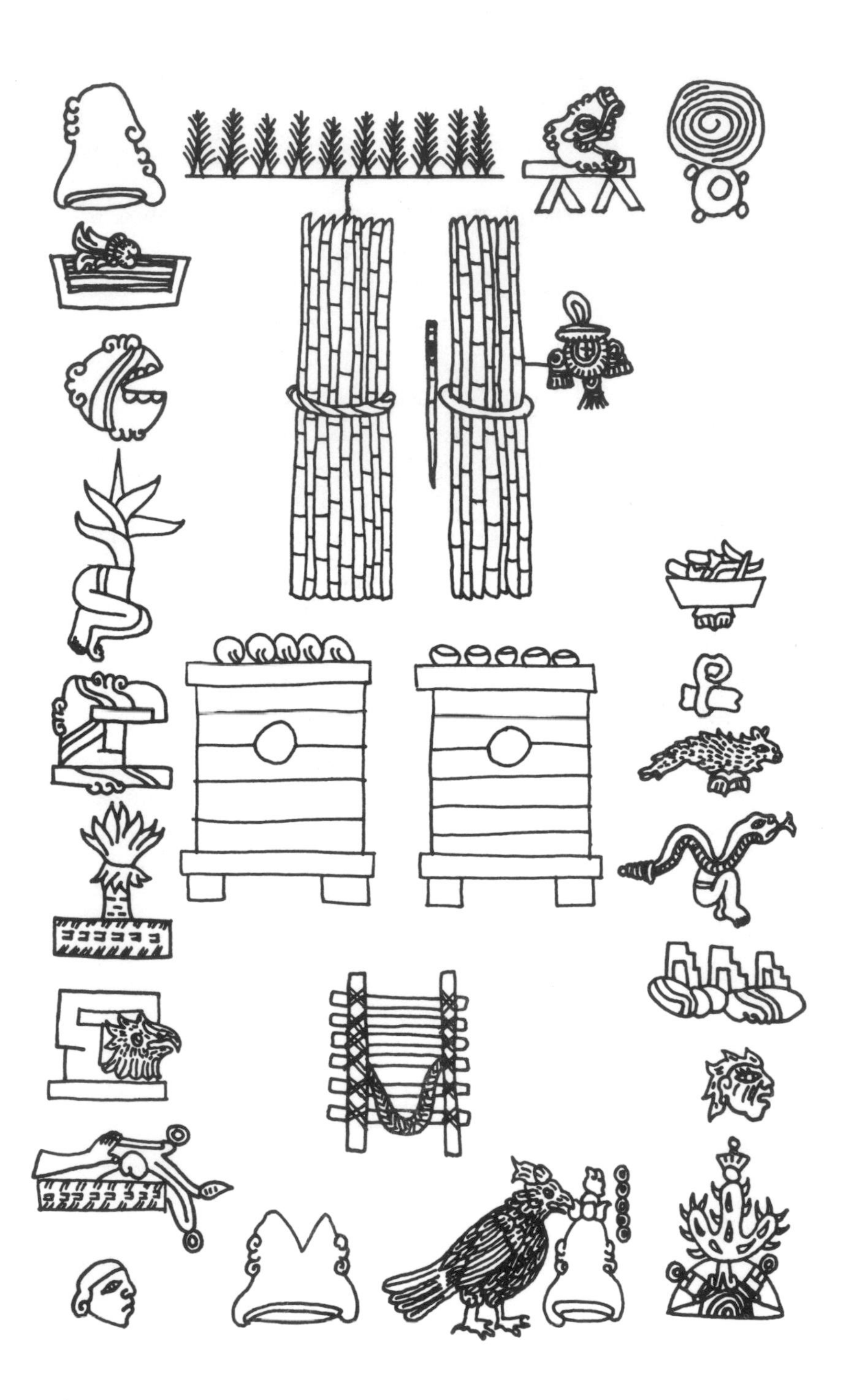

of Moteczuma, was put in command of the expedition down past the boundaries of Tlaxcala and Huexotzinco to the province of Tepeacac where the little birds sang four hundred songs.[11]

There was no secret in their march. They moved at last on the plain with all their equipment and camped on a hill, setting up their shades against the sun, carrying wood for fires, and water for cooking and drinking.

Strangely, they saw no one watching them. They sent their listeners and their watchers and their runners to the towns scattered over the plain and the hills to see how many men were armed and waiting. But the spies came back with surprising reports:

"There are no guards, no defenses built up. It is as if these towns had never been notified."

They divided their troops. Without opposition some marched to the town of Tecamachalco, perched high against a ridge above the green plain. Some marched to Acatzinco, low in the fertile valley, where they saw mountains stand distant and blue in the afternoon light. Some marched to Quauhtinchan, which claimed all the towns of the province though it had been overcome long since by Mexico-Tlatelolco. Around its lush green lands stood the hills and ridges streaked with white limestone and shadowed with dark areas of trees. Some went on to Tecalli, where the high sweet wind blew from the sun-paled marble and limestone hills. And some near the sharp hill of Tepeacac watched the town where the merchants had been killed.

Still no masked and plumed dancers came singing into battle. Under the great sun there was quietness.

"At the quarter moon we will attack in the middle of the night. By daybreak the five towns will be ours."

In the strange time of waiting there was no word from the listeners and watchers and runners. The quarter moon came. The troops marched in the silent midnight and found no one to fight against them.

In the morning the messengers arrived from the high hill of Tepeacac.[12]

"Rest your arms. We offer you tribute of corn and beans and chilli, sandals, palm mats to sleep on, thin cloth and deer-skins, captive slaves for sacrifice. We are on your trade route south. As often as you pass through here you will find food."[13]

When the returning Tenochca with their prisoners reached home, the old men and the speakers, the old eagles, and the images of the gods were lining the road on both sides to welcome them. Bright with pleated paper headdresses, with belts of little gourds and leather thongs, carrying bowls of pine incense, the officials addressed them:

"Welcome, sons, to Mexico-Tenochtitlan, to the city in the midst of the lake reeds where the water animals croak, and the flying birds are caught twittering in nets over the marshes."[14]

Victors and prisoners went first to the temple of Huitzilopochtli.

"Here in time the knife will be put to your breast," the prisoners were promised. "Welcome—and let it be a comfort that you come not by any cowardly act of women but by the deeds of men, and here a memory of you will remain forever."

To the words meant to be heartening, the conquerers added the divine drink, the fermented honey water of the maguey, the milk-white pulque.

From the temple they went to the Speaker-king.

"Welcome," said Moteczuma Ilhuicamina to the prisoners. "Take gifts of mantles and sandals and food."

Then after the long march from Tepeacac, prisoners and captors rested.

Together, holding shields and roses in their hands, and pipes to lift sweet-smelling smoke like incense before the market altar, they went forth later to dance. They gave to Huitzilopochtli a sweeping round fan of white feathers in a wooden box. They ate earth before him.

Moteczuma himself came out as the wooden beat of a new teponaztli sounded in the square.

And the king danced in the market place.[15]

The treaty, when it was completed, was an agreement on market privileges. Moteczuma Ilhuicamina, under whose direction the trading interests of Mexico-Tenochtitlan were reaching farther all the time and assuming more intricate organization, determined the provisions clause by clause.

"You will set aside a convenient place for our merchants so that going and coming they will always have it to use. You will guard them against attack and offence."

He too would make his promises.

"Our merchants will take to your market precious stones, plumes, clothing, slaves, rare birds brought from the ends of the world."

Section by section the agreement went on, clearly understood.

"You will see that all foreigners, from however far they come, those that go to Xoconochco and Guatemala over the whole earth, will receive help from you. When foreigners wish to live in your land, assign them fields so that they can help make your city noble and great. These merchants make a city rich and give food to the poor and to all the people."

The lists of imports they could expect from far away went on—metals of many kinds, cacao, and skins of mountain cats.

"It is my will," said Moteczuma, "that you build up a great market in which all the merchants of the land will stop."

The lords of Tepeacac returned to their town rejoicing, thinking of Moteczuma Ilhuicamina not as their ruler but as their friend and ally.[16] In the face of the business future that opened before them it seemed unimportant that they would have to send tribute to the high country every eighty days and that Coacuech, a collector from Mexico-Tenochtitlan, would live among them as representative of its tlatoani, and as the calpixque, Keeper of the Tribute House.[17] It seemed unimportant too that nothing had been said about boundaries between the lands owned by the towns which had been taken between midnight and morning. Now that they were all tributary in Mexico, ancient rivalries between them seemed ended.

Quauhtinchan, however, remembered her earlier glory as the main town of the area.

"Now we are one, without boundaries," said her citizens. "We are one—and are named Quauhtinchan."

The men from Tepeacac came again to the high country. They sought out Axayacatl, who had commanded their conquerers.

"We of Tepeacac come humbly. Is your land and ours all the property of Quauhtinchan? Where shall we gather the white corn and the black corn? Fix our boundaries; set our landmarks. This is all we ask."

"I have heard you. I have understood. It shall be done," promised Axayacatl.

There was no objection from Moteczuma or Tlacaelel. In the year One Reed three men came from Mexico-Tenochtitlan to set the boundaries, and quiet the dispute among the conquered towns. It did not seem important enough to them to pace out the lines so that their footprints could be marked upon a map. They did not walk. They only climbed a hill and pointed with their fingers, naming the hills that should be the frontiers. It was as if they knew that before long their decision would not be important even to the people of Quauhtinchan. Already people were moving to the market town. Let boundaries be set and ignored. Let people plant where they would. It no longer mattered.[18]

In Mexico-Tenochtitlan the task of years was finished. The aqueduct from Chapultepec was ready at last. With two channels so that one could remain in use whenever the other was being cleaned and repaired, it would carry clear water to the city in the marsh.

Nezahualcoyotl came over from Texcoco to turn the water

into it for the first time. His skill had given shape to the dream the Tenochca had struggled toward since the days when the old and feeble king of Azcapotzalco had given the islanders the water rights to the springs on the Hill of the Grasshopper. In giving the Hungry Coyote the place of honor, Moteczuma recognized that the new aqueduct was as much a result of their friendship and alliance as their conquests had been.

Nezahualcoyotl set his crowbar to the rock and sod that closed the upper end of the aqueduct. The head of water, thicker than a man's body, moved along the channel.

All the way from its source the captive prisoners from Tepeacac went before it, hurrying it along, drawing blood in sacrifice before the water.[19]

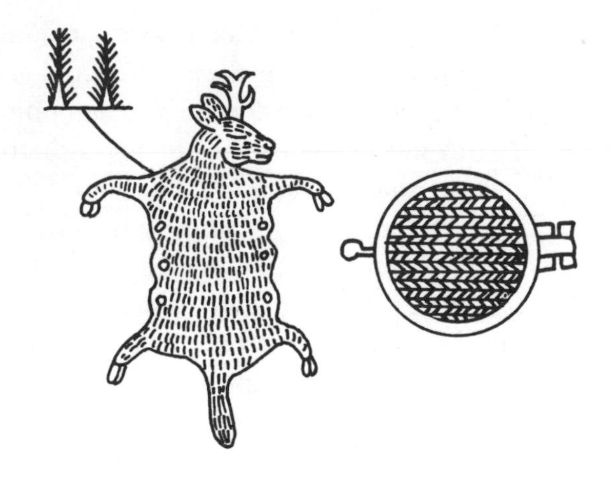

XIX

Sandals of Conquest and Return

IN THE LAKE TOWNS stone hammers beat upon stone. In One Reed a new stage was begun in the never-ending work on the temple of Huitzilopochtli in Mexico-Tenochtitlan.[1] The Texcocans too were completing their own temple to the Hummingbird on the Left.[2] Nezahualcoyotl sent to his friend Moteczuma.

"We will need prisoners for sacrifice when the temple is dedicated," he said.

Even he who worshipped the God of the With and the By who did not ask for blood knew that the warrior god of the sun must be fed. But this was a time of peace.

The two friends worked out a plan. Towns of the highland country were chosen to be spied out and attacked. But that there should be no break in the alliance, soldiers from the country of the great sun should be brought up to do the fighting, and the towns to be attacked should be forewarned.

Naked fighters came from the Totonaca country and from Cuextlan carrying their white banners for the first time into battle by the highland lake. And the temple of Huitzilopochtli in Texcoco was dedicated with the blood of the prisoners foreign soldiers took in Tzompanco for Texcoco.[3]

Workmen began to hew stone for the walls of a ball court

where the nobles of Texcoco and Tenochitlan could play, striking the rubber ball with hip and thigh, and kings could bet a city on the game. The ball would fly high through stone rings, and honor be given to Tonatiuh, the Sun, and to Xolotl, god of the Evening Star sinking to the land of bones.[4]

Tlatelolco too was building the House of the Serpent and the Place of the Skull and a temple to Huitzilopochtli.[5] Even the conquered Chalca came to Moteczuma.

"Let us build high like a mountain the temple which we left abandoned."

"It is good that it be done," said Moteczuma.[6]

From the busy centers of tribute collection a report came to the king.

"Cuetlaxtlan has not sent in its quarterly tribute. There is no word from the collector there."

Moteczuma commissioned two men among the merchants who travelled that way to seek out the representative of the king and send back a report on the interrupted business relations with the town in the hot country.

They did not return, nor did the other merchants with whom they travelled. Instead a man came from the market of Tepeacac with gossip that had reached that busy center with travelers from the country of the great sun. It was retold in Tenochtitlan with horror.

Xicotencatl and other officials from Tlaxcala visiting in Cuetlaxtlan had said to One Water Day, Ce Atonal,

"Why do you pay tribute to Mexico-Tenochtitlan? Let them come again with arrows and obsidian-toothed clubs against you! We will defend you."

The Cuetlaxteca had listened. And when the envoys and merchants had come from the high country, they had locked them in a room, built a fire of chilli, and suffocated them with the smoke.

"The odor of burning chilli hung in the town for many days," reported the news gatherer from the market of Tepeacac.

He went on with added horror. When the Cuetlaxteca entered the room at last to remove the dead bodies, they slit them up the back, stuffed them with straw, and set them on icpallis of authority in mockery. They put white feather fans on their heads like crowns and held hot cocoa to their lips. Mockingly they said,

"You are welcome. Did you come with demands for feathers and cocoa?"

Moteczuma, the Angry One, the Archer of the Sky, heard the story.

"For this the whole town of Cuetlaxtlan will die," he said.

"It is a rich town," Tlacaelel reminded him. "Let us leave half the population alive. Let us not cut off our tribute, but double it. Let mantles be woven for us not of ten arms' length but twenty. Let chalchihuitl stones come as tribute, not only green but white. Let big snakes be delivered to us alive. Let us receive white skins of lions and tigers."

The anger of Moteczuma was quieted as they discussed the possibilities.

Then down from the hot country once more marched fighters ready for battle. Messengers went from the Mexica-encircled Tlaxcala to the Cuetlaxteca whom they had encouraged to revolt.

"Delay the moment of battle as much as possible," they said. "We are gathering our forces and will attack the Mexica from the rear."

But the Mexica did not wait for the battle array to form with the order and pattern of a dance. They sent no envoys to deliver the shield and arrows, the paint for war and death. Swift and certain, they carried fire and obsidian points to Cuetlaxtlan.[7]

Xicotencatl had no time to bring in his own troops from the rear. The allies shouted the names of their own towns as they fought—Tenochtitlan, Texcoco, Tlacopan . . . The air was filled with the names of towns from the high country and the sound of wooden drums and shell trumpets. And war was like fire in a field of dry grass.

Then the macehuales and the mayaques, the farmers and the laborers, cried out at last,

"Why do you kill us? What blame have we, the poor people? We have not injured you. Why do you not seek our lords and rulers? They have brought us death. As for us, do we not give you our tribute? Does not all that you get come from our sweat and work? If they give mantles, did they weave them? If they give cacao and plumes and fish and gold, are we not the ones who give them to our conqueror Moteczuma?"

The Mexica laid down their arms.

"Speak," they ordered.

"We would have you kill our lords, and spare us. They were the ones who conspired with the Tlaxcalteca. All that they give you comes from us. And we will still give you tribute."[8]

The Mexicans hesitated.

"We have no authority to kill except in battle," they said. "But bring your leaders forth."

The macehuales sought them out in the caves where the stone images of the gods were kept, and where sacrifices were made.

At last Ce Atonal and his companion Tepetecutli, the two leaders of Cuetlaxtlan, stood before the Mexica.

"Guard them well. Moteczuma will send word what shall be done with them."

The Mexica went up again through the pass in the hills and came to their own city.

"The common people of Cuetlaxtlan were not to blame for the revolution," they reported. "Their rulers conspired with Tlaxcala, and live only to eat and drink and play games, all at the cost of the common people. They pray that you will do justice and see that their rulers are killed."

Moteczuma called his brother, the warrior priest.

"The rulers of Cuetlaxtlan are images of the gods—rulers and priests. Do we offend the gods if we kill them?"

"They have offended Huitzilopochtli," said Tlacaelel. "The macehuales plead justice, and we need not deny it to them."

Authorized by Moteczuma, Archer of the Skies, and by his brother the priest of Cihuacoatl, the executioners went back down to the neighbors of the sea. Carefully the punishment was made to fit the crime, and the knife slit the backs of the rulers of Cuetlaxtlan. Now the song of victory could sound again: "Where now is Water Day?"[9]

The Mexica supervised the election of two new rulers, and appointed a new tax collector.

Within a few days the lines of burdenbearers began to appear in the high country, bringing the beauty of gold and silver and jewels and plumes, bringing thick and heavy-muscled snakes for sacrifice to Huitzilopochtli, squatting before the god to eat earth.

Moteczuma confronted them.

"Those who have come as slaves will not be sacrificed," he said. "My sons from Cuetlaxtlan, do not listen to the Tlaxcalteca. If they speak to you, remember we are here."

The people of Tlaxcala looked bitterly on their neighbors —Tepeacac and Cuetlaxtlan and the other cities that the alliance had conquered.

"They inform against us, hoping for favor from the Tenochca, hoping to keep our traders from competition with theirs," they said.

Xicotencatl, who had missed his moment of action, waited for another time and another ally. The circle around his city was complete, shutting him off from the sea of the sky, from the cotton of the coast country, from cocoa and salt. At the moment there was nothing for him to do. The Tlaxcalteca must learn to like their beans and deer meat without salt.[10]

Once more the never-ending pattern repeated like the sequence of suns, with the pallor of bones already white in the southern day.

Merchants passing south through Coaixtlahuaca and Oaxaca were warned by macehuales in the fields.

"Do not keep on to the south. We have been ordered to kill the traders that pass this way—as we did those others."

And they took them into the woods and showed them bones of men who had been killed several years before when they were coming from the coast country with red paint for shields, and shell trumpets, and gold dust. A trader from Chalco took word to Tenochtitlan about the bones in the woods.

"We will find prisoners to sacrifice at the dedication of the completed pyramid to Huitzilopochtli," suggested Moteczuma to his brother.

Again the troops marched south with vengeance, and slaves came up from the distant land.

"But the temple is not finished." said Tlacaelel. "The supporters of the sky are not in place. The Chalca and the Xochimilca and the other builders still work on the sides which have been assigned to them and swarm like ants over the face of the building. Let us wait."

In this pause of war and sacrifice they pondered the problem of feeding the gods. Now there were revolutions rather than new conquests, prisoners thin with the long march from the hot country.

"We cannot wait until we are provoked into another war," said Tlacaelel. "And these prisoners, thin and tough, provide hard bread for the gods. Shall we offer food without flavor to Huitzilopochtli—men of a strange and unknown tongue?"

The two men considered other aspects of the situation that had developed in recent years for their city.

"We must find a market where the gods may buy their food," said Tlacaelel, "a nearer market than these coastlands we now control, for they are far away and our armies cannot stand these constant long marches."[12]

The solution was clear to both men. Victims must again be provided by the enemies within the house—enemies encircled now, eating their food without salt. Xicotencatl was willing to engage again in the formal war. Month by month his fighting men and those of the neighboring towns[13] would take their turn in meeting the lake towns on assigned fields of battle.

"Only the slaves and workmen went to the old war of flowers in Chalco," one remembered who cherished the ancient records.[14]

"Let this war be for the sons of nobles," said Tlacaelel. "Thus they may win their insignia, thus prove themselves men. They will go to this war joyously, as men go to their marriage."

"Tell them the honors they can win," said Moteczuma.

And Tlacaelel roused the Tenochca to battle.

"Do you seek bracelets and jewels in the market? Now you can seek them in another market, for when you return from this war of flowers the king, who stands beside me, will offer you gifts—bracelets, lip and nose plugs, colored plumes and gold, arms and shields and incense bowls. Those who do not go, though they be kings' sons, will be known as men of little heart. They will labor on the public works. They will not be permitted to wear cotton garments. We will not go out to meet them with roses and cocoa.

"But the brave will be known. In this market they will buy honor and rank—and the right, though they may be the sons of concubines, to rule over sons of a legitimate wife who have not gone to war. The king will still eat alone, but when he is done, the brave will have food from what remains. And through all time men will remember them."

They went with gladness to the war so that gods might not die and the Fifth Sun might not end, as gods had died and times had ended before.

The men who went from Chalco remembered a more ancient war of flowers, one which they had fought with the Mexica and which in the end was real.[15]

And in Tlaxcala men said,

"Is this a war of flowers? We fight with hate."[16]

But in Tenochtitlan and the other lake cities the long journeys into the lands of the great sun to do battle with the neighbors of the sea seemed to be ended.

Moteczuma Ilhuicamina, Archer of the Skies, who had listened to the song of Huitzilopochtli, and with blood and sweat brought home the shining chalchihuitl stones, pondered a new expedition. He called to him his brother, the Priest of the Snake Woman, Cihuacoatl.

"Let us equip our men with arms and send them to find the seven caves from which we came, to find whether Coatlicue, She of the Skirt of Snakes, the mother of our god, still lives."[17]

Tlacaelel hesitated.

"Forgive me that I always seem to put my reasoning above yours," he said. "But one does not seek the gods with armies. Those whom we send must go not to conquer but to know."

They spoke of a dim past, floating between human and divine—of how Coatlicue of the Serpent Skirt had miraculously given birth to Huitzilopochtli and of how Huitzilopochtli had slain four hundred. Already it was not clear whether they were his sisters, or fighting men, or stars, or whether a man, or an image carried on the shoulders of men, or a warrior striding the sky, had led the Tenochca to the place in the marshes, and more recently, to the land of the great sun.

"Our ancestors came from a place which was one of rest, where people did not grow old and were never hungry. When they left, it turned into a place of thorns. Even the rocks became pointed and the plants pricked, and the trees grew spines. It will be best to call the priests and those who know magic and send them to seek this land."

Moteczuma called the man who knew best the histories in the painted books—Eagle Snake, keeper and guardian of the image of Huitzilopochtli. Old and bent, he appeared before the king.

"What do you know from your books of the land from

which our ancestors came—the place where Huitzilopochtli lived, the place of the seven caves?"

"It was a happy land," the old man replied, "that land of Aztlan, that hill in the middle of the water. There were ducks and waterbirds and fish—birdsong and the shade of trees. Our people went in canoes among gardens. But when they left, all was changed. The very plants began to bite."

The blunt king who liked to talk to business men and builders and craftsmen listened silently to the old priest.

"It must be true. It is what my brother told me," he said.

He left it to the priests, and to those who knew magic, to seek the ancient place, and the ancient mother if she should be found. But he gave them gifts to take to her, such as a tribute town might send—mantles, and women's clothing, and gold, and precious green stones, cocoa and vanilla and plumes.

They took the treasure and went away. Eighteen days later they came again. The king listened in wonder to what they told him. He saw, as clearly as if he had been there, the moment when with their magic they had turned to birds and flown over the distances to the lake where an old man paddled a canoe among gardens.

"We have been sent by Moteczuma and his co-ruler Tlacaelel Cihuacoatl," they had called to him.

"Who is Moteczuma and who is Tlacaelel Cihuacoatl?" he had replied.

The king listened humbly.

"Where are the ones who went away from here?" the old man on the lake had asked the Tenochca.

"We do not know them. They are dead."

"And who is guardian and keeper and father of Huitzilopochtli?"

"Eagle Man—and Huitzilopochtli speaks to him."

"And what did he say to you when you left?" the old man had asked.

"He did not send us. We were sent by the king and his co-ruler."

The old man paddled them across the lake to the sandy hill where the mother of the Humming Bird on the Left still lived. He went lightly up the steep slope of the hill, and youth came upon him as he climbed.

But the Tenochca who followed went with heavy feet, sinking into the sand.They went slowly, step by step, as a warrior prisoner might climb the steps of the pyramid to the sun. They stopped and were helpless.

And the ancient mother of their god came to them, a woman mourning until the return of her warrior child, as women in Mexico-Tenochtitlan mourned the men who had gone to war. Like them she waited unwashed, saving for the day of return what beauty of age might be hers. It was not strange to Moteczuma to hear that it was so.

They had given her his gifts—

"For they belong to Huitzilopochtli," they told her.

"He wears cloth like this—and eats this food and drinks this cocoa?" she asked. And she was comforted for his long absence. "But because of these foods and this rich cocoa," she warned them, "you are weak. Because of them you could not climb this hill."

Like the old man she asked for those who had come from the seven caves.

"We do not know those leaders of the calpullis," they said.

But they gave her the names of the kings of Mexico-Tenochtitlan.

"And now Moteczuma is king," they ended. "The city is rich and free. The roads to the coast and the sea are open and safe."

"My heart is quiet," the ancient mother of the warrior god had answered, the goddess of the serpent skirt. "My son will come to me again. He took two pairs of sandals—one to go away and one to return. He said that he would conquer many cities in their order, and in the same order would lose them. Let him come soon . . ."

Back to the goddess of earth, the ancient mother . . .

The priests and sorcerers laid gifts before Moteczuma that she had sent to Huitzilopochtli, her son—not jewels, but a mantle and breechcloth of maguey fiber, such as the poor wore, and the soldiers on the march to the hot lands by the sea. And the old man had gathered flowers and vegetables that grew in the gardens by the ancient lake—beans and chilli and tomatoes—and sent them to the unknown Moteczuma and his brother Tlacaelel.

The king who had sent jewels received the simple gifts from the hands of these men, and accepted trustingly all that they had said. He addressed his envoys to the goddess as he would address his envoys to a southern city, returning with their report of strange and distant roads.

"Rest now. You have done well."

And he commanded that the plain fiber mantle and breechcloth be sent to the temple of Huitzilopochtli, as the gift of his ancient mother, who remembered that he had taken one pair of sandals to stride forth to victory, and another to return in defeat.

XX

Obsidian Knife

MOTECZUMA ILHUICAMINA, Archer of the Skies, stood in the young orchard at Huaxtepec.

In the heavy air was the sweetness of white magnolia—the heart flower that only nobles could carry. The cacao was in bloom. And the spices that would be put in foaming cocoa were sun hot around him—the soft richness of vanilla, and the flowers whose spiced fragrance would go not only into the drink of nobles, but into medicines to sooth the throat, to cure the sick; whose petals would wrap ground medicines into sweet smelling capsules; and whose leaves would be dried for teas.

Vine and shrub and tree were heavy with blossom. And only three years had gone by of the seven that the gardeners from the coast country had said would be needed for the gardens of the king to flower and bear fruit.[1]

The gardeners stood on the flowering hill.

"These trees do better in this climate than in the coast country," they said in a matter-of-fact way.

The king stood beside them among the flowers. Here was life—strong under the sun. But always life had turned to death around him.

He seemed to hear the weeping of a young goddess of love who had plucked and broken a flower and the wailing of an old goddess of earth who carried in her cradle an obsidian blade of sacrifice and death.[2]

He wept at life, and knew that he would die.

He turned to his brother Tlacaelel.

"Note well what I say to you. These blooms have come early because in a few days I reach my end. Let us take these flowers and cover my body when it is time."

He took his brother apart and spoke to him quietly.

"Who in this land can rule as well as you? When I die, my brother, it is you who must take command, in the line of men who have been like merchants and travelers one after another on a long road."[3]

Tlacaelel was quiet and the two men thought of their sons. Not far away younger members of Tlacaelel's family were ruling in Yacapichtla with their lives settled into pattern.[4] Moteczuma himself had chosen a life of trades and crafts for his sons, knowing that kings eat the bread of sadness. Perhaps his daughter Atotoztli, Water Bird, could rule when he was dead, helped by her husband Tezozomoc, the son of Itzcoatl. Or perhaps their sons Axayacatl or Tizoc or Ahuizotl, young men who had already gained glory in battle.[5] There were travelers enough who could take their place in the line of rule.

"Two kings have taken my counsel. What greater power do I seek? I am old for a new burden to be put on my shoulders," he thought.[6]

But now he did not argue the point with his brother. He spoke to give him peace.

"I am grateful," he said.

Moteczuma Ilhuicamina looked a last time at the green distances of his mother's country. Elsewhere he had been a stranger and a foreigner.

When his mother had taken him a prisoner from the universe an obsidian knife had cut the cord. Now again the black blade waited in the cradle of age and death.

The two men returned to Tenochtitlan.

And now Moteczuma, Archer of the Sky, went into the Dark House.

Its walls closed around him with a kind of safety and peace at last, there in the house of Cihuacoatl, the Snake Woman, whom his brother served. Like a merchant returning from a long journey he was within the walls of the ancient earth mother, who was not only the Snake Woman but Chantico, guardian of his own house and hearth fire. The dark and the night were about him.[7]

His friend Nezahualcoyotl came to him, carrying a fan, like the god of merchants who went before them on far roads. He came with a song to his friend who had no time for song.

"I lift my song to give joy to Moteczuma
In the Dark House here in Mexico.
The old kings left you this city where the ahuehuetl trees grow.
Do you weep, Oh Moteczuma, because you still keep your throne?"[8]

Neither his icpalli of power, nor new word of conquest[9] comforted him. He reached out to his friend.

"Moteczuma weeps because you visit the city,
Because you come to visit your sick friend, oh Nezahualcoyotl.
In the house of blackness where the books were made,
Books such as you make and cherish,
You visit your friend, who is sick, oh Nezahualcoyotl.
Where the books open their petals of light,
Only among the pictures of your books
Will this city of Tenochtitlan endure."

In the face of death, Nezahualcoyotl, who had sung in youth of fading flowers, comforted him now with permanence.

"The flowers of green chalchihuitl stones
Will live in your hands."

And to him who would rather have his sons know how to paint books than to be rulers, Nezahualcoyotl added in further consolation,

"You have painted the land beside the water
Like a sky."

The silent king who had spread his rule to the neighbors of the sea, died on the island in the highland lake where the mists lay on the marsh grass and the night birds flew over.

Tlacaelel, Warrior Priest of the Snake Woman, had the body carried out of the dark house of the ancient mother and placed on the pyramid of Huitzilopochtli, Warrior God of Sun and Sky, god of the sandals of conquest and return.

He spoke for his brother the last time.

"The burden which our king has carried is laid down," he announced to the nobles of Mexico-Tenochtitlan.[10]

The body of the Speaker-king was bathed in water sweet with flowers. The rulers of the lake towns gathered, and envoys came over the roads of war and tribute. Slaves were killed and jewels offered for the king's last journey.

Then they carried his body across the square to his own house.[11] Knees to chest and wrapped in his graveclothes he was buried in the courtyard. Like a merchant home from far markets he slept beside his own hearth.

Notes

CHAPTER I

[1] This repeated admonition is from the *Crónica Mexicayotl*, Par. 2 and 3. The same source, Par. 134-150, gives this symbolic and legendary account of the Moteczuma Ilhuicamina. See also genealogical table.

The following sources also give the name of Miahuaxihuitl of Cuauhnauac as the mother of Huehue Moteczuma: *Historia de los Mexicanos por sus Pinturas*, *Orígen de los Mexicanos*, *Annales de Chimalpahin*, *Pablo Nazareo*. She is described as from Cuauhnauac but her name given as Mihuaxochitl by Torquemada and Clavijero. This name is also given her by Veytia, but she is described as from Azcapotzalco. Mengin's tabulation from the *Codex Mexicanus* has her from Azcapotzalco but names her Ayauhcihuatl. The following sources, like the others, mention Huitzilihuitl as the father, but do not mention the mother: Tezozomoc, Durán, *Codex Mendoza*, *Leyenda de los Soles*, *Relación de la Genealogía*, Motolinía. The completely divergent report of Moteczuma as the son of Chimalpopoca is given by Ixtlilxochitl, the *Codex Xolotl*, and the *Anales de Cuauhtitlan*. The latter composite source also has passages in which he is the son of Itzcoatl. In Par. 138, however, there is a confused reference in an incomplete and unrelated sentence to the daughter of an unnamed person from Cuauhnauac.

[2] The traditional answers to the marriage makers according to Sahagún, Lib. VI, cap. 23, Ed. Robredo, Vol. II, p. 152.

[3] Durán I, pp. 53, 55.

[4] An explanation of the metaphorical use of these terms to express danger may be found in Sahagún, Lib. VI, cap. 43, Ed. Robredo, Vol. II, p. 245. This sheds light on their use in the *Crónica Mexicayotl*. A discussion of the metaphorical language of the Aztecs is contained in Garibay, *Historia de la Literatura Náhuatl*, Vol. I, 445-448. Belief in witchcraft and *nagualismo* is mentioned by Sahagún, Lib. X, cap. 9 (Ed. Robredo, Vol. III, p. 33; Dibble and Anderson, Book 10, p. 31); also IV: 11 (Ed. Robredo, Vol. 1, p. 324; Dibble and Anderson, Books 4 and 5, p. 42). It was discussed in 1629 by Hernando Ruiz de Alarcón, "Tratado de las Supersticiones y Costumbres Gentílicas que Oy Viuen Entre Los Indios Naturales Desta Nueua España," *Anales de Museo Nacional de México*, Primera Época, Vol. VI, 1900, pp. 133-134, with special reference to the animal counterpart of the *nagual*. Recent studies in Mexico of modern *nagualismo:* William L. Wonderly, "Textos en Zoque sobre el Concepto del Nagual," *Tlalocan*, Vol. II, No. 2, 1946, pp. 97-195; Roman Cervantes y Cristóbal, "Los Nahuales en Oaxaca," *Anuario de la Sociedad Folklórica de México*, 1950, pp. 471 ff; Virginia Rodríguez Rivera de Mendoza, "El Nahual en el Folklore de México," *Anuario de la Sociedad Folklórica de México*, Vol. VII, 1951, pp. 123-37.

[5] Again the words used by the chronicler come weighted with connotation. Yoalli Ehecatl, Wind of Night, is used for Tezcatlipoca according to Spence, p. 138. It is also used for Tonacatecutli, says Seler in his commentary on the Aubin, p. 38, who describes it as a phrase of prayer which does not identify any particular god. Tonacatecutli is the same as Ometecutli — Lord of our

Subsistence and Twofold Lord, as Spence translates the Nahuatl. In this connection it is interesting to note also the song in the *Historia Tolteca-Chichimeca* (*Anales de Quauhtinchan*), par. 195, which calls upon "Ometeotl, El Creador Tezcatlanextia" — Twofold God, the Creator, the Resplendent Mirror.

[6] See *Anales de Cuauhtitlan*, Par. 28 for the *chalchihuitl* swallowed by the mother of Quetzalcoatl, and *La Leyenda de los Soles*, Par. VI, for the shooting of arrows at Chimalman by Mixcohuatl before the conception of Quetzalcoatl.

[7] The symbolism of the *chalchihuitl* stone and the use of the *chalchihuitl* necklace as used in the Códices *Bologna*, *Borbonicus*, and *Vaticanus B*, is analyzed by Seler in his commentary on the latter codex, pp. 23, 24. He shows that the necklace, the round *chalchihuitl* symbol, the footprints from the place of the twofold creating gods, and the quetzal feather, are all related to the birth of a warrior. He discusses this symbolism also in his commentary on the *Fejérváry-Mayer*, pp. 10, 184. The concentric circles on the shield of Tlazolteotl as Teteoinnan, Mother of the Gods, in the *Florentine Codex*, a *chalchihuitl* form, are analyzed as a sex symbol by Spence, pp. 157-158.

[8] See all the addresses made in connection with the newborn child, Sahagún Lib. VI, cap. 32-35, Ed. Robredo, Vol. II, pp. 190-209.

[9] From Spanish translation in Sahagún, Ed. Robredo, Vol. V, p. 151. (Anderson and Dibble, Book 2, p. 213.)

[10] From Garibay's Spanish translation of the same song, *Poesía Indígena*, p. 21.

[11] *Historia de los Mexicanos por sus Pinturas*, p. 229, says his father gave him this name later "because his father was señor against the will of many." See also later chapters in this biography for opposition also to Moteczuma Ilhuicamina in Tenochtitlan.

[12] This name, not uncommon among the Aztecs, is mentioned by the *Crónica Mexicayotl* and by Chimalpahin. The *Mexicayotl*, Par. 139, emphasizes the lack of cotton in Tenochtitlan and Torquemada, Tomo. I, p. 104, says that after this marriage, cotton came to Tenochtitlan. The procession toward Huitzilihuitl in the *Telleriano-Remensis* might be interpreted as coming from Cuauhnauac and its king, whom the *Mexicayotl* calls Ozomatzin, but whom Torquemada names as Escoaci as does the *Historia de los Mexicanos por sus Pinturas*. Pablo Nazareo spells this name correctly as Itzcoatl. In that case the woman seated behind Huitzilihuitl would probably be Miahuaxihuitl, here a painter of books. She is painting the glyph for Ilhuitl, day, as Dibble points out in another connection in his commentary on the *Códice en Cruz*, p. 17.

[13] The meaning of the Ilhuicamina glyph is so analyzed by Clark in his commentary on the *Codex Mendoza*, Vol. I, p. 10. It occurs in the Codex in Folio 7v. The gods of air and rain are Quetzalcoatl and Tlaloc; of fire, Xiuhtecutli; of the House of Red Dawning, Tlahuizcalpantecutli; of the Smoking Mirror, Tezcatlipoca; of the earth and the skirt of snakes, Coatlicue; of the land of the dead, Mictlantecutli; of love, the Flower Feather, Xochiquetzal.

An interesting variation on the night sky glyph of Ilhuicamina is shown in the *Codex Aubin of 1576* (*Histoire de la Nation Mexicaine*) under date 5 Reed (1471).

The *Códice Azcatítlan*, Sheet XVIII, shows the sky glyph, and also the crown glyph and nose plug, all used for Moteczuma Ilhuicamina. The *Telleriano-Remensis*, mentioning that Moteczuma Ilhuicamina was the first to wear this turquoise band, relates it to the crown of Tonacatecutli. Seler in his commentary on the *Aubin Tonalamatl* derives it from the frontal band of Xiuhtecutli or Xiuiteotl, the fire god, p. 75. Dibble commenting on its use for Moteczuma Ilhuicamina in the *Códice en Cruz*, 13 Stone, 1440, says it came to have a reference to a *tecuhtli* and is so used in place names such as the Mendocino's representation of Tecuhtepec. In the *Xolotl* the glyph used for Moteczuma Ilhuicamina seems to be a variation on the frontal band or crown glyph, perhaps from the front view.

[14] Chimalpahin and the *Codex Mexicanus* give this year, Ten Rabbit, 1398. The *Historia de los Mexicanos por sus Pinturas* gives the date as seventy-five years after the foundation of Tenochtitlan.

[15] Chimalpahin mentions the hour of sunrise. However, though the time of day was carefully noted by the priests as Sahagún makes clear (Lib. VI, cap. 36, Ed. Robredo, Vol. II, p. 210) it is likely that the hour of sunrise had more symbolic than literal meaning, for Ixtlilxochitl (*Historia Chichimeca*, p. 82) says Nezahualcoyotl was born at sun-up, to the great pleasure of his father, and Chimalpahin has Moteczuma's half brother Tlacaelel also born at sunrise. See below. For lords of the day and night hours see Seler's commentary on the *Aubin Tonalamatl* and Robelo, *Diccionario de Mitología Nahuatl*, p. 124, (Horas). The relation between the turquoise crown and Xiuiteotl, the fire god and patron of the sunrise hour, might be a further reason for accrediting the birth of important individuals to this hour.

[16] For the elements brought together from the *tonalamatl*, or ceremonial calendar, for the forecasts of the life of the newborn child and the selection of the date for his dedication to Chalchihuitlicue, of the Skirt of Jade, see Gillmor, *Flute of the Smoking Mirror*, pp. 9-15, with notes.

CHAPTER II

[1] Sahagún, Lib. 10, cap. 22 (Ed. Robredo, Vol. III, p. 64; Dibble and Anderson, Book 10, p. 80); Pomar, pp. 54-55; Tezozomoc, pp. 228, 261, 262, 265, 271; Durán I, pp. 41-42. The lake activities are shown in a pictorial map drawn about 1555, for Alonso de Santa Cruz, map maker for the King of Spain, and published in facsimile by the University of Uppsala, Sweden. It is reproduced by Ola Apenes, *Mapas Antiguos del Valle de México*, Universidad Nacional Autónoma de México, 1947, and in his article on the continuing use of the old lake techniques in modern times, "The Pond in our Back Yard," *Mexican Life*, Vol. XIX, no. 3, March, 1943, pp. 15-18, 60. That it was drawn by a Mexican Indian was established by the studies in *Planos de la Ciudad de México* by Manuel Toussaint, Federico Gómez de Orozco, and Justino Fernández. S. Linne makes a detailed study of it and of the life it shows and includes a color reproduction of it in *El Valle y la Ciudad de México en 1550*. Ethnographical Museum of Sweden, Stockholm, New Series, Publication No. 9, 1958.

[2] Sahagún, Lib. I, cap. 20 (Ed. Robredo, Vol. I, pp. 46-47; Anderson and Dibble, Book 1, p. 21).

[3] Chimalpahin, 10 Rabbit, 1398, who identifies his mother as Cacamacihuatl. Explanation of his name from Alonso de Molina's *Vocabulario*, tlacaellelli. See also Chap. I, note 15. Barlow, "La Fundación de la Triple Alianza," *Anales del Instituto Nacional de Antropología e Historia*, Vol. III, 1947-48, pp. 152, identifies the town as near Tlalnepantla, and thus as a Tepanecan town.

[4] Durán I, p. 59; Tezozomoc, p. 236; *Códice Ramírez*, p. 41.

[5] The chinampa technique is described by Apenes, "The Pond in our Back Yard," *Mexican Life*, loc. cit.

[6] Tezozomoc, p. 228.

[7] Chimalpahin under these dates.

[8] Durán I, p. 60.

[9] Itzcoatl's position as tlacatecatl under Huitzilihuitl is mentioned by Chimalpahin, 6 Reed, 1407, and 1 Reed, 1415. However, the *Anales de Cuauhtitlan*, Par. 138, has Chimalpopoca as tlacatecatl under Huitzilihuitl. For Itzcoatl's family connections see genealogical table and Chap. IV, note 8.

[10] The towns, except Cuauhnauac (Cuernavaca) were within the Valley of Mexico. See *Anales de Cuauhtitlan*, Par. 142, 148-149; Ixtlilxochitl, *Historia Chichimeca*, p. 79; *Anales Mexicanos: México-Azcapotzalco*, 12 Rabbit, 1426, p. 1; *Crónica Mexicayotl*, Par. 169-174; *Anales de Tlatelolco*, Par. 76 ff., with Mengin genealogical table; *Códice Xolotl*, Sheet V, with Dibble commentary and genealogical table.

[11] For these and other details relating particularly to Texcoco during Nezahualcoyotl's youth, see the more extended discussion and notes in Gillmor, *Flute of the Smoking Mirror*. For Nezahualcoyotl's family relationships with Tenochtitlan see genealogical table.

[12] The date of the accession of Chimalpopoca varies in the sources. The date 3 House, 1417, is given by the text of the *Codex Mendoza* though the line in the drawing connects him with the following year, 4 Rabbit. The year 3 House is also given by the *Aubin Codex of 1576*, *Anales de Cuauhtitlan*, *Anales de Tula*, *Hidalgo*, *Anales de Tlatelolco*, Par. 54, *Mapa de Tepechpan*.

The date 13 Rabbit, 1414, is given by the *Códice en Cruz* and the *Telleriano-Remensis*. The date 1 Reed, 1415, is given by Chimalpahin; *Anales de Tlatelolco*, Par. 257 (reporting from one of its two traditions); *Crónica Mexicayotl*.

The date given by Ixtlilxochitl gives a wider variation — 8 House, 1409. The *Historia de los Mexicanos por sus Pinturas* gives the date as ninety-four years after the founding of Tenochtitlan.

Durán, Tezozomoc, and the *Códice Ramírez* give no date.

Chimalpopoca's accession followed directly upon the death of Huitzilihuitl according to all these sources except the *Anales de Tlatelolco*, Par. 256, which says Mexico-Tenochtitlan had been without a ruler for four years.

For family relationships of Chimalpopoca see genealogical table.

The table follows the following basic sources in making Chimalpopoca the son of Huitzilihuitl: *Crónica Mexicayotl*, *Annales de Chimalpahin*, *Leyenda de los Soles*, *Codex Mendoza*, Durán, Tezozomoc, *Códice Ramírez* Ixtlilxochitl in both the *Historia Chichimeca* and the *Relaciones*, *Codex Xolotl*. Another group, however, make him the son of Acamapichtli and the brother of Huitzilihuitl and Itzcoatl: *Historia de los Mexicanos por sus Pinturas*, *Orígen de los Mexicanos*, *Relación de la Genealogía*, Torquemada, Clavijero, Veytia, Motolinía, and Mengin's table based on the *Codex Mexicanus*. The *Anales de Cuauhtitlan*, in one of its combined sources, makes him the son of Acamapichtli, but the father of Itzcoatzin and Moteczuma. Ixtlilxochitl and the *Códice Xolotl* also make him the father of Moteczuma.

[13] Itzcoatl is mentioned as tlacatecatl under Chimalpopoca by the *Crónica* Mexicayotl, Par. 161, and by Chimalpahin, 1 Reed, 1415. But Cf. Chapter III.

[14] Sahagún, Lib. VII, cap. 5 (Ed. Robredo, Vol. II, p. 263; Anderson and Dibble, Book 7, Chap. 4, p. 14).

[15] Durán I, p. 62.

[16] Chimalpopoca's part in getting water rights and material and labor for an aqueduct is recounted in Durán I, pp. 62-64; Tezozomoc, p. 237; and the *Códice Ramírez*, pp. 42-43. The latter source says the request was an intentional provocation to war on the part of Tenochtitlan.

[17] Chimalpopoca's support of Tezozomoc in these demands is indicated on Sheet VII of the *Códice Xolotl* and Dibble's interpretation, p. 90. See also Ixtlilxochitl, *Relaciones*, pp. 146-148.

[18] The death of Ixtlilxochitl and flight of Nezahualcoyotl took place in 4 Rabbit, 1418, according to Ixtlilxochitl, *Historia Chichimeca*, p. 93, and Chimalpahin, and in the next year 5 Reed, 1419, according to the *Anales de Cuauhtitlan*, Par. 140. The *Códice en Cruz* might indicate the date 7 House, 1421, if Dibble's tentative identification of the event pictured there is correct. The *Anales de Tlatelolco*, Par. 269, gives 13 Reed, 1427, as the date. The 1418 date seems more probable since it is backed up by the Texcoco sources. They have him go directly to Tlaxcala after his father was killed, and put his period of residence in Tenochtitlan later. The *Anales de Cuauhtitlan* have him taken directly to Itzcoatl. The conversation here is from the *Anales de Cuauhtitlan*, Par. 150, the only source mentioning Moteczuma Ilhuicamina's part in this night rescue.

[19] The date of Tezozomoc's death as given in the different sources has only a one year variation from 12 Rabbit, 1426, to 13 Reed, 1427. The 12 Rabbit date is given by Chimalpahin, *Anales de Tlatelolco*, *Anales Mexicanos: México-Azcapotzalco*, *Crónica Mexicayotl*. The 13 Reed date is given by Ixtlilxochitl, the *Codex Xolotl*, and the *Anales de Cuauhtitlan*.

The presence of Moteczuma Ilhuicamina and Nezahualcoyotl at his funeral is established by Ixtlilxochitl, *Relaciones*, p. 193, and by the *Códice Xolotl*, Sheet VIII, even their relative position in line being indicated.

[20] Ixtlilxochitl, *Relaciones*, p. 189.

[21] The ceremonial details preceding and during the funeral are described by Ixtlilxochitl as the ancient Toltec rite, *Relaciones*, pp. 191-196. As he describes Tezozomoc's funeral at Azcapotzalco he takes the details of procedure almost word for word from Gómara, pp. 383-389, to whom he pays tribute for accuracy. Sahagún gives burial customs and beliefs concerning the dead in Apéndice, Lib. III, cap. 1 (Ed. Robredo, Vol. I, pp. 283-288; Anderson and Dibble, Book 3, p. 39). It is to be noted, however, that these elaborate usages did not grow up in Mexico-Tenochtitlan until after the time of Moteczuma Ilhuicamina.

It is of interest that the description of funeral customs by codices and chroniclers has been confirmed archaeologically by excavations of the Aztec period of Coaixtlahuaca in the state of Oaxaca by Ignacio Bernal, "Exploraciones en Coixtlahuaca, Oaxaca," *Revista Mexicana de Estudios Antropológicos* Tomo X, 1948-1949, pp. 5-76. A picture of a wooden mask encrusted with turquoise is included in this report and the funeral customs thus verified are summarized on p. 25, and include "la forma de doblar al muerto, de envolverlo en un petate, de amarrarlo, de pintar el petate o las tiras que lo sujetaban, de poner una máscara," etc.

[22] This detail from Sahagún.

[23] The number mentioned by Gómara, though Sahagún emphasizes the necessity for blankets and clothing to pass the wind of knives.

[24] This detail is mentioned by both Gómara and Sahagún. Sahagún mentions that the chalchihuitl was described as the heart of the dead person.

[25] Ixtlilxochitl says this mask was used only for kings.

[26] See Note 19.

[27] This detail is Gómara's.

[28] Gómara mentions the dog as guide and Sahagún explains that a white or black dog would refuse to go into the river to protect the color of its fur. Little clay dog heads are still found at Acolman where the old dog market of the Aztecs was located and often show the red spot on the nose which was put on dogs of other colors once a year to make them ceremonially red.

[29] Garibay, *Poesía Indígena*, p. 75.

[30] Garibay, *Poesía Indígena*, p. 110. Ixtlilxochitl mentions the singing. These particular songs are employed here as perhaps of the same type of mourning song, though Garibay says the first one is perhaps of Otomí origin, absorbed

by the Nahuatl or Aztec speaking people, and the second refers to a later Tezozomoc.

[31] The warning described by Ixtlilxochitl, *Historia Chichimeca*, p. 108; *Relaciones*, p. 194. Tlacateotzin of Tlatelolco also warned Nezahualcoyotl.

[32] Detail given by Ixtlilxochitl and Sahagún.

CHAPTER III

[1] *Anales Mexicanos: México-Azcapotzalco*, p. 49; Ixtlilxochitl, *Relaciones*, pp. 194-195; *Historia Chichimeca*, p. 108.

[2] Ixtlilxochitl, *Historia Chichimeca*, p. 108, gives this number counting from the death of Tezozomoc in the month Tlacaxipehualiztli, the day 1 Vulture, in his Texcoco dating, the year 13 Reed. This would bring the count to the month Tecuilhuitontli, the little feast of the lords.

[3] These and other details of the fiesta of this month are given by Sahagún, Lib. II, cap. 26 (Ed. Robredo, Vol. I, pp. 154-157; Anderson and Dibble, Book 2, pp. 86-90).

[4] The conversation is reported by Ixtlilxochitl, *Historia Chichimeca*, pp. 108-109 and *Relaciones*, pp. 197-198; *Anales de Cuauhtitlan*, Par. 143. I follow the dating of the *Historia Chichimeca* as indicated in Note 2. In the *Relaciones* the conspiracy is instituted immediately after Tezozomoc's death.

[5] A *jacal*, says the *Anales de Cuauhtitlan*, and Ixtlilxochitl emphasizes the speed of building.

[6] This remark by Maxtla is given by Ixtlilxochitl, *Relaciones*, p. 201, and is related by Dibble in his commentary on the *Códice Xolotl*, p. 105, to the sequence of glyphs on Sheet VIII containing, after the speech-scroll, a child (with the idea of "younger"); the glyph of Xolotl, a dog head; a skull; a glyph of Chimalpopoca; and one of Tenochtitlan. The conversation is between Maxtla and his counsellor Chichincatl, as is clearly indicated by their glyphs and the speech scrolls. It is an interesting example of the way conversation can be indicated by the codices.

[7] This remark is quoted by the *Anales de Tlatelolco*, Par. 258, and his fear of war mentioned.

[8] Durán, II, pp. 284-285.

[9] *Anales Mexicanos: México-Azcapotzalco*, p. 50.

[10] Both conversations given by *Anales Mexicanos: México-Azcapotzalco*, pp. 49-50.

[11] *Anales de Cuauhtitlan*, Par. 236, for this violent gesture by Chalco. See also *Codex Mendoza* where the event is pictured at end of Chimalpopoca's reign.

[12] In the *Anales de Cuauhtitlan*, Par. 143; *Crónica Mexicayotl*, Par. 161; and *Annales de Chimalpahin*, 1 Reed, he is described as Chimalpopoca's tlacochcalcatl and in the *Anales de Tlatelolco*, Par. 258, as tlacatecatl. For this last, contrast Chap. II, Note 13. His identification as Chimalpopoca's son is by the Tenochtitlan group — Tezozomoc, p. 238; Duran I, p. 65.

[13] *Anales Mexicanos: México-Azcapotzalco*, p. 50.

[14] The *Anales Mexicanos: México-Azcapotzalco* has Chimalpopoca make the suggestion, though Ixtlilxochitl has it made by his counsellor, an interesting example of frequent reversal of speaker in the conversations reported in different sources.

[15] The motive is so analyzed by Ixtlilxochitl, *Historia Chichimeca*, p. 111.

[16] The death of Chimalpopoca is placed in this month — Hueytecuilhuitl — by Ixtlilxochitl, *Relaciones*, p. 203. These fiesta details are given by Sahagún, Lib. II, cap. 27. (Ed. Robredo, Vol. I, p. 159; Anderson and Dibble, Book 2,

p. 92). It has not been pointed out, however, until the present biography, how both Chimalpopoca and the Tepanecas utilized the procedures of the fiesta to carry out their own intentions.

[17] *Anales Mexicanos: México-Azcapotzalco*, p. 50.

[18] Ixtlilxochitl, *Historia Chichimeca*, p. 111. Pomar, p. 12, says only a king could represent Huitzilipochtli in Texcoco.

[19] The description of costumes and face painting in the fiesta dance of this month is given Sahagún, Lib. II, cap. 27 (Ed. Robredo, Vol. I, p. 161; Anderson and Dibble, Book 2, p. 94). Chimalpopoca's costume, corresponding with remarkable exactness, is shown in the *Códice Xolotl*, Sheet VIII. Dibble's commentary on the *Xolotl* follows Ixtlilxochitl in referring to it as a warrior or dance costume, but, though Ixtlilxochitl refers to the month, neither he nor Dibble mentions that it is the costume of this fiesta. It is significant also that Sahagún goes on to mention that the Señor (in the Robredo translation) or Moteczuma (in the Anderson and Dibble version) danced in this fiesta. Thus Chimalpopoca's participation would not in itself show intention of suicide aside from his own recorded statement.

[20] *Anales Mexicanos: México-Azcapotzalco*, p. 50. Both Sahagún in the account cited and the description of this particular occasion emphasize the elaborate skirts.

[21] *Anales Mexicanos: México-Azcapotzalco*, p. 50.

[22] Ixtlilxochitl, *Relaciones*, p. 200, and the *Anales Mexicanos: México-Azcapotzalco* give the differing reports.

[23] This effort of Moteczuma to stop the dance is mentioned by Ixtlilxochitl, *Relaciones*, p. 200; and *Historia Chichimeca*, p. 112.

[24] Durán II, pp. 175, 287.

[25] This use of the cage is mentioned by Durán II, p. 172, who says that the girl representing Xilonen, to be sacrificed as part of this month's festival, was so prevented from running away. The cage is also shown as part of this fiesta in the *Códice Florentino* (No. 27, illustrating Book II, chap. 27, and reproduced by Anderson and Dibble after Paso y Troncoso). Here two prisoners are shown inside of it. The imprisonment of Chimalpopoca in the cage is mentioned by Ixtlilxochitl in both the *Relaciones* and the *Historia Chichimeca, loc. cit.*, and is shown by *Códice Xolotl*, Sheet III, and by the *Codex Mexicanus*, Sheet LXI. The latter source draws it below the date of Chimalpopoca's death, his dead body with a rope around his neck being shown above.

[26] Ixtlilxochitl, *Historia Chichimeca*, pp. 112-113.

[27] Ixtlilxochitl, *Historia Chichimeca*, p. 115; and *Relaciones*, p. 203.

[28] This gift of tamales is described by Ixtlilxochitl, *Relaciones*, p. 202, and is shown in the closely related *Xolotl*, Sheet VIII, where the conversation between Nezahualcoyotl and the farmer as he is given them shows Chimalpopoca's glyph between the speech scrolls. This emphasis on the tamales is interpreted by Ixtlilxochitl apparently as showing that Chimalpopoca was being starved in his cage. However, the gift of tamales would be appropriate to the festival of this month as the descriptions of Sahagún and Durán already referred to, make clear.

[29] Ixtlilxochitl, *Historia Chichimeca*, p. 118.

[30] The Calmecac was then of zacate — grass — according to the *Anales Mexicanos: México-Azcapotzalco*, p. 50.

[31] Ixtlilxochitl, *Historia Chichimeca*, p. 119.

[32] *Anales Mexicanos: México-Azcapotzalco*, p. 50.

[33] Ixtlilxochitl, *Historia Chichimeca*, p. 119, names the place specifically as the Huitzcalli. Sahagún, in the Apéndice of Book II (Ed. Robredo, Vol. I, p.

222; Anderson and Dibble, Book 2, p. 170) mentions among the late buildings of the great temple of Mexico the twenty-fourth called the Huitznahuac Calmecac, and the service with incense.

[34] Again the parallels between the rituals for Chimalpopoca and sacrificial procedure become clear when the account of the former in *Anales Mexicanos: México-Azcapotzalco*, p. 50, is compared with the ceremony, not for this month, but specifically for the representative of Huitzilopochtli in Sahagún, Lib. III, cap. 1, 3a parte (Ed. Robredo, Vol. 1, p. 263; Anderson and Dibble, Book 3, p. 7).

[35] Acolnahuacatl and Tzacualcatl, whose names are given by the *Anales Mexicanos: México-Azcapotzalco*, are listed as members of the council which had opposed sending stone and men to build the aqueduct by Tezozomoc, pp. 237-238. That Moteczuma was with their messengers is implied by the *Anales Mexicanos: México-Azcapotzalco*, "se retiraron los enviados de México, dirigiendose *todos* á Calmecac."

[36] These remarks given by Ixtlilxochitl, *Historia Chichimeca*, p. 120, and *Anales Mexicanos: México-Azcapotzalco*, p. 50.

[37] Sahagún, Lib. II, cap. 27 (Ed. Robredo, Vol. I, p. 166; Anderson and Dibble, Book 2, p. 100). The dating given by Ixtlilxochitl and the correlation of these closing events in Chimalpopoca's life with the festival details of the Little Feast of the Lords and the Great Feast of the Lords establishes the time covered as this two-month period. Ixtlilxochitl, *Relaciones*, p. 203, gives the date of Chimalpopoca's death at the day Ten Flower in the month Hueytecuilhuitl, in the year corresponding to 1427. The same year — 13 Reed — is given by the *Códice en Cruz*, the *Codex Mendoza* and the *Codex Mexicanus*.

The following group of sources are not in significant disagreement when they give the date as 12 Rabbit, 1426: Chimalpahin, *Crónica Mexicayotl*, *Anales de Tlatelolco*, *Telleriano-Remensis*, *Mapa de Tepechpan*, and *Anales Mexicanos: México-Azcapotzalco*.

At wider divergence are the *Aubin of 1576* which gives 10 Stone (1424) and the *Anales de Cuauhtitlan* which gives 1 Stone (1428).

The following sources say that Chimalpopoca was killed by the Tepaneca: Ixtlilxochitl, *Historia Chichimeca*, p. 119; Tezozomoc, p. 238; *Códice Ramírez*, p. 44; Durán I, p. 65; *Anales Mexicanos: México-Azcapotzalco*, p. 50; *Crónica Mexicayotl*, Par. 176, 185; *Anales de Cuauhtitlan*, Par. 143, 160, 236; Chimalpahin, *Aubin of 1576*. It is clearly implied in the *Anales de Tlatelolco*, Par. 258. The *Codex Mexicanus* shows Maxtla and the cage below the dead Chimalpopoca with associated symbols of war. Ixtlilxochitl's *Relaciones* in contrast to the account in his *Historia Chicimeca* say that Chimalpopoca died of starvation during his imprisonment by Maxtla. Torquemada discusses the whole situation as reported in sources available to him and believes that he carried through his intention of suicide, Vol. I, p. 126. He bases his belief on two painted histories, one from Coatlichan and the other apparently from Tenochtitlan; also on a family tradition recounted by a descendant of Chimalpopoca. In describing the painting from Coatlichan, however, he says Chimalpopoca was in a cage, strangled, and nearby was the name sign of Maxtla who held him in prison. This could equally well be interpreted as in accord with the larger group of histories and as indicating that Maxtla had him strangled, rather than that he hanged himself. Torquemada also mentions a Texcocan history.

The *Orígen de Los Mexicanos*, p. 271, and Motolinía, *Memoriales*, p. 7, mention the Culhua as enemies of the Tenochca and enmity between them as occasion for Maxtla's intervention. Don Pablo Nazareo, p. 118, says Chimalpopoca was condemned to death for treason against the Mexicans and his descendants deprived of honors forever.

CHAPTER IV

[1] These varying reports are given by the sources. Ixtlilxochitl, *Historia Chichimeca*, p. 112, has Maxtla order that he be allowed to sacrifice himself according to plan, but in the *Relaciones*, pp. 200-201, has him continue to dance with Chimalpopoca, share in the killing of Acamapichtli during the night, and be killed by the Tepaneca when they imprisoned Chimalpopoca. The *Anales Mexicanos: México-Azcapotzalco*, p. 50, says only that he died during the night. The *Anales de Cuauhtitlan*, Par. 143, says that he committed suicide. He was killed by the Tepaneca with his father according to Tezozomoc, p. 238, while they were sleeping, adds Duran I, p. 65. He was strangled with Chimalpopoca according to the *Anales de Tlatelolco*, Par. 258. Perhaps he is the figure, whose identity leaves Barlow perplexed, shown dead with the dead Chimalpopoca in the *Azcatítlan*, Sheet XVI.

[2] *Anales Mexicanos: México-Azcapotzalco*, p. 50.

[3] *Crónica Mexicayotl*, Par. 177. Also Antonio de León y Gama, "Descripción de la Ciudad de México," p. 11. Other sources so far brought to light do not include him in the list of rulers.

[4] This agreement is mentioned by the *Anales de Cuauhtitlan*, Par. 236, the motivation, however, being analyzed as fear of the Tepaneca who had already killed Chimalpopoca. Pablo Nazareo, p. 118, also mentions agreement.

[5] Durán I, p. 67; *Códice Ramírez*, p. 45. The speech is condensed in the present work.

[6] *Orígen de los Mexicanos*, pp. 271-272, which mentions that his father chose him as legitimate heir, and also the opposition to him on the grounds that his mother was from Cuauhnauac.

[7] Don Pablo Nazareo de Xaltocan, pp. 121-122, gives her name as Chichimecacioatzin, daughter of Cuauhtototzin of Cuauhnauac. This seems to be the only information we have about Moteczuma's wife, the "Chichimecan Woman." *The Crónica Mexicayotl* gives the name to his daughter. The lack of information on the personal relationships within his family contrasts with the details preserved about the legitimate wife, the concubines, and the children of his relative and friend in Texcoco, Nezahualcoyotl. See Gillmor, *Flute of the Smoking Mirror*.

[8] The variant tradition that makes him a son of Huitzilihuitl is found in Tezozomoc, p. 239; Ixtlilxochitl, *Relaciones*, p. 203, *Historia Chichimeca*, p. 79. Several other relationships are given in the composite *Anales de Cuauhtitlan*, Par. 138, 145, 151. The present work follows the majority of the sources in making him the son of Acamapichtli and the Tepanecan vender of herbs or slave girl. If the custom of electing brothers in their turn as Tlatoani of Tenochtitlan, mentioned by the *Relación de la Genealogía*, p. 253, had been followed, he would thus have succeeded Huitzilihuitl. His failure to do so need not be credited to his mother's humble position, however, since the election of the Beloved Grandchild of Tezozomoc held obvious political advantages. Furthermore, since Acamapichtli's legitimate wife proved barren, the daughters of the principal leaders of Tenochtitlan had been brought to him to provide children in her place, and none of them were actually in the legitimate line. It should be noted here, however, that Pomar, p. 25, speaking of Texcoco where the succession was by inheritance, said it was the only type of inheritance barred to a son not in the legitimate line, and the constant emphasis on Itzcoatl's lowly inheritance may indicate the same barrier to election in Tenochtitlan. This is also indicated in Tlacaelel's

speech to young men going to the War of Flowers with Tlaxcala. See Chap. XIX.

[9] This speech is from *Anales de Cuauhtitlan*, Par. 145.

[10] This speech given by Durán I, pp. 67-68; Tezozomoc, p. 239; *Códice Ramírez*, p. 46. It is somewhat condensed here.

[11] Tezozomoc, p. 239. Itzcoatl's reign began in 10 Stone, 1424, according to Durán I, p. 69, and the *Códice Ramírez*, p. 46; in 11 House, 1425, according to the *Aubin of 1576;* in 12 Rabbit, 1426, according to *Telleriano-Remensis;* in 13 Reed, 1427, according to Chimalpahin, *Códice en Cruz*, *codex Mendoza* (text), *Anales de Tlatelolco* (Par. 259), *Crónica Mexicayotl* (Par. 187), and Ixtlilxochitl. The latter in the *Historia Chichimeca*, p. 201, says he died in 1440 "having reigned almost fourteen years," and in the *Relaciones*, says he died in 1441 and "governed fourteen and a half years." The date 1 Stone, 1428, is given by the *Anales de Cuauhtitlan* (Par. 145), *Mapa de Tepechpan*, *Codex Mexicanus*, and *Codex Mendoza* (beginning year sign on Itzcoatl sheet).

[12] *Orígen de los Mexicanos*, pp. 271-272. This confused reference to Moteczuma Ilhuicamina's flight to Huexotzinco does not make the time clear. He is described as the obvious successor to Itzcoatl and as taking flight to avoid his enemies. When Itzcoatl dies, Moteczuma is called back from Huexotzinco. Yet he is described as being there at the same time as Nezahualcoyotl, which puts at least one period there at the beginning of Itzcoatl's reign, an idea supported by the *Anales de Cuauhtitlan*, Par. 158-164, which describes Nezahualcoyotl's presence there during the conferences. After the Tepanecan wars began they were both active in the war, and Nezahualcoyotl immediately afterward was reinstated in the rule of Texcoco, and Moteczuma given increasing honors and influence in Tenochtitlan. The period of exile then must have been early in Itzcoatl's reign, and Moteczuma's later journey there purely optional.

[13] For the alliances described below see *Anales de Cuauhtitlan*, Par. 158-164, and *Anales Mexicanos: México-Azcapotzalco*, pp. 59-60. The statement of the Acolhua, from the latter source, is to be noted for its emphasis on land as a motive in these early wars.

[14] For this preliminary campaign by Nezahualcoyotl, and the Tlaxcala alliance see Gillmor, *Flute of the Smoking Mirror*, Chap. VI, and notes. The Tlaxcala alliance is mentioned by Ixtlilxochitl, *Historia Chichimeca*, p. 139, and *Relaciones*, p. 217, the Texcoco source. It is also mentioned by the *Anales de Cuauhtitlan*, Par. 165, though the date is given as 3 Rabbit, 1430. It is possible that the date read by the compiler of these records as a day sign, 1 Stone, was in fact a year sign. This would bring the alliance to 1428. It is an interesting fact that the Tlaxcala source, Muñoz Comargo, does not mention Nezahualcoyotl's stay in that city, nor the alliance for this preliminary march.

[15] *Anales Mexicanos: México-Azcapotzalco*, p. 51. This is one of the earliest instances of their paired responsibility. See further discussion of this in later chapters.

[16] This remark of the Mexicans, given in *Anales Mexicanos: México-Azcapotzalco*, p. 51, is interesting in showing the emphasis on food supplies in the early expansion of the Mexica from their island home.

[17] Names translated by Chavero's footnote to *Anales Mexicanos: México-Azcapotzalco*, p. 52.

[18] *Anales Mexicanos: México-Azcapotzalco*, pp. 53-54.

CHAPTER V

[1] *Anales Mexicanos: México-Azcapotzalco*, p. 54, gives this remark and the following conversation with the Acolhua and with Nezahualcoyotl. This source gives the names of the young men who accompanied Moteczuma to Totopillatzin (Bird, with the nobility suffix) from Tlatelolco; Tepoltomitzin, the Destroying Cat, and Telpoch-chillilicatl, the Restless Youth, both from Tenochtitlan. (Chavero interpretations of names). Ixtlilxochitl, *Historia Chichimeca*, p. 146, omits Tepoltomitzin from the list and uses the shortened Telpoch for Telpoch-Chillilicatl, making him simply the Youth. In his *Relaciones*, p. 222, he mentions the same two. In *Relaciones*, p. 314, he mentions only Moteczuma by name among three, and in *Relaciones*, p. 489, names two of the three, the Youth becoming now only another "caballero." Torquemada, Vol. I, p. 137, mentions two companions of Moteczuma giving their names as Tepolomichin and Tepuchtli, the latter going for the warm clothing, a detail mentioned only by him. *The Annales de Chimalpahin*, 1 Stone, gives the same three names.

[2] Ixtlilxochitl, *Relaciones*, pp. 222, 314, and 489, gives this background for public opinion in Texcoco.

[3] This conversation given by Ixtlilxochitl, *Relaciones*, p. 222.

[4] Ixtlilxochitl, *Historia Chichimeca*, p. 146, mentions the brother.

[5] This interpretation based on Tepanecan source, the *Anales Mexicanos: México-Azcapotzalco*, p. 55.

[6] Ixtlilxochitl, *Relaciones*, p. 223.

[7] For details of life in the Calmecac see Pomar, pp. 26-29; Sahagún, Apéndice del Lib. III, cap. 8 (Ed. Robredo, Vol. I, pp. 296-298; Anderson and Dibble, Book III, pp. 63-65).

[8] The *Annales de Chimalpahin* under 4 Stone (1444) gives this relationship between Coateotl and Moteczuma. Ixtlilxochitl, *Historia Chichimeca*, p. 147, and the *Anales Mexicanos: México-Azcapotzalco*, p. 56, describe him as from Tlalmanalco. Chimalpahin describes him under 1 Stone (1428) as from another division of Chalco: Itzcahuacan-Tlacochcalco-Atenco. The political subdivisions of the Chalco area and jurisdiction were highly complicated.

[9] The excursions to Huexotzinco, including all the conversation, are described by the *Anales Mexicanos: México-Azcapotzalco*, p. 56. Torquemada, Vol. I, p. 138, also reports this episode.

[10] For details of the festival see Sahagún, Book II, cap. 33 (Ed. Robredo, Vol. I, pp. 187-192; Anderson and Dibble, Book II, pp. 124-129). The quoted lines about the identity of the sacrificial victim and Mixcoatl in this fiesta of Quecholli come from the Anderson and Dibble translation, p. 129. For symbolism of arrow and fire drill see Sahagún's Cantos VII and XIX and Seler's notes to these ritual songs, Ed. Robredo Vol. V, pp. 83, 184. The songs above are given in Anderson and Dibble, Book 2, pp. 209, 214.

[11] An account of this fiesta as it was given for Camaxtli in the Tlaxcala-Huexzotzinco area is given by Durán II, pp. 126-134; Motolinía, *Memoriales*, pp. 74-78.

[12] *Historia de los Mexicanos por sus Pinturas*, p. 217.

[13] Motolinía, *Memoriales*, p. 301.

[14] The names so translated by Chavero in his notes to the *Anales Mexicanos: México-Azcapotzalco*, p. 52, are respectively Cahualtzin and Citlalcohuatzin. They are mentioned in that location as among the group that went to Azcapotzalco, again on p. 57, when they came to Chalco, and on p. 58 when Moteczuma later accuses them in Tenochtitlan. See below.

[15] The lighting of the fires is mentioned in the *Anales Mexicanos: México-Azcapotzalco*, p. 57. The connection of the festival of Mixcoatl with the

lighting of fires is explained in the *Historia de Los Mexicanos por sus Pinturas*, pp. 214-215. See also Seler's note, p. 184, on Sahagún's Canto XIX, Ed. Robredo, Vol. V.

In spite of the step by step correspondence of the plans for sacrificing the prisoners with the details of the festival of the month Quecholli, the relationship has not heretofore been pointed out.

[16] This particular speech is added by Torquemada, Vol. I, p. 139, to those given by the *Anales Mexicanos: México-Azcapotzalco*, pp. 57-58, which are otherwise followed here.

[17] This follows the Chalco source — the *Annales de Chimalpahin*, 1 Stone (1428). The *Anales Mexicanos: México-Azcapotzalco*, p. 58, also seem to imply that only the two guards were killed, and mention Coateotl later at the conference called by Maxtla in Chalco, p. 62. Torquemada appears to know nothing of the later events in Coateotl's life which these two sources mention and says he was killed with all his family except for one son who escaped to Yacapichtlan and one daughter who went to Mexico. The *Codex Mexicanus* shows a cage with two dead men in front of it in the year 10 House (1437). The Chalco glyph is attached, both to the cage and to the date. Mengin in his commentary interprets this in spite of its late date as referring to this episode. It is interesting to note the Aztec inscription below which Mengin interprets as "Le proprietaire du jardin s'en retourne et arrive." He says the sense is obscure. It is possible that the Nahuatl commentator confused the Coateotl of this episode with another man of the same name — a gardener killed by an ungrateful stepson whom he had rescued and reared. See Chimalpahin under dates 9 Rabbit (1410) and 5 Reed (1419) for the account of the gardener.

[18] *Anales Mexicanos: México-Azcapotzalco*, p. 58.

[19] This detour to Texcoco is only mentioned by Ixtlilxochitl, *Historia Chichimeca*, p. 147, a Texcoco source. The report Moteczuma gave in Tenochtitlan is from the *Anales Mexicanos: México-Azcapotzalco*, pp. 58-59.

[20] Chalco's last minute effort to establish friendship again with Texcoco is mentioned only by the Texcoco source Ixtlilxochitl, *Relaciones*, pp. 224, 315.

[21] The argument between the peace and war parties in Azcapotzalco is from the *Anales Mexicanos: México-Azcapotzalco*, pp. 59-60.

[22] The arguments between the peace and war parties in Tenochtitlan are from Tezozomoc, pp. 240-246; Durán I, pp. 69-75; *Códice Ramírez*, pp. 46-50; *Anales Mexicanos: México-Azcapotzalco*, p. 59. Durán and the *Códice Ramírez* describe the alignment as between the common people who were for peace, and the leaders who were for war. Tezozomoc has the division between the young who were for war, and the old for peace. The missions of Tlacaelel to Azcapotzalco are also described by these sources in connection with the arguments.

The absence of Moteczuma during these Tenochtitlan discussions is to be noted. The Tenochtitlan sources do not mention him or his whereabouts. However the Texcoco source, Ixtlilxochitl, *Relaciones*, p. 224, says he stayed in Texcoco after his release from Chalco, and though his appearance to report in Tenochtitlan is specifically described by the *Anales Mexicanos: México-Azcapotzalco*, the indication that Texcoco was his headquarters through this time is borne out by his being under Nezahualcoyotl's orders during the later battle. See next chapter.

CHAPTER VI

[1] For Xayacamachan's earlier support see Ixtlilxochitl, *Historia Chichimeca*, pp. 135-136; *Códice Xolotl*, Sheet VII, with Dibble commentary, p. 92, and

Sheet X, with Dibble commentary, p. 112; also Chap. V of the present work, with notes. For his presence during the battle with Azcapotzalco see Ixtlilxochitl, *Historia Chichimeca*, p. 150, and *Anales Mexicanos: México-Azcapotzalco*, pp. 60-61.

[2] Garibay, *Poesía Indígena*, p. 106. Garibay quotes the Spanish note on the original Nahuatl manuscript of this poem as saying that it refers to a later occasion, but for showing the reaction of a Huexotzincatl when he reached the high lake, and as an example of the poetic expression of the same period, it seems suitable for quotation here.

[3] Ixtlilxochitl, *Relaciones*, pp. 226-228, for positions assigned and for conversation about the white armor. Also *Historia Chichimeca*, p. 150, for positions.

[4] Both the above references and the *Anales Mexicanos: México-Azcapotzalco*, p. 61, state that Moteczuma was assigned to his position by Nezahualcoyotl. The reference to flowers takes on added significance in the light of León Portilla's study in *Filosofía Nahuatl* where he analyzes flowers and song as expressing eternal truth.

[5] Ixtlilxochitl, *Historia Chichimeca*, p. 150.

[6] Itzcoatl, *Historia Chichimeca*, p. 150; *Relaciones*, p. 227.

[7] *Anales de Cuauhtitlan*, Par. 164.

[8] Ixtlilxochitl, in *Relaciones*, pp. 225-227, and *Historia Chichimeca*, p. 149, tells of dangers of attack from these directions. The military separation of the Tenochca peace party is described by Durán I, p. 76; Tezozomoc, p. 247.

[9] Garibay, *Poesía Indígena*, pp. 79-80.

[10] Durán I, 76.

[11] For Itzcoatl's drum, Durán I, p. 76. It was the custom of the señor of Texcoco to start a battle with a drum, according to Motolinía, *Memoriales*, p. 297.

[12] The "médico" left in command is mentioned by *Anales Mexicanos: México-Azcapotzalco*, p. 61. His name indicates that he was young. Motolinía, *Memoriales*, p. 298, speaks of the presence of "surgeons" to treat the wounded as customary. Nonohualco was not far from Tlatelolco, nor from Acozac where Moteczuma is to be found a little later. Alfonso Caso in his study of *Los Barrios Antiguos de Tenochtitlán y Tlatelolco*, p. 40, locates Acozac as bounded on the north by the present day street of Sirio; to the east by Galena, to the south by the edge of the island and marshes, more or less along Camelia, and to the west by a line between Soto and Zarco, also the edge of the island.

[13] Jacques Soustelle, *La Vie Quotidienne des Aztèques*, p. 240, in his discussion of the methods of declaring and waging war among the Aztecs, emphasizes the fact that they deliberately deprived themselves of the advantage of surprise. This is a good case in point.

[14] Chavero in his note to the *Anales Mexicanos: México-Azcapotzalco*, p. 61, considers this to be Ixtlahuacan, one of the pueblos of the Valley of Mexico. However, since the name is given more completely, it is interesting to consider the possibility that it might be Coaixtlahuaca of the Oaxaca region, conquered later by the Tenochca, and possessing legends that they had once penetrated to Tenochtitlan.

[15] Durán I, p. 77; Tezozomoc, p. 247.

[16] His name, Mazatl Nahualli, Deer Mask, is given by *Anales Mexicanos: México-Azcapotzalco*, p. 61. Torquemada refers to him simply as Mazatl, Deer, and says he surrendered to Moteczuma and at Moteczuma's hand he died, Vol. 1, p. 141. Veytia, in *Tezcoco*, p. 144, and *Historia Antigua de México*, Vol. II, p. 137, also gives this report of his death.

[17] The following Texcoco sources give this report: Ixtlilxochitl, *Historia Chichimeca*, pp. 150-151; *Relaciones*, p. 228. Veytia, *Texcoco*, p. 144, and *Historia Antigua de México*, Vol. II, p. 137. Torquemada, p. 142, has him

killed in his sweat bath by the victors but does not state by whom specifically.

[18] *Historia de los Mexicanos por sus Pinturas*, p. 230, gives this story, saying that the Tenochca had refused to listen to overtures for peace unless Maxtla were killed.

[19] This Tlatelolco point of view is given by the *Anales de Tlatelolco*, Par. 58.

[20] This report is given by Mexico-Tenochtitlan, Azcapotzalco and Chalco sources: Tezozomoc, p. 255 ff. and Durán I, p. 81 ff. have him ruling in Coyohuacan later. The *Crónica Mexicayotol*, Par. 189, *Anales Mexicanos: México-Azcapotzalco*, p. 62, and *Annales de Chimalpahin*, 1 Stone and 2 House, say he fled there. The picture in the *Codex Mexicanus*, Sheet LXII, shows the death of Maxtla, with a rope around his neck, in 3 Rabbit (1430) but groups with it all the events of the war with the Tepaneca by showing glyphs of the towns involved, including one of Coyohuacan. It is thus not clear in this picture which town he died in. Sometimes Maxtla of Azcapotzalco and Maxtla of Coyohuacan are handled almost as if they were distinct persons, as in the *Anales de Tlatelolco*, Par. 260.

[21] Interconnections of the gods and fiestas of Azcapotzalco and Chalco give ritualistic as well as personal associations to Moteczuma's vision. The chief fiesta of Azcapotzalco and other Tepanecan towns was Xocotl huetzi (Motolinía, *Memoriales*, p. 61, and Durán II, p. 291) and was given in honor of Xiuhtecutli, god of fire, according to Sahagún, Lib. II, cap. 10 and 29 (Ed. Robredo, Vol. I, pp. 97-99, 169-174; Anderson and Dibble, Book 2, pp. 17-19, 104-109). He was the same as Huehueteotl, Old God. The god of fire of the Tepaneca is named by the *Historia de los Mexicanos por sus Pinturas*, p. 218, as Ocotecli, who through a series of steps is related by Seler in his commentaries on Sahagún's Cantos (Ed. Robredo, Vol. V, pp. 88, 107-108) to Amimitl, the arrow or lance of Mixcoatl, god of the Chalca. Moteczuma's vision (*Anales Mexicanos: México-Azcapotzalco*, p. 61) is described as from the devil by the post-conquest writer, but the meaning is clearly Huitzilopochtli, god of the Mexica. That the conquests by the Aztecs were not only of cities but of gods is indicated by the already described plan of the peace party to carry Huitzilopochtli to Azcapotzalco, and by Motolinía, *Memoriales*, p. 295, who describes the acceptance of the conquering god, sometimes by peaceful agreement, along with arrangement of tribute.

The burning of the temple is the usual way of describing a conquest in the codices. Codex representations of the conquest of Azcapotzalco include: *Vaticanus* 3738 and the *Telleriano-Remensis* which give date as 12 Rabbit, 1426; *Mapa de Tepechpan* which by a figure of Itzcoatl attached to the date 1 Stone (1428) and a speech scroll connected to a shield and arrow between a glyph of Azcapotzalco and of Maxtla indicates the declaration of war, and by the burning pyramid with the place glyph of Azcapotzalco (an ant on sand) shows the victory (figs. 54, 55, 59); *Codex Mexicanus*, Sheet LXII, 3 Rabbit (1430) which shows the place glyphs and glyphs of leaders in the battle; *Codex Mendoza*, which shows the place glyph and burning pyramid first among the conquests of Itzcoatl; *Códice Azcatítlan*, Sheet XVII, and "Una Nueva Lámina del *Mapa Quinatzin*," fig. A2, p. 113, with date on the latter, 13 acatl (1427), written in Nahuatl; *Códice en Cruz* which shows war in 1 Stone (1428).

Dates given by other sources for the fall of Azcapotzalco are 1 Stone, 1428, by *Anales Mexicanos: México-Azcapotzalco*, pp. 61-62 (where next year begins); Ixtlilxochitl, *Historia Chichimeca*, p. 151, *Anales de Tlatelolco*, Par. 260; *Crónica Mexicayotl*, Par. 189. The date 2 House, 1429, is given by the *Annales de Chimalpahin* and by the *Anales de Tlatelolco*, Par. 58, (in contrast with Par. 260). The year 3 Rabbit, 1430, is given by the *Anales de Cuauhtitlan*, Par. 171.

[22] Tezozomoc, p. 249.
[23] *Anales de Cuauhtitlan*, Par. 155; Durán II, p. 218; Ixtlilxochitl, *Historia Chichimeca*, p. 151, and *Relaciones*, p. 229; Sahagún, Lib. I, cap. 19 (Ed. Robredo, Vol. I, p. 44; Anderson and Dibble, Book 1, p. 19).
[24] Durán I, p. 78; Tezozomoc, p. 249.
[25] Durán I, p. 78; Tezozomoc, p. 248.
[26] Durán I, p. 78; Tezozomoc, p. 249.
[27] This phrase from *Historia Tolteca-Chichimeca*, Par. 123. The particular assignments of land after the conquest of Azcapotzalco including that to Moteczuma are given by Durán I, pp. 79-80, and Tezozomoc, pp. 253-254. The most complete description in the early sources of land law and the calpullis is given by Zurita, pp. 86-91 and 141-145. He mentions (p. 90) the dignity of the oldest relative who is chosen to keep the painted records, changing them to keep them up to date, and showing which family cultivated a given plot and what was not cultivated and should be reassigned. He points out to Philip II that much trouble resulted from ignorance of the rules governing ownership of the calpulli land, and the authority of the elder relative who had original charge of its assignment to particular families. The colors used to record the three types of land assignment are given by Torquemada, Vol. II, p. 546. T. Esquivel Obregón, Vol. I, pp. 369-374, discussing the land law of the Aztecs says that these maps were used to establish property lines in Spanish colonial times. An illustration of the way water rights held over into colonial times is given in the documents translated as "The Titles of Tetzcotzinco" by Byron McAfee and R. H. Barlow, *Tlalocan*, Vol. II, No. 2, 1946, pp. 110-126. Ixtlilxochitl, *Historia Chichimeca*, pp. 169-171, gives types of land ownership, including assignment of conquered lands.

For further discussion of land law see Kohler, pp. 47-52; Mendieta Nuñez, pp. 42-48; Orozco y Berra, Vol. III, pp. 257-258; Monzón, *El Calpulli en la Organización Social de los Tenochca;* Kirchoff, "Land Tenure in Ancient Mexico," *Revista Mexicana de Estudios Antropológicos*, Tomo XIV, Primera Parte, 1954-1955, pp. 351-361.
[28] A phrase which Sahagún says was current to mean that it was well deserved, and also won by sweat and work. Sahagún Lib. VI, cap. 41, Ed. Robredo, Vol. II, p. 230.

CHAPTER VII

[1] This attempt to incite the conquered Azcapotzalco to rebellion is recorded by Tezozomoc, pp. 254-255, and Durán I, pp. 81-82.
[2] These negotiations are described by Tezozomoc, pp. 256-260; Durán I, pp. 83-89; *Anales Mexicanos: México-Azcapotzalco*, p. 62.
[3] For sequence of these campaigns see *Anales de Cuauhtitlan*, Par. 165-167. For towns related to Azcapotzalco by the marriages of Tezozomoc's children see Chap. II, note 10. For Moteczuma's part in subduing Huexotla see Torquemada, Vol. I, Lib. II, cap. 38, p. 143.
[4] Xalatlauhco and Atlapulco.
[5] The list of towns represented at this meeting is given in *Anales Mexicanos: México-Azcapotzalco*, p. 62. This source though mentioning Coateotl puts the meeting at another house. Tezozomoc, p. 259, puts it at the house of Cacamatl though Cuateotl was already there. Durán I, p. 86, says it was at a community house of Toteociteuctli and Coateotl. The *Annales de Chimalpahin*, under 2 House (1429) places it at house of Cohuacacatzin, who was

Tlacaelel's brother-in-law according to the relationships described by that source. The speech of Coateotl is as given in Durán and Tezozomoc.

[6] This procedure for messengers and ambassadors described by Torquemada, Vol. II, p. 535.

[7] *Annales de Chimalpahin*, 9 Rabbit (1410). (See genealogical table.)

[8] The time of day is mentioned by *Anales Mexicanos: México-Azcapotzalco*, p. 62.

[9] The boundary was at Temalacatitlan, says Durán I, p. 89, reporting this scouting expedition. Tezozomoc, p. 257, puts it before the conference at Chalco instead of after.

[10] Tezozomoc, pp. 256-257; Durán I, pp. 83-84.

[11] Tezozomoc, p. 261; Durán I, pp. 90-91.

[12] This interchange is given by Tezozomoc, p. 257, and Durán I, p. 89. However, Tezozomoc, p. 261, shows Maxtla and Cuecuex with reversed attitudes.

[13] The particular festival identified by Durán I, p. 89. He and Tezozomoc, pp. 262-264, recount what happened on this occasion, the latter giving the list of delegates from Tenochtitlan. Additional details of the fiesta of Xocotl uetzi from Sahagún, Lib. II, cap. 10 and 29 (Ed. Robredo, Vol. I, pp. 97-99, 169-174; Anderson and Dibble, Book 2, pp. 17-18, 104-109). Characterization of Huehue Zacan based on later episode of his life recounted in *Crónica Mexicayotl*, Par. 250.

[14] Tezozomoc, p. 265; Durán I, p. 91.

[15] The meeting with the three men is recounted by Tezozomoc, pp. 264-266, and Durán I, pp. 91-92. Tezozomoc later (p. 271) makes it clear that their nets were not for fishing but for catching ducks. The use of bird nets is shown on the map of Alonso de Santa Cruz (1555) and their present day use on Lake Texcoco described and photographed by Ola Apenes, "The Pond in our Backyard," loc. cit.

[16] Moteczuma's part in the distribution of arms mentioned by *Annales de Chimalpahin* under 2 House (1429).

[17] Tezozomoc has Tlacaelel refer to the historical parallel (p. 266). Durán I, p. 94, has Tlacaelel and his bird hunter friends collect scalps, a change which does not fit the old tradition nor the later fears in Xochimilco. See below. Durán I, pp. 115-116, recounts the earlier basket-of-ears episode, referring to an old picture. It is described also in the *Historia de los Mexicanos por sus Pinturas*, p. 226.

[18] It is to be noted, however, that Durán II, p. 169, says women did dance at this fiesta.

[19] The detail that Moteczuma killed the Otomí soothsayer at Ajusco (Axochco) is given by the *Annales de Chimalpahin* under date of 3 Rabbit (1430). The detail that Maxtla wept is given both by Chimalpahin and by the *Anales Mexicanos: México-Azcapotzalco*, p. 62, and the latter mentions that Moteczuma and Nezahualcoyotl were fighting at Ajusco at the time. There are both a town and a mountain called Ajusco, the latter being on the way to the towns where the fleeing Coyohuaque went. Otomí connections of the Tepanecan gods explain the presence of the Otomí priest; for example, see Sahagún, Vol. V, Canto XI, and Seler commentary, Ed. Robredo, pp. 107-108; Anderson and Dibble, Book 2, p. 211. See also references on subject given in Chap. VI, note 21.

[20] *Anales Mexicanos: México-Azcapotzalco*, p. 62; *Crónica Mexicayotl*, Par. 190. Torquemada, Vol. I, p. 145, who has already reported Maxtla dead, describes this as the flight of the Señor de Coyohuacan, not naming him.

[21] Tezozomoc, p. 271, gives the list of the places where Tlacaelel was given land allotments. Two well known places among them were Copilco and Mixcoac.

[22] The awarding of titles after the victory over Coyohuacan is described by

the *Annales de Chimalpahin*, 4 Reed (1431); Tezozomoc, pp. 268-269; Durán I, pp. 97-98. *The Annales de Chimalpahin*, 6 Reed (1407) and 1 Reed (1415) mention Itzcoatl's position as tlacatecatl under Huitzilihuitl and Chimalpopoca — showing earlier use of the title. See Chap. II, note 13, and Chap. III, note 12.

A note apparently inserted by Sahagún himself in one of the speeches he records (Sahagún, Lib. VI, cap. 14, Ed. Robredo, Vol. II, p. 107) describes these two offices and their close relation to each other and sheds much light on the closely paired relation of Tlacaelel and Moteczuma from this point in their lives forward:

> "For this business of executing justice there were two principal persons, one who was noble and a person of the palace, and the other a captain and valiant person who was of warfare. Also over the soldiers and captains were two principal persons who commanded them, the one who was tlacatecatl and the other tlacochtecutli; the one of the said persons was noble (pilli) and the other a leader in things of war, and always they paired a noble with a soldier for these offices. Also for captains general in things of war they paired two, one noble or magnanimous and of the palace, and the other valiant and skilled in war; the one of these was called tlacatecatl and the other tlacochcalcatl; these had authority in all the things of war and in ordering everything that concerned the military."

These paired titles were thus used at different levels of administration — and in lower classes as also indicated by Sahagún. See Note 29 below.

In addition to this close pairing of activities implicit in their offices it is interesting to speculate how far oral transmission may have affected the ultimately written records, and increasingly stylized the remarkable parallels in the lives of the half brothers.

Both born at sunrise on the same day, they both follow messenger roles — Moteczuma to Texcoco and Chalco, and Tlacaelel to Azcapotzalco. They both take part in the battle of Azcapotzalco, but the Texcocan sources mention Moteczuma only and the Tenochtitlan sources mention Tlacaelel only. In later chapters it will be seen that Tezozomoc and Durán, both Tenochtitlan sources, often reverse the role of the two men in their accounts of the same incidents, Tezozomoc making one the initiator of an idea, the other the follower, and Durán reversing the pattern. Such reversal is characteristic of oral transmission.

Duplication of role and reversal of role are often found in American Indian twin myths. Gladys Reichard discusses duplication and multiple selves as applied to twins in her *Navaho Religion: A Study of Symbolism*, pp. 54-55 and in her concordance to that work under "Twins," pp. 483-484; also in her *Navajo Medicine Man*, p. 15. There are many sets of "twins" in Navajo mythology, chief among them the warrior culture heroes, one of whom is a child of the sun and both of whom visit the sun and return with a turquoise arrow. Alfred Métraux, in his "Twin Heroes in South American Mythology," *Journal of American Folklore*, April-June, 1946, p. 114-123, mentions the widespread myth of twins, half-brothers, or partners, who after a series of miraculous deeds climb to the sky by means of a chain of arrows and become Sun and Moon. The blowgun-carrying twins of the *Popol Vuh: The Sacred Book of the Ancient Quiché Maya*, nearer to Aztec territory than are the myths described by Reichard and Métraux, have similar features. Reversal of names is mentioned by Métraux, p. 116. Miraculous births are characteristics of twin legends.

The attaching of mythological characteristics to prominent persons is seen in contemporary times by the way Soviet folklore makes Lenin and Stalin demigods holding the sun in their hands, sending it above the tundra.

(Nelly Schargo Hoyt, "The Image of the Leader in Soviet 'post-October' Folklore" in *The Study of Culture at a Distance*, edited by Margaret Mead and Rhoda Métraux, University of Chicago Press, 1953, pp. 234-242.)

Modern study of folklore process shows reduplication and reversal of role as common types of folktale change. See Antti Aarne, "Leitfaden der vergleichenden Marchenforschung," *FF Communications* No. 13, Hamina, 1913; quoted in Stith Thompson, *The Folktale*, Dryden Press, New York, 1946, p. 436.

It is significant that what we know of Tlacaelel is through words — not through pictures, though pictures could have contributed to the confusion by using the day-name, necessarily the same for both men. A period of oral explanation of lost pictures and of tradition had preceded the writing of the chronicles which describe him, when these processes of change would have been at work. The glyph in the *Códice Xolotl* which Beyer suggested might have been his (Hermann Beyer, "El Jeroglífico de Tlacaelel," *Revista Mexicana de Estudios Antropológicos*, Tomo IV, Núm. 3, Sept.-Dec., 1940, pp. 161-164) is not so identified by Dibble in his later study of this codex. It would be interesting if the small crowned figure back of Moteczuma Ilhuicamina on Lámina XVIII of the *Códice Azcatítlan* could be interpreted as Tlacaelel, but Barlow's commentary on this figure (p. 121) does not attempt to identify him at all. Clark suggests in his commentary on the *Mendoza* that the figure shown in the *Telleriano-Remensis* in 1465 and 1467 may be Tlacaelel. See also Chap. XIII, note 49.

This suggestion that the study of the processes of oral change might shed light on the relationship of Moteczuma and Tlacaelel is not designed to cast doubt on the historicity of either of them, though it might sound like support of Torquemada (Vol. I, p. 171) in his doubt of the existence of Tlacaelel. He identified him not with Moteczuma but with Itzcoatl.) The sources which do tell about him contain more than twin-like reflection and continue telling of him after Moteczuma's death; furthermore they include sources from Tenochtitlan, Azcapotzalco, and Chalco. *The Crónica Mexicayotl* gives a long list of his descendants into Spanish times. There seems no doubt in the material now available that Tlacaelel was one of the most important figures of Aztec history. But the relationship between him and Moteczuma may have been emphasized and stylized in terms already familiar in twin myths in North and South America.

[23] Sahagún, Lib. VI, cap 3, Ed. Robredo, Vol. II, p. 53.

[24] Sahagún, Lib. VI, cap. 14, Ed. Robredo, Vol. II, p. 103.

[25] *Ibid.*

[26] See *Codex Mendoza*, Folio 64, and Clark commentary for dress of tlacatecatl and other ranks. Also Sahagún, Lib. VIII, cap. 9; Ed. Robredo, Vol. II, pp. 295-297; Anderson and Dibble, Book 8, pp. 27-28. Also Torquemada, Vol. II, pp. 542-544.

[27] See note 22. The titles were kept in the family connection.

[28] Durán I, p. 98.

[29] Sahagún, Lib. II, cap. 27; Ed. Robredo, Vol. I, p. 166; Anderson and Dibble, Book 2, p. 100. See also Sahagún, Apéndice Lib. III, cap. 5, 6; Ed. Robredo, Vol. I, pp. 291, 293; Anderson and Dibble, Book 3, p. 53, with note.

[30] Tezozomoc, p. 270; Durán I, p. 98.

[31] Durán I, pp. 99-100, for this raid.

[32] This phrase and mention of the common land from Durán I, pp. 100-101.

Dates for his conquest of Coyohuacan are given as 1429 by the *Anales de Tlatelolco* and Chimalpahin; as 1430 by the *Anales Mexicanos: México-Azcapotzalco*—and by inference in the *Anales de Cuauhtitlan* where the sequence of Tepanecan wars following the fall of Azcapotzalco is grouped under this date of 3 Rabbit; as 1431 by the *Crónica Mexicayotl;* Ixtlilxochitl,

Relaciones, groups it with a number of other campaigns in 1428 apparently, since he describes the battle of Xochimilco as in the year following them — 1429, p. 230.

Aside from the sources which give dates for the sequence of conquests of Tepanecan towns, lists without dates are given by a number of sources and are important for the consideration of the order. In connection with the sequence of Coyohuacan, Xochimilco, and Cuitlahuac, taken in that order in the present work, the same order is followed by Tezozomoc; Durán; the *Códice Ramírez;* Torquemada; Ixtlilxochitl in the *Historia Chichimeca;* and in the *Relaciones* with the accompanying "Pintura de México" (pp. 229-230 and 258-261) *La Leyenda de los Soles;* and the *Anales de Cuauhtitlan*, Par. 165-167; *Mendocino;* and *Nueva Lámina del Mapa Quinatzin.* The reverse order is given in the following lists: *Anales de Cuauhtitlan*, Par. 237; *Carta de Pablo Nazareo de Xaltocan;* and *Anales de Tlatelolco*, Par. 7.

Modern studies of order in the conquests have been made by Barlow, "La Fundación de la Triple Alianza," *Anales del Instituto Nacional de Antropología e Historia*, Tomo III, 1947-1948, p. 153; by Isabel Kelly and Angel Palerm (in *The Tajín Totonac*, Part I, Appendix B, pp. 265-317), and by Wigberto Jiménez Moreno in a series of unpublished maps.

It seems clear that disturbed times and fighting went on in all the cities of the Valley of Mexico for several years following the fall of Azcapotzalco.

CHAPTER VIII

[1] The main accounts of the conquest of Xochimilco are to be found in Tezozomoc, pp. 272-277; Durán I, 104-116.

[2] The word that Tezozomoc uses is "vassals." However, in Molina's *Vocabulario* (1571) among the Nahuatl words so translatable is *mamaloni*, which conveys the idea of burden bearing, a term which fits better into the Aztec pattern, and which was probably closer to the original sources Tezozomoc used—the so-called Crónica X.

[3] Sahagún Lib. IX, cap. 17 (Ed. Robredo, Vol. II, pp. 387-389; Dibble and Anderson, Book 9, pp. 79-82) gives the details about the gods of the workers in precious stones at Xochimilco.

[4] The name of the place was Chiquimoltitlan, from *chiquimolin*, gossiper; the connective *-ti;* and *-tlan*, the suffix, place of.

[5] The sources give different emphases on leaders who participated in this war. Tezozomoc and Durán agree in having Tlacaelel in command. Ixtlilxochitl (*Relaciones*, p. 231) claims that Nezahualcoyotl was there "sin llevar ningún Mexicano" but immediately before (p. 230) has described Nezahualcoyotl, Moteczuma, and Itzcoatl, as participating in the series of campaigns of which this was certainly part, and says Nezahualcoyotl went to Mexico when they had fiestas and decided on the Xochimilco campaign, a decision which he says was made by Nezahualcoyotl and Itzcoatl (*Historia Chichimeca*, p. 152). The *Anales de Cuauhtitlan*, Par. 167, names Xochimilco as seventh among the conquests of Nezahualcoyotl, but in the next paragraph, referring to the whole series of conquests listed in the "Relación del Cantar" says that those who waged the war included also Itzcohuatzin, and the kings of Cuauhtitlan and Huexotzinco. Torquemada (Vol. I, pp. 148-149) refers only to Nezahualcoyotl and Itzcoatl. Moteczuma as tlacatecatl was a member of the council described in the last chapter, and thus participated in council decisions, and presumably shared in the battle. Itzcoatl, however, from the time of the battle of Coyohuacan apparently stayed in Tenochtitlan — the Tlatoani, the

Speaker, rather than a warrior.
[6] Tezozomoc, p. 276.
[7] Durán I, p. 110.
[8] See list of places where land was assigned in Tezozomoc, p. 277.
[9] Ixtlilxochitl, *Historia Chichimeca*, p. 158; *Relaciones*, pp. 326-327.
[10] Tezozomoc, p. 276; Durán I, pp. 113-114.
[11] Durán I, p. 114.
[12] Tezozomoc, p. 277. Sunday excursionists in the Floating Gardens seldom realize that their presence there was permitted by treaty, and the custom has continued for more than five hundred years.

The date of conquest is given by Ixtlilxochitl, *Relaciones*, p. 230, as 1429, by Chimalpahin as 1430 (3 Rabbit) though he says there was fighting in the previous year 2 House. The untranslated *Otomí Codex of San Mateo Huichapan* which Dr. Alfonso Caso was kind enough to let me look at in his office and which he is making a study of, shows a glyph of a temple with a plant in 1436 which may well refer to Xochimilco since in 1437 the glyph is clearly that of Cuitlahuaca.

See also Chap. VII, note 32, for sources on order of conquests.

CHAPTER IX

[1] Ixtlilxochitl, *Relaciones*, pp. 231-232, says this part of the Texcocan campaign waited until after the conquest of Xochimilco. He says Itzcoatl and Moteczuma took part in it.
[2] See Sahagún, Lib. III, Apéndice, cap. 4-5 (Ed. Robredo, Vol. I, pp. 288-293; Anderson and Dibble, Book 3, pp. 49-55) for speeches of teachers and customs of the telpochcalli, including the connection with the cuicacalco, or house of song. The speech quoted here is based on the Spanish translation of the Robredo edition. The Anderson and Dibble translation into English gives an opposite interpretation to the sentence about the hearts: "Perchance in him we may enclose and set in place our hearts" (p. 51). Pomar, pp. 27 ff. indicates that going to the house of song was part of the training in both this school and the Calmecac, which was the school for nobles. The Mixcoacalli, also a house of dance, seems not to have been part of the school system, but for adult singers of the city who as time went on gathered to dance and sing, in appropriate regional costume, according to the customs of different parts of the Aztec domain. Sahagún, Lib. VIII, cap. 14, par. 7 Ed. Robredo, Vol. II, pp. 312-313; Anderson and Dibble, Book 8, p. 45).
[3] Sahagún, Canto IX (Ed. Robredo, Vol. V, pp. 98-99; Anderson and Dibble, Book 2, p. 210).
[4] Muñoz Comargo, p. 155.
[5] For the festival of Quecholli, and particularly the sacrifices to Mixcoatl (Comaxtli) see Chapter V with notes 10 and 12. Torquemada (Vol. II, p. 299) shows that both Mixcoatl and Xochiquetzal were honored in this month. He speaks of Mixcoatl in Tenochtitlan and Tlaxcala, and Xochiquetzal in other places, and describes it as everywhere the month of lovers. Durán (II, pp. 192-198) places the fiesta to Xochiquetzal and the farewell to the roses as extending through the preceding month Uepachtli.
[6] Seler analyzes the attributes of Xochiquetzal in his commentary on the *Vaticanus B*, pp. 237, 188-189.
[7] Torquemada (Vol. II, p. 299) says that they did go into battle. They were called *maqui*, the *entremetidas*, those placed between or interspersed.
[8] From the *Telleriano-Remensis*.

[9] For reference to temple and image of Mixcoatl at Cuitlahuac see *Anales de Cuauhtitlan*, Par. 186. For connection of Cuitlahuac with cult of Mixcoatl in his form of Comaxtli, see *Historia de los Mexicanos por sus Pinturas*, p. 217.

[10] Tezozomoc, pp. 278-281, specifically says that the girls were demanded for the *cuicoyan*, the place of song, and that the people of Cuitlahuac replied that "to give their sisters and daughters carnally was not right." Durán in his account of this war (I, pp. 117-124) softens the whole situation and considers that the Mexicans were asking the girls to go to a festival properly chaperoned by their fathers and brothers.

[11] Durán I, p. 120.

[12] Pomar, p. 27.

[13] Sahagún, Lib. III, Apéndice, cap. 6 (Ed. Robredo, p. 293; Anderson and Dibble, Book 3, p. 57) tells about the problem of graduation. Durán (I, p. 120) says the boys in this battle were twenty-four years old; the *Códice Ramírez*, (p 60) that they were from sixteen to eighteen. Torquemada (Vol. I, p. 149) apparently thinking of the boys as considerably younger than this, doubts the whole story that Cuitlahuac could have been conquered by boys "tan a lo niño." The idea, according to Tezozomoc and Durán, was Itzcoatl's and designed to belittle the fighting ability of Cuitlahuac.

[14] The *Anales de Cuauhtitlan* (Par. 180 ff.) makes it clear that the war with Cuitlahuac did not end with this battle. According to this source the first attempt was in 7 Rabbit (1434). Two years later the Texcocans got around to helping. In 8 Reed the Cuitlahuaca came to Mexico pretending to belong to the Mexicans. In 1 House (1441) the pretended image of Mixcoatl was brought to Mexico. This all took seven years. Torquemada says the battle lasted seven days. Durán and Tezozomoc put the battle a few days before Itzcoatl's death. It began in 1432 according to *Anales Mexicanos: México-Azcapotzalco*. The defense was destroyed in 1433 according to Chimalpahin. The date 1437 is shown by *Otomí Codex of San Mateo Huichapan*. See also Chap. VII, note 32.

[15] That the Festival of Quecholli came in November is supported by the many sources that mention the entrance of Cortés into Mexico-Tenochtitlan in 1519 as being in November and in the month of Quecholli; these sources are listed and analyzed by Alfonso Caso, "Correlación de los Años Azteca y Cristiano," *Revista Mexicana de Estudios Antropológicos* III, Núm. 1, Enero-Abril, 1939, pp. 11-45, — particularly pp. 25-28 on this point. In his tables correlating Christian and Aztec months he shows, however, the sliding dates of the months' beginnings. See "El Calendario Mexicano," *Memorias de la Academia Mexicana de la Historia*, XVII, No. 1, 1958, pp. 41-96. Durán II, p. 297, says that this festival was in November. It is described as the festival of the fourteenth month of the Aztec year by Sahagún, Durán, and Torquemada. The birds, songs, and other details used at the end of this chapter are from Torquemada, Vol. II, p. 299.

CHAPTER X

[1] Durán I, pp. 53-55.

[2] Durán I, p. 115.

[3] The details of this war with Cuauhnauac are from Torquemada, Vol. I, p. 149. The conquest is mentioned by the *Aubin Codex of 1576* as in 9 Stone (1436); by the *Codex of Cuauhtlancingo*, and the *Annales de Chimalpahin* as in 12 Reed (1439); by the *Anales de Cuauhtitlan*, Par. 171, as in 3

Rabbit (1430); and by the *Anales de Tlatelolco*, Par. 264, as in 6 House (1433). It is included among the place glyphs of Itzcoatl's conquests in the *Codex Mendoza*, and in Ixtlilxochitl's *Pintura de Mexico* (in *Relaciones*) Yauhtepec is listed in the same area, though Cuauhnauac is not mentioned. The *Anales de Cuauhtitlan*, Par. 237, includes Cuauhnauac among the conquests of Itzcoatl. *La Leyenda de los Soles* mentions Xiuhtepec and Cuauhnauac among the conquests of Itzcoatl, but repeats them and adds Tlachco in the reign of Moteczuma.

Regarding the assignment of tribute, the *Codex de Cuantlancingo* and the *Aubin Codex of 1576* mention that the tribute was for two years; the *Annales de Chimalpahin* say for only one. The *Anales de Cuauhtitlan*, Par. 224, assigns it specifically to Texcoco. The room in the royal house there is mentioned by Ixtlilxochitl, *Historia Chichimeca*, p. 180, and shown in the *Mapa Quinatzin*.

[4] Xolotl, god of the evening star, to whom Quetzalcoatl was Precious Twin, went down to get the bones for the creation of man. He was one of the gods of the ball court as pictured in the codices. For Maxtla's flight to Tlachco, the modern Taxco, see Chap. VII, note 20. His death "on the ball court" is mentioned in *Annales de Chimalpahin* under 4 Reed (1431).

[5] *Telleriano-Remensis*, Commentator on 4th trecena.

[6] *Anales de Cuauhtitlan*, Par. 186. The suffix of respect is *-tzin*. The wife from Cuauhnauac is the only one mentioned in the basic sources. See *Carta de Pablo Nazareo*, pp. 121-122.

[7] Only during that thirteen-day period beginning with the day 1 Death could they remove their collars, says Sahagún, Lib. IV, cap. 9 (Ed. Robredo, Vol. 1, p. 321; Dibble and Anderson, Book 4, p. 34). The slave collar is shown in the *Florentine Codex* and also in the *Codex Borbonicus*, Sheets 16 and 20.

[8] For clarifying discussion of relationships of Cihuacoatl see Caso, *La Religion de los Aztecas*, p. 30, and *The Aztecs: People of the Sun*, pp. 52-56. An interesting point is her relationship to La Llorona, the Wailing Woman, a legend widespread in modern times. Sahagún, Lib. I, cap. 6, describes her characteristics, and in Lib. VIII, cap. 1, describes how she wailed in the streets in the reign of the second Moteczuma. (Ed. Robredo, Vol. I, p. 18, and Vol. II, p. 289; Anderson and Dibble, Book 1, p. 3, and Book 8, p. 3.) For construction of the temple to her in the reign of Itzcoatl, see *Anales Mexicanos: México-Azcapotzalco*, p. 59, and Torquemada, Vol. I, p. 150.

[9] From Spanish of Garibay, *Poesía Indígena*, p. 16. See also Seler's comments on this song, Sahagún, Ed. Robredo, Vol. 5, pp. 124-126. An English translation also in Anderson and Dibble, Book 2, p. 211.

[10] Veytia, *Tezcoco en los Ultimos Tiempos de sus Antiguos Reyes*, p. 17, says these were continued by the later Texcocan rulers.

[11] Torquemada, Vol. I, pp. 145-146, gives these details of the coronation. However, the *Anales de Cuauhtitlan*, Par. 172, 177, says he was crowned in Mexico itself in 4 Reed, 1431, and established himself in Texcoco in 6 House, 1433. The 4 Reed date is also given by the *Annales de Chimalpahin*, *Códice en Cruz*, and *Anales de Tlatelolco*.

[12] *Anales de Tlatelolco*, Par. 262.

[13] Pomar, p. 31.

[14] Phrases from *Anales de Tlatelolco*, and from the "Tratado del Principado y Nobleza del Pueblo de San Juan Teotihuacan" respectively.

[15] Ixtlilxochitl, *Historia Chichimeca*, p. 158; Veytia, *Tezcoco en los Últimos Tiempos de sus Antiguos Reyes*, p. 165.

[16] Ixtlilxochitl, *Historia Chichimeca*, pp. 151, 154.

[17] For examples of threefold alliances see Gillmor, *Flute of the Smoking Mirror*,

pp. 18, 39-40, 43, 86, 136, 148; also threefold military strategy in battles of Azcapotzalco and Cuauhnauac.

[18] The division according to Ixtlilxochitl, *Historia Chichimeca*, p. 154, and Zurita, p. 74, although Zurita qualified by saying that in the case of tribute from a few towns the three powers divided equally. Torquemada (Vol. I, Lib. II, cap. 40, p. 146) agrees that Tlacopan got a fifth but says that of the remainder Texcoco took one third and Tenochtitlan two thirds. Division of tribute from the towns in the valley of Mexico and later conquests is shown in *Anales de Cuauhtitlan*, Par. 224-233; *Mapa Quinatzin; Historia del Señorio de Teotihuacan*, No. 3 in Ramírez, *Anales Antiguos de México y sus Contornos*. Division of land by Itzcoatl in 1438 is referred to by "Manuscrito Americano No. 4 Biblioteca Real de Berlin" in Peñafiel, *Colección de Documentos para la Historia Mexicana*, Vol. 1.

[19] Ixtlilxochitl, *Historia Chichimeca*, p. 154; Veytia, *Tezcoco en los Últimos Tiempos de sus Antiguos Reyes*, p. 163. For the military arrangement, Zurita, p. 74.

[20] This conference and agreement took place in 8 Reed (1435) according to the *Anales de Cuauhtitlan*, Par. 183, and the *Anales de Tlatelolco*, Par. 264, though the *Annales de Chimalpahin* puts the conquest in 4 Reed, 1431. Details are described in the *Ordenanza del Cuauhtemoc*, translated by Silvia Rendón, *Philological and Documentary Studies*, Vol. II, No. 2, Middle American Research Institute, Tulane University of Louisiana, New Orleans, 1952. The account of this dispute was written down and a new copy of the carefully kept map made in 1523 after a night conference in which Cuauhtemoc in the presence of his soldiers of rank commanded that the old land and water rights be guarded. Torquemada (Vol. I, p. 157) mentions the construction of a wall between Tenochtitlan and Tlatelolco. A wall is also mentioned in the *Ordenanza*.

[21] This account of a battle between Tenochtitlan and Texcoco is from Ixtlilxochitl, *Historia Chichimeca*, pp. 161-164. Since it is given only by this Texcoco source, it is doubted, along with the corresponding account by the Tenochtitlan sources of a victory later over Texcoco (See below—Chap. 12), by Chavero in his notes to Ixtlilxochitl, *Historia Chichimeca*, pp. 162, 164; also by Ramírez in his note to Durán I, p. 130; and by Orozco y Berra in his note to Tezozomoc, p. 284. It has been believed that these accounts all refer to the same war, the opposite claims to victory being due to the vanity of the two contesting cities. I treated it as one war in my earlier book, *Flute of the Smoking Mirror*, p. 90 (with notes).

I am increasingly convinced, however, that there were two wars, both formal, to establish the dignity of each city in the alliance, both following, as the sources describe, the coronation of one king by the other. Not the claim to victory but the wars themselves might well be credited to the vanity of each city. This would be consistent with the view of war as the "judgment of the gods" pointed out by Soustelle. It would be consistent also with the speech accredited to Nezahualcoyotl by Ixtlilxochitl, *Historia Chichimeca*, p. 163, and the speech accredited to Tlacaelel by Durán I, p. 128.

[22] Ichtecuachichtli was killed by the boy Teconatltecatl, according to Ixtlilxochitl, *Historia Chichimeca*, p. 163, the Texcocan source. This source, careful to mention Moteczuma's name wherever he was an ally of Nezahualcoyotl, so conspicuously leaves him unmentioned in the account of this particular battle, that the significance of the omission seems to support the interpretation given here.

[23] The book burning and the type of history the books contained is described by Sahagún, Lib. X, cap. 29, Par. 12 (Ed. Robredo, Vol. III, pp. 137-138; Dibble and Anderson, Book 10, p. 191). It is interesting that the later burning of Aztec books by the Spaniards was not unprecedented.

[24] *Anales de Tlatelolco*, Par. 235.

[25] The visits by Nezahualcoyotl and by Moteczuma are described by the *Annales de Chimalpahin*, under the respective dates. For the phrasing about Nezahualcoyotl's companions I am indebted to the Spanish translation (in manuscript) by Silvia Rendón. The French translation of the same passage by Rémi Siméon does not give these details. Moteczuma's desire to be away from Tenochtitlan, mentioned in Chimalpahin's account in an obscure and confusing way as if he wished to escape threatened war — an attitude inconsistent with all the rest of his life — is illuminated by the *Orígen de los Mexicanos*, pp. 271-273, which tells of the opposition to him personally in Tenochtitlan at this time.

[26] Durán I, p. 123.

[27] Durán I, p. 123, who gives this date, though he says a less trustworthy painting gives the date 1445. The date 13 Stone (1440) is given as the date both for the death of Itzcoatl and the accession of Moteczuma by the *Telleriano-Remensis*, *Mapa de Tepechpan*, *Annales de Chimalpahin*, *Anales de Cuauhtitlan*, *Códice en Cruz*, *Crónica Mexicayotl*, and one tradition of the *Anales de Tlatelolco* (Par. 57-59), *Anales Mexicanos: México-Azcapotzalco*, text of *Codex Mendoza*, and Ixtlilxochitl, *Historia Chichimeca* (p 201).

The dates 12 Reed (1439) for the death of Itzcoatl and 13 Stone (1440) for the accession of Moteczuma are given by one tradition of the *Anales de Tlatelolco* (Par. 265).

The *Códice Ramírez* says Itzcoatl began to reign in 1424 and reigned twelve years, which would make his death in 1436. The *Aubin Codex of 1576* gives 1437 for the death of Itzcoatl and 1438 for the accession of Moteczuma.

The *Códice Cuantlancingo* gives 1 House (1441) for the death of Itzcoatl, and 2 Rabbit (1442) for the accession of Moteczuma. The *Codex Mexicanus*, Sheet LXIV, also puts the death of Itzcoatl in 1 House (1441). The accession of Moteczuma is drawn immediately next to it, with possible reference to the same year or to the following year. The *Otomí Codex of San Mateo Huichapan* gives the dates for the two events as 1440 and 1441.

CHAPTER XI

[1] Durán I, p. 124.

[2] *Orígen de los Mexicanos*, pp. 271-273.

[3] *Códice Ramírez*, p. 62.

[4] Durán I, p. 124, says the common people shared in this election, but Sahagún, who lists very specifically the groups permitted to be electors in Lib. VIII, cap. 18 (Ed. Robredo, Vol. II, p. 321-322; Anderson and Dibble, Book 8, p. 61) does not include them, nor does Zurita, pp. 73-82. The *Códice Ramírez*, pp. 62-63, and Torquemada, Vol. I, pp. 150-151, speaking of Moteczuma's election in particular, do not include them.

[5] The *Códice Ramírez*, p. 66, describes this as the attitude of Tlacaelel at the time of the election of Moteczuma's successor, and says that "as at other times he never wanted to accept kingship." Since this was the most recent time when such a choice would have been in order, it seems safe to mention it here.

[6] So described for identification purposes by Durán I, p. 124.

[7] This was frequently done, says Sahagún, Lib. VIII, cap. 18 (Ed. Robredo, Vol. II, p. 322; Anderson and Dibble, Book 8, p. 62).

[8] The characteristics listed are those given by Sahagún as prerequisites for

election, and by the *Códice Mendocino* as Moteczuma's characteristics in particular.

[9] Torquemada, Vol. I, p. 150.

[10] Sahagún, Lib. VI, cap. 13; Ed. Robredo, Vol. II, pp. 95-97—the speech made when the newly elected señor is not present. It is spoken by some principal person, friend or relative.

[11] *Orígen de los Mexicanos*, p. 273.

[12] This and the following speeches in the series are from Sahagún, Lib. VI, cap. 10, 11, 12; Ed. Robredo, Vol. II, pp. 82-95 — a speech used to notify a señor recently elected, a speech made by a second orator to express happiness in his election, and the reply by the one elected. The prescribed positions and garb are all described by Sahagún, who also gives the information that the elected individual would later always have an orator by his side ready for an emergency, pp. 94-95.

[13] The fact that the propitious day in the ceremonial calendar was considered before the crowning of a king is mentioned by Sahagún, Lib. VIII, cap. 18 (Ed. Robredo, Vol. II, p. 322; Anderson and Dibble, Book 8, p. 61). The choice of 1 Crocodile for Moteczuma I (and also Moteczuma II) is mentioned by Ixtlilxochitl, *Historia Chichimeca* (p. 306). However, the *Crónica Mexicayotl* gives the day as 3 Serpent whose position as third day would have helped the bad luck of its week 1 House, according to Sahagún, Lib. IV, cap. 28; Ed. Robredo, Vol. I, p. 347; Dibble and Anderson, Book 4, p. 96. For year see Chap. X, note 27.

[14] The fortune belonging to this particular day and the thirteen-day week it initiated is given by Sahagún, Lib. IV, cap. 1 (Ed. Robredo, Vol. I, pp. 305-307; Dibble and Anderson, Book 4, pp. 1-4).

[15] Sahagún, Lib. IV, cap. 1 (Ed. Robredo, Vol. I, p. 307; Dibble and Anderson, Book 4, p. 4). Also for quick reading of relations between the trecenas of the Tonalamatl and the directions and gods, see table by Ola Apenes. For survey of characteristics of gods see Spence, *Gods of Mexico*. The bird masks accompany the day signs in the codices *Borbonicus*, *Borgia*, and *Aubin*.

[16] Directional connections analyzed by Seler in commentary on *Codex Féjerváry-Mayer*, particularly for this day on p. 204.

[17] Seler, *Féjerváry-Mayer* (p. 50), mentions this calendar association of the Fire God; and the abundance of the week this date initiates is described by Sahagún, Lib. IV, cap. 38 (Ed. Robredo, Vol. I, p. 360; Dibble and Anderson, Book 4, p. 127). Rabbit years, however, had quite a different meaning and were believed to be associated with famine. See Sahagún, Lib. VII; Ed. Robredo, Vol. II, cap. 9, p. 267; Anderson and Dibble, Book 7, chap. 8, p. 23. The *Anales de Cuauhtitlan*, Par. 180, show the same association in the year 7 Rabbit (1434) during Itzcoatl's rule. The tragic year 1 Rabbit which particularly gave emphasis to the belief was, of course, in 1454, and is described below in Chapter XIII.

[18] They held these positions in the year immediately following Moteczuma's coronation according to the *Anales de Cuauhtitlan*, Par. 186, 1 House (1441), and presumably were in the council which Sahagún describes as installed at the coronation of a new king. However, new appointments could be made, as we see Moteczuma's brother Huehue Zacatzin serving as tlacatecatl later, *Crónica Mexicayotl*, Par. 248 ff.

[19] It is immediately following the installation of Moteczuma as king that Tezozomoc starts giving Tlacaelel the title of Cihuacoatl (p. 282). Up to this time he has always coupled his name with his post as tlacochcalcatl. An interesting discussion of the position of Cihuacoatl as sometimes held by the tlatoani himself and as becoming separate in the time of Moteczuma

Ilhuicamina is given by Miguel Acosta Saignes in his study of "Los Teopixque," particularly on pp. 176 ff. It is a further aspect of the twin-like aspects of the two half-brothers.

[20] Details of coronation ritual from Sahagún, Lib. VIII, cap. 18 (Ed. Robredo, Vol. II, p. 321-325; Anderson and Dibble, Book 8, pp. 61-64) and from Zurita, p. 77. For Moteczuma's coronation in particular, *Códice Ramírez*, pp. 62-63; Durán I, p. 125; *Telleriano-Remensis.*

[21] For this and the following prayers, Sahagún, Lib. VI, cap. 9, Ed. Robredo, Vol. II, pp. 77-81.

[22] *Telleriano-Remensis.*

[23] *Códice Ramírez*, Lamina 12, shows Nezahualcoyotl, identified by his glyph, passing the crown to Moteczuma, identified by his.

[24] Zurita, p. 78.

CHAPTER XII

[1] A day was studied and selected for the election festival according to Sahagún, Lib. VIII, cap. 18, Par. 3 and 4 (Ed. Robredo, Vol. II, p. 324; Anderson and Dibble, Book 8, p. 64). For those elected in the trecena which began with 1 Dog, the preferred date was 4 Reed, the fourth day of the trecena, says Sahagún, Lib. IV, cap. 25 (Ed. Robredo, Vol. I, pp. 343-344; Dibble and Anderson, Book 4, pp. 87-89). We cannot say what the date was for Ilhuicamina, since we do not know the date of his election, and the day 1 Crocodile on which he was crowned would have been thirteen trecenas earlier — 169 days before 1 Dog, and 173 days before 4 Reed. It is improbable that they would wait for the election festival that long. Four days of fasting after 1 Crocodile would bring us through 5 Serpent and then the fiesta could begin on 6 Death.

[2] Durán I, p. 125, for this speech, much condensed as usual in the present work.

[3] Tezozomoc, p. 283.

[4] Tezozomoc, p. 282.

[5] Durán I, p. 128. This situation is one in which the reversal of role between Tlacaelel and Moteczuma is apparent in the main Tenochtitlan sources. Tezozomoc has Moteczuma initiate the action against Texcoco. Durán and the *Códice Ramírez* have Tlacaelel suggest it, the latter in the reign of Itzcoatl (pp. 61-62).

[6] Durán I, p. 130.

[7] *Anales de Tlatelolco*, Par. 262, for this help.

[8] The details given here for this feigned war in which Tenochitlan is described as victorious are from Durán I, pp. 124-132, and Tezozomoc, pp. 282-286. The victory is also so described by the *Códice Ramírez*, pp. 61-62, and the *Annales de Chimalpahin* give the Chalco viewpoint under date of 4 Acatl (1431), these two sources thus putting it in the reign of Itzcoatl. If there were actually two wars as suggested in Chapter X, note 21, and as treated in the present work, these two sources must be considered as confusing them with each other, or as confusing the attack on Texcoco in the "feigned war" with the earlier "mopping up" operations against the opposition to Nezahualcoyotl's return already described, and participated in by both Moteczuma and Nezahualcoyotl. Acosta, *Historia Natural y Moral de las Indias*, pp. 541 ff., puts it after the Cuitlahuac victory; Torquemada, Vol. I, p. 149, doubts that it happened.

[9] Tezozomoc, p. 287, and Durán I, p. 133.

[10] Tezozomoc, p. 288.

[11] Tezozomoc, p. 289, and Durán I, pp. 135-136. Tlacaelel sends a message to Coateotl in much more threatening terms in the *Anales Mexicanos: México-Azcapotzalco*, p. 65, than in these two sources.
[12] Durán I, pp. 137-139.
[13] Their ages given by Durán I, p. 138; the distribution of arms by the officials by Tezozomoc, p. 291. For military training in the schools see Chap. IX, note 2.
[14] *Códice Ramírez*, p. 63.
[15] Tezozomoc, p. 293. The two gods were associated. For example, note the discussion of the tenth trecena of the Tonapahualli by Sahagún, Lib. IV, cap. 21 (Ed. Robredo, Vol. I, p. 339; Dibble and Anderson, Book 4, p. 77); and the movable feast in this trecena — the eleventh movable feast — Sahagún, Lib. II, cap. 19 (Ed. Robredo, Vol. I, p. 115; Anderson and Dibble, Book 2, p. 38). Durán speaks of the festival of Xocotl — but the relation is to events in the later phase of the war when Tlacahuepan died.
[16] Tezozomoc, p. 294; Durán I, pp. 144-145.
[17] *Anales de Cuauhtitlan*, Par. 186.
[18] *Ibid.*
[19] *Anales de Cuauhtitlan*, Par. 92, gives the account of the man who went to his death so that his sons might have noble status and an inheritance from Huehue Moteczuma — in this case Tepotzotlan.
[20] This is the phrasing of the Seventh Relación of the *Annales de Chimalpahin* under 4 Stone, 1444. The Third Relación (Silvia Rendón tr.) gives the date as 1446 and says he was killed in battle. The *Anales Mexicanos: México-Azcapotzalco* puts his death in the later phase of this war in 11 Stone, 1464.

In grouping the events of this chapter I follow the dating of Chimalpahin who has the capture of Tlalmanalco in 1443. He is the Chalco source, discussing the loss of this part of the Chalco domain, and the death of a Chalco leader — from Itzcahuacan, he says, though the *Anales Mexicanos: México-Azcapotzalco* have him from Tlalmanalco. The governmental relationships of the various Chalco divisions need more study than has so far been given. The Tepanecan identification of Coateotl with Tlalmanalco would make his murder consistent with the resentment felt by Tepanecan cities against the first of their subject towns to yield. Cf. the night raid of Coyohuacan on conquered Azcapotzalco.

Durán and Tezozomoc handle their material topically instead of chronologically and group all the events of the Chalco war right through the final victory in 1465. For the later phase of it see Chap. XVII where I handle it in chronological position. It is because of the topical handling of these Crónica X sources that they treat Coateotl mistakenly as alive when Tlacahuepan jumps to his death, at a date clearly identified by a number of sources, including Chimalpahin, as in the later period.

CHAPTER XIII

[1] This fact given by Torquemada, Vol. I, p. 156.
[2] Ixtlilxochitl, *Historia Chichimeca*, p. 217, 210-212.
[3] The description is Torquemada's phrase, Vol. I, p. 155.
[4] Ixtlilxochitl, *Historia Chichimeca*, pp. 214-215. In the *Mapa de Tepechpan* his death is shown in 3 Reed. The marriage would thus have been a little later in the same year or in the following year 4 Stone.

[5] For the speeches at a marriage, Sahagún, Lib. VI, cap. 23, Ed. Robredo, Vol. II, p. 154.

[6] Torquemada, Vol. I, p. 156.

[7] The grasshopper plague is engagingly pictured in the *Codex Mexicanus*, Sheet LXIV, where a grasshopper nestles in the branches of a stalk of corn attached to the date 6 Rabbit (1446). It is also pictured in the *Aubin Codex of 1576* on this date, and mentioned by Chimalpahin, by the *Anales Mexicanos No. 1* (No. 7 in *Anales Antiguos de México y sus Contornos*) and by the *Anales Mexicanos: México-Azcapotzalco*. The *Códice de Cuantlancingo* lists it in the following year, 7 Reed.

[8] Torquemada, Vol. I, p. 157.

[9] Torquemada (Vol. I, pp. 157-158) describes the building of the dike, the direction by Nezahualcoyotl, and the fact that both he and Moteczuma put their hands to the work along with the macehuales. The order to kill Huehue Zacan "who went singing and singing, playing and playing" during the building of the dike is described by the *Crónica Mexicayotl*, Par. 249-250. Those who "went singing" were considered as giving evidence of drunkenness, says Sahagún, Apéndice, Lib. III, cap. 6 (Ed. Robredo, Vol. I, p. 293; Anderson and Dibble, Book 3, p. 57); and drunkenness was by law punishable by death. The death sentence could only be given by the king according to Moteczuma's own laws, according to Durán I, p. 216. These facts help to explain Moteczuma's action.

[10] Mentioned by the *Anales de Tlatelolco*, Par. 266, in year 10 Rabbit (1450). The dike begun the previous year in 9 House would not yet be finished.

[11] Veytia, *Historia Antigua de México*, Vol. II, pp. 216-217, gives this description of the dike, and puts its construction in 1446. Document 1169 in the Latin American Library of the University of Texas gives the same date and width and says it was nine miles long. Torquemada describes it as three leagues long but four arm-spreads wide.

[12] *Orígen de los Mexicanos*, p. 273; *Anales de Cuauhtitlan*, 11 Reed (1451), Par. 188; *Anales de Tula*, same date; *Historia de los Mexicanos por sus Pinturas*, p. 230.

[13] Ixtlilxochitl, *Historia Chichimeca*, p. 205.

[14] In 11 Reed, 12 Stone, 13 House, say the *Anales de Tlatelolco*, Par. 266.

[15] Ixtlilxochitl, *Historia Chichimeca*, p. 206.

[16] Ixtlilxochitl, *Historia Chichimeca*, p. 206, mistakenly dates this eclipse as 1454 instead of 12 Stone, 1452. For note on exact dating in Julian count and according to Caso correlation see Gillmor, *Flute of the Smoking Mirror*, pp. 125 and 169, note 19. Details of sacrificial procedures from Sahagún, Lib. VII, cap. 1 (Ed. Robredo, Vol. II, p. 255; Anderson and Dibble, Book 7, p. 2). The *Otomí Codex of San Mateo Huichapan* shows an eclipse in 1455, mistakenly named 3 Reed instead of 2 Reed.

[17] *Annales de Chimalpahin*, Relación III, 11 Reed (1451), typescript translation by Sylvia Rendón, *Seis Relaciones Históricas . . .*

[18] Veytia, *Historia Antigua de México*, Vol. II, p. 217, mentions a rebellion of Chalco — actually so far conquered only in certain sections. In the Chalco source, the *Annales de Chimalpahin*, we see that war was going on all through this period. From the time it began in 1453 it never stopped, and never was there such fighting before, says Chimalpahin.

[19] For details of the Feast of the Lords, Sahagún, Lib. II, cap. 27 (Ed. Robredo, Vol. I, pp. 158-166; Anderson and Dibble, Book 2, pp. 91-100). For the freeze which came during the feast of the lords in this particular year, *Anales de Tlatelolco*, 13 House (1453), Par. 266. The *Historia de los Mexicanos por sus Pinturas* describes the lake freezing during the "feast of bread," in the 128th year after the founding of Tenochtitlan (p. 230). The *Aubin Codex of 1576* shows hail in the year 13 House. The snow pictured in the

Telleriano-Remensis and *Vaticanus B* is earlier in 7 Reed (1447).

[20] See Chapter III for Chimalpopoca's dance in this festival. Sahagún in his discussion of this festival says Moteczuma (the younger, of course) danced or not as he chose.

[21] This comparison is from Durán II, p. 286, in his discussion of the feast.

[22] Sahagún, Canto XVI (Ed. Robredo, Vol. V, p. 158; Anderson and Dibble, Book 2, p. 213). This is also included by Garibay, *Poesía Indígena*, p. 23.

[23] It was offered to Cinteotl, says Sahagún, and the song already quoted mentions Tlalocan, the land of Tlaloc, the rain god.

[24] "Anales Mexicanos No. 1: No. 7 in *Anales Antiguos de México y sus Contornos* — Ramírez. Entry under 13 House.

[25] These details of the earthquake that came in the year 13 Reed are from *Anales de Tlatelolco*, Par. 266.

[26] "Titles of Tetzcotzinco." Translated and annotated by Byron McAfee and R. H. Barlow, *Tlalocan*, Vol. II, No. 2, 1946, pp. 110-127. These water rights granted by Nezahualcoyotl were confirmed after the Spanish conquest.

[27] *Leyenda de los Soles*, p. 126.

[28] Nezahualcoyotl gave the order to the Texcocans for Moteczuma, say the *Annales de Chimalpahin* under 1 Rabbit (1454). When the subject is taken up again in 13 Rabbit (1466) it is emphasized that the aqueduct had taken thirteen years to build. For its completion see Chapter XVIII.

[29] *Anales de Tlatelolco*, Par. 267, 1 Rabbit.

[30] *Anales de Cuauhtitlan*, Par. 188, 1 Rabbit.

[31] Tezozomoc, p. 364.

[32] *Annales de Chimalpahin*, VII, 11 Reed through 1 Rabbit. Also *Relacion* III (Silvia Rendón translation), 1 Rabbit. The *Aubin Codex of 1576* shows a buzzard plucking at a man, and the compiler of the *Anales de Cuauhtitlan*, Par. 188, refers to a similar painting among his sources.

[33] *Historia de los Mexicanos por sus Pinturas*, p. 230.

[34] Tezozomoc, p. 366, and *Anales de Tlatelolco*, Par. 267 (2 Acatl).

[35] Torquemada, Vol. I, p. 158; Veytia, *Historia Antigua de México*, II, p. 217.

[36] Durán I, p. 248; Tezozomoc, p. 366. Tezozomoc has them leave after the feast of the lords.

[37] Durán I, p. 248: Sahagún, Lib. VIII, cap. 1 (Ed. Robredo, Vol. II, p. 279; Anderson and Dibble, Book 8, pp. 1-2).

[38] A phrase used by *Anales Mexicanos: México-Azcapotzalco*, p. 63, 12 Stone (1452). In this year 1 Tochtli (1454) also "there was much hunger and because of this it was said that they endured much fire" (p. 66). A similar phrase is used by Durán I, p. 245, when he says the earth burned like fire and refers to the fire that came from the ground and parched the plants.

[39] The *Annales de Chimalpahin* and the *Anales de Cuauhtitlan* both mention the coyotes. The *Anales de Tlaxcala No. 1* (No. 16 of Ramírez, *Anales Antiguos de México y sus Contornos*) says many dogs fed themselves with the arms of a child. The *Otomí Codex of San Mateo Huichapan* in 1454 shows a wolf or coyote eating a person's leg.

[40] Tezozomoc, pp. 363-364; Durán I, pp. 242-244. Both of these sources describe it as the colonization of Oaxaca, and put it after, rather than before, the Mexican conquests to the south, though in the time of Moteczuma Ilhuicamina, and with the intention of making the conquest secure. I place it at the time of the famine instead, on the following grounds: (1) Durán and Tezozomoc use a topical rather than a chronological order, putting the famine of 1 Rabbit (1454) after campaigns of Coaixtlahuaca, Cotaxtla, etc., which occurred in the late '50's and '60's. (2) Tezozomoc himself moves from his account of the colonization of Oaxaca to his account of the famine of 1 Rabbit with a transitional sentence — "In this time came a very sterile year." (3) This colonization expedition is in the pattern of the migrations

of the famine years. (4) The places mentioned as welcoming these colonists were nearer Coaixtlahuaca than Oaxaca. See note 45. (5) The colonies could account for the Mexica in the area at the time the Coaixtlahuaca campaign. (See next chapter.)

[41] *Anales de Tlatelolco*, Par. 267, 2 Reed.

[42] Durán I, p. 248; Tezozomoc, p. 367; Torquemada, Vol. I, p. 158.

[43] Tezozomoc, p. 368. Chimalpahin, *Relacion* III, 1 Reed (Silvia Rendón trans.).

[44] *Anales de Tecamachalco*, 2 Reed — a confused entry which seems to refer to a contested settlement before the actual conquest of Tepeacac eleven years later.

[45] The people who came with help were people from Cuauhtochpan, Tuchtepecas and Teotlitlecas, says Tezozomoc, p. 364. Durán gives the places as Teotlilan, Tochpan and Cuauhtochco. They were in the northern part of the present state of Oaxaca.

[46] *Annales de Chimalpahin*, 2 Reed.

[47] These wars of flowers in the 1300's are referred to by the *Anales de Cuauhtitlan*, Par. 131, 132, and by Chimalpahin in *Relación* V (1 Stone — 1324) and VI (1387), Silvia Rendón translation.

[48] *Anales de Cuauhtitlan*, Par. 59.

[49] *Códice Ramírez*, p. 66. This fact suggests that the small seated and crowned figure back of Moteczuma Ilhuicamina on Sheet XVIII of the *Códice Azcatítlan*, which Barlow in his commentary (p. 122) does not attempt to explain, might be Tlacaelel — indeed "a power behind the throne" with kingly insignia permitted. Apparently he was the only one who wore a crown in time of peace, though Durán I, p. 214, says in war the great señores wore one as representatives of the king. Compare, however, the *Mendoza* picture of a row of "alcaldes" with crown and speech scroll like Tlatoanis, each with a small crowned figure seated back of him. The small figures are called *tectli* and are described in the Spanish text as young men who are present with the "alcaldes" at hearings, learning matters of law.

[50] Ixtlilxochitl, *Relaciones*, p. 321.

[51] Ixtlilxochitl, *Historia Chichimeca*, pp. 206-208, dates this war of flowers specifically as part of the famine situation of 1454. It should be noted, however, that the war of flowers apparently became expedient again in the period following the conquests at a distance, since the difficulty of bringing prisoners for sacrifice from remote places is mentioned by Ixtlilxochitl, *Relaciones*, p. 321, and by Durán I, pp. 238-241. Durán speaks of the Huaxteca and the coasts as already subject areas — and even includes Michoacan, which, in fact, was not conquered at all.

[52] Sahagún, Canto III (Ed. Robredo, Vol. V, pp. 32-37; Anderson and Dibble, Book II, p. 208); Garibay, *Poesía Indígena*, pp. 9-10.

[53] Inanimate objects have no plural forms in Nahuatl. But mountains, stars, and skies have their plural forms since they are thought of as animate.

[54] See note 52. The translation is that of Anderson and Dibble. For the phrases for the land of the dead see discussion in Seler's notes, Sahagún, Ed. Robredo, Vol. V, pp. 48-49; and Garibay's notes, *Poesía Indígena*, p. 181.

[55] The directional associations of the Year Bearers in this fiesta are given by Durán II, p. 296, and the throwing of the corn to the directions by Durán II, p. 195. The colors are listed in the same order in both references, and on p. 195, the red corn (el morado) is specifically related to the direction called *amilpan*, which Molina defines: *Amilpampa ehecatl* — viento meridional — south wind. The directional association of the year bearers is the same in Sahagún, Lib. VII, cap. 8 (Ed. Robredo, Vol. II, pp. 266-267; Anderson and Dibble, Book 7, chap. 7, p. 21). The ceremonial details of this sacramental festival of the mountains are from Durán II, pp. 195-198 and 295-296; Sahagún, Lib. II, cap. 32 (Ed. Robredo, Vol. I, pp. 185-187;

Anderson and Dibble, Book 2, pp. 121-123); Torquemada, Vol. II, pp. 279-280.

[56] The ceremonial details of the sacrifices on the hills and mountains are given by Durán as they were carried on in the time of Moteczuma II and Nezahualpilli (Vol. II, pp. 135-146 and 199-207). *El Origin de los Mexicanos*, p. 273, states that the sacrifices on the hills were first started by Moteczuma I in the time of famine. For the ahuehuetl tree as the drum of water, see Durán II, p. 212.

[57] Durán II, p. 205.

[58] "Anales Mexicanos No. 2: Anónimo en lengua Mexicana." (No 8 in *Anales Antiguos de México y sus Contornos* — Ramírez.)

[59] Ceremonial details of binding of the years from Sahagún, Lib. VII, cap. 9-13 (Ed. Robredo, Vol. II, pp. 267-274; Anderson and Dibble, Book 7, Chap. 8-12, pp. 23-32). They are pictured in the *Codex Borbonicus*.

[60] *Anales de Tlatelolco*, Par. 267, 2 Reed; Durán I, p. 249; Torquemada, Vol. I, p. 159.

[61] Tezozomoc, p. 228.

[62] *Anales de Tlatelolco*, Par. 267, 2 Reed.

[63] *Anales de Tecamachalco*, 2 Reed.

[64] Durán I, p. 249.

[65] Tezozomoc, pp. 368-369; Durán I, pp. 249-251. Durán says both brothers were included in the portrait. Tezozomoc speaks of only one but has Tlacaelel say, "La obra me ha cuadrado muy mucho." Remnants of sculpture on the cliffs of Chapultepec are still to be seen, but these have been credited to the time of Moteczuma II by Dr. Ignacio Alcocer, *Apuntes Sobre la Antigua México-Tenochtitlan*, pp. 91-95, and more recently by H. B. Nicholson, "The Chapultepec Cliff Sculpture of Motecuhzoma Xocoyotzin" *El México Antiguo*, IX, 1959, pp. 379-444.

CHAPTER XIV

[1] Most of the already established relations between these towns and Mexico-Tenochtitlan have been treated in the preceding chapters. It might be noted here that Ixtlilxochitl, *Historia Chichimeca*, p. 196, discusses Nezahualcoyotl's conquest in the direction of Tulancingo, and on p. 46 describes earlier expansion under Nopaltzin even before Chichimecan administration had moved from Tenayuca to Texcoco. This is also described by Torquemada, Vol. I, p. 66. The *Códice Xolotl* Sheet VII shows Tulancingo still allied with Texcoco in the time of Ixtlilxochitl, Nezahualcoyotl's father (Dibble's commentary, p. 94). The *Códice Azcatítlan* on Sheet XVIII shows an interesting glyph of the conquest of Tulanzingo by Nezahualcoyotl.

The relation of the merchants with Cholula and Quetzalcoatl indicated in Sahagún, Canto XIV (Ed. Robredo, Vol. V, p. 137; Anderson and Dibble, Book 2, p. 212) has been pointed out by Acosta Saignes in his study of "Los Pochteca." He also shows their relation to the gulf coast in a tabulation of like characteristics.

Both the *Anales de Tlatelolco*, Par. 251, and the *Anales de Quauhtinchan*, Par. 355, place the conquest of Quauhtinchan in 10 Rabbit, and in the latter source Lam. xxv shows the glyph of the conquering king as Cuauhtlatoa who carries off the wife of the defeated ruler, as is also described in the text. This date can be identified as 1398 or, in the next cycle of fifty-two years, as 1450. Barlow chooses the earlier date and thinks the name of the king is confused with an earlier one. See "Un Problema Cronológico: La Conquista de Cuauhtinchan por Tlatelolco," *Tlatelolco a Travês de los Tiempos*,

X, Num 4, 1948, pp. 43-47. Wigberto Jiménez Moreno would add forty years to correlate the Mixteca dates; and the earlier date of 1398 would thus become 1438, within the reign of Cuauhtlatoa. His tabulation of date equivalents correlates the system of the *Historia Tolteca Chichimeca (Anales de Quauhtinchan)* with that in Tenochtitlan and Texcoco, "Cronología de la Historia de Vera Cruz," *Revista Mexicana de Estudios Antropológicos*, Tomo XIII, Núm. 2-3, 1952-1953, pp. 311-313.

[2] This and the following speeches are from Sahagún's accounts of the departure of the merchants, Lib. IV, cap. 17-19; Ed. Robredo, Vol. I, pp. 332-337; and Lib. IX, cap. 2 and 3, Vol. II, pp. 341-353; Dibble and Anderson, Book 4, pp. 61-71, and Book 9, pp. 3-16. The conversation between the merchants and the king is described by Sahagún as between Moteczuma II and Ahuitzotzin, but see Note 5 for speeches of Tlacaelel about Moteczuma Ilhuicamina's similar relation to the merchants.

[3] Description of market at Coaixtlahuaca from Durán I, p. 188.

[4] Jiménez Moreno (*Códice de Yanhuitlán*, p. 9) quotes Lehman in identifying Atonal with Dzahuindanda, whose name means Rain Day in Mixtec. Using the Nahuatl name Atonal, Water Day, Torquemada, Vol. I, p. 159, mentions his expanding conquests and growing rivalry with Moteczuma Ilhuicamina. The Oaxaca authority, Fr. Francisco de Burgoa, Vol. I, p. 319, using the Mixtec name, reports that the "painted traditions" said he reached the environs of Mexico in a northward expedition. It should be noted that Rain and Water are different day signs, however.

[5] This speech was made by Tlacaelel years later to Ahuitzotl when he was urging him to follow a course like that of Moteczuma Ilhuicamina. (Tezozomoc, p. 521.) Soustelle points out the importance of the crafts and the export of manufactured goods (*La Vie Quotiedienne des Aztèques*, p. 86). The articles of trade preceding and following this period are outlined by Sahagún from the Tlatelolco standpoint, Lib. IX, cap. 1 (Ed. Robredo, Vol. II, p. 339; Dibble and Anderson, Book 9, pp. 1-2).

[6] Sahagún, Lib. IV, cap. xvi (Ed. Robredo, Vol. I, p. 331; Dibble and Anderson, Book 4, p. 59) and Lib. IX, cap. 3 (Ed. Robredo, Vol. II, p. 347; Dibble and Anderson, Book 9, pp. 9-13).

[7] See directionally oriented *Fejérváry-Mayer*, and Seler commentary, p. 204.

[8] He appears with Xiuhtecuhtli as presiding deity over the thirteen-day week which begins with One Snake. See for example *Codex Borbonicus*, Ninth Week.

[9] It is interesting to compare this detail from Sahagún with the ceremonial use of cut paper in modern Mexico as described by Bodil Christensen, "Notas Sobre La Fabricación del Papel Indígena y su Empleo Para 'Brujerías' en la Sierra Norte de Puebla," *Revista Mexicana de Estudios Antropológicos*, Tomo VI, Núm 1-2, 1942, pp. 109-124.

[10] Chantico's connection with the hearth and fire and the transformations of the *nagual* are analyzed by Spence, *Gods of Mexico*, pp. 280-283.

[11] Sahagún, Lib. IX, cap. 3 and 5 (Ed. Robredo, Vol. II, pp. 348, 359; Dibble and Anderson, Book 9, pp. 10, 25).

[12] Sahagún, according to the Spanish translation gives two different orientations. He describes the north as the left hand and the south as the right hand of the earth in Lib. IX, cap. 3, Ed. Robredo, Vol. II, p. 348, and a little farther on in the same discussion of the activities of the merchants (cap. 8, p. 366) reverses the relation. Dibble and Anderson, Book 9, p. 10, note 4, consider the second interpretation correct. Seler in his commentary on the *Fejérváry-Mayer*, p. 132, points out the Aztec use of the "left of the sun" as meaning the south and the "right of the sun" as meaning the north, a relation he adopts with reference to the directional connotations for Huitzilopochtli and

which would agree with Sahagún's first set of relations if we think of a person on earth facing the rising sun with north to his left; and the sun as facing him with the north to its right.

[13] The detail that it was without knots is from Torquemada, Vol. II, p. 57. Other details from Sahagún's discussions of the merchants, *loc. cit.*, and in his discussion of the gods, Lib. I, cap. 19 (Ed. Robredo, Vol. I, pp. 42-45; Anderson and Dibble, Book 1, pp. 17-20). Meanings suggested for the name Yacatecuhtli are summarized by Anderson and Dibble — Lord at the Vanguard. He of the Long Nose, the Leader. Jiménez Moreno suggests, however, that Yacatecuhtli is derived from *acatl* — the reed the merchants carried — by the process of palatalization analagous to *yolotl* from *olotl* -heart, rather than being derived from *yacatl* -nose.

[14] For discussion of the philosophical point of view represented by this attitude of Nezahualcoyotl and this god, see Caso, *La Religión de los Aztecas*, p. 8.

[15] See Ixtlilxochitl, *Historia Chichimeca*, pp. 175-176, for description of the judgment rooms at Texcoco, and pp. 219-222, for this particular case. See also Pomar, p. 30.

[16] Sahagún, Lib. IV, cap. 19 (Ed. Robredo, Vol. I, p. 336; Dibble and Anderson, Book 4, p. 69).

[17] Sahagún, Lib. IX, cap. 5, Ed. Robredo, Vol. II, p. 357. Dibble and Anderson, Book 9, p. 22, mention several birds.

[18] Sahagún, Lib. IX, cap. 6 (Ed. Robredo, Vol. II, pp. 360-361; Dibble and Anderson, Book 9, pp. 27-32); Seler *Fejérváry-Mayer*, pp. 66-67.

[19] The account of the attack on the traders and the resulting hostilities is given by Tezozomoc, pp. 334-338, and Durán I, pp. 188-193.

[20] This detail from Torquemada, Vol. I, p. 160. See also this biography Chap. 13, note 40.

[21] This preliminary embassy is recorded only by Torquemada.

[22] It is interesting to note that this list of towns given by Tezozomoc, p. 335, and the shorter list given by Durán I, p. 189, do not include the Cuetlaxtlan (now Cotaxtla) area, although in their topical rather than chronological handling the conquest of Cuetlaxtlan preceded that of Coaixtlahuaca, and they are supported in this order by the *Carta de Pablo Nazareo*. However, a long list of sources put the conquest of Coaixtlahuaca first — the first big distant campaign after the famine. The following put it in 5 Rabbit (1458): Chimalpahin; *Anales de Tlatelolco* (Par. 268); *Anales de Tula; Anales de Cuauhtitlan* (Par. 189) — though in Par. 238 this source lists conquest of Cuetlaxtlan before that of Coaixtlahuaca. The *Anales Mexicanos: México-Azcapotzalco* have it begin in 5 Rabbit but end in 8 House three years later. Dibble interprets the *Códice en Cruz* as indicating war in 5 Rabbit and thinks it is the war of Coaixtlahuaca (pp. 51-52). The *Historia de los Mexicanos por sus Pinturas* has it go on for three years from 136 to 139 years after the founding of the city, and puts it before the conquest of Cuetlaxtlan. Ixtlilxochitl, without dating, lists Coaixtlahuaca before Cuetlaxtlan on pp. 260, 320, 492 of his *Relaciones*. Torquemada has it begin in the fertile year following the famine but because of the preliminary defeat of the Tenochca continue another year before a successful conclusion. The *Otomí Codex of San Mateo Huichapan* shows for the year 1458 a warrior standing on a design of serpents which may be the Plain of Serpents — Coaixtlahuaca. The *Mendocino* shows Coaixtlahuaca as the second of Huehue Moteczuma's conquests with Cuetlaxtlan well toward the end. Orozco y Berra in an attempt to coordinate sources has a preliminary defeat in 1454 and victory in 1463.

Modern attempts to sort out the chronology of these conquests include those of Isabel Kelly and Angel Palerm, who follow the Crónica X order because of the amount of circumstantial detail this group of sources — Durán and Tezozomoc — give (*Tajín-Totonac*, Part I, p. 271); R. H. Barlow, "Conquistas de Los Antiguos Mexicanos," *Journal de la Société des Américanistes*, Nouvelle Série, xxxvi, 1947, pp. 215-222, who rejects the order of the Crónica X sources and accepts the order of the majority of the sources. Wigberto Jiménez Moreno, "Síntesis de la Historia Precolonial del Valle de México," *Revista Mexicana de Estudios Antropológicos*, Tomo XIV, Primera Parte, 1954-1955, pp. 234-235, also rejects the Crónica X order and has Huehue Moteczuma Ilhuicamina's "big push" start south from Matamoros Izucar, the farthest point of Itzcoatl's conquest, and go on "to Coaixtlahuaca, from there to the Chinantla-Icotepec to a place named Tlacatepetl, from there to Cotaxtla, threatening finally Orizaba."

This is the order I follow in this biography, following the majority of the dated sources rather than the Durán-Tezozomoc order. I appreciate the advantage of this topical arrangement they chose, however, in bringing pattern into what must otherwise be a confusion of detail involving constant comings and going from Tenochtitlan as men departed on foot for constant new conquests and constant new rebellions during the ten-year period of Moteczuma's big push. In view of the amount of human detail, conversation, etc., which they included, their topical arrangement was almost necessary.

[23] Sahagún describes this in the time of Ahuizotl and speaks of it as a regular custom, Lib. IX, cap. 5 (Ed. Robredo, Vol. II, p. 359; Dibble and Anderson, Book 9, p. 24).

[24] For these customs, Tezozomoc, p. 311.

[25] Pomar, p. 23. This is a Texcoco source.

[26] Torquemada recounts this preliminary defeat, Vol. I, p. 160.

[27] This legend described by Burgoa, p. 320, as of an earlier time and attached to a ruler of the name Rain Day. See above, Note 4.

[28] Torquemada in his account of the campaign gives this detail.

[29] This comparison is made both by Durán and Torquemada in their accounts of this campaign.

[30] The "hochones" says Durán I, p. 190.

[31] *Anales de Cuauhtitlan*, Par. 67. Spinden in his "Indian Manuscripts of Southern Mexico," *Annual Report of the Smithsonian Institution for 1933*, pp. 429-451, discusses the Toltec origins of the Mixtecan manuscripts and calendar, and the historical Quetzalcoatl's adaptation of the latter from the earlier Maya calendar. Also see Alfonso Caso's calendar studies of the Mixtecan codices: "El Mapa de Teozacoalco," *Cuadernos Americanos*, Vol. 47, No. 5, 1949, and "Explicación del Reverso del Codex Vindobonensis," *Memoria de El Colegio Nacional*, Tomo V, Núm 5, pp. 9-46. Caso's study of dates recorded on bone and stone in "El Calendario Mixteco" *Historia Mexicana*, Vol. V, 4, Núm 20, pp. 481-497, concludes that the Toltec calendar was adopted by the Mixtecs toward the end of the tenth century (p. 488). The Teozacoalco study (p. 31) mentions in one of the dynasties of Tilantongo a king named "10 Rain-Tlaloc-Sun," born in 1424 and married to "5 Wind — Wreath of Cacao Flowers." In view of Gay's comment (Vol. I, p. 150) that the señores of Coaixtlahuaca were appointed by Tilantongo, it would be interesting if this Ten Rain were our Atonal or Dzhuindanda, whose numerical coefficient has been lost from his date name. In that case the Tall Woman could be called by her own very poetic name, instead of by the descriptive term applied to her in Tenochtitlan. (*Anales de Cuauhtitlan*, Par. 189.)

[32] Costume of women of the Mixteca as given by Sahagún, Lib. X, cap. 29, Par. 10 (Ed. Robredo, Vol. III, pp. 133-134; Dibble and Anderson, Book 10, pp. 187-188). The beads in the necklace are those listed as part of a necklace in an offering in Coaixtlahuaca in the late Aztec level — Ignacio Bernal,

"Exploraciones en Coixtlahuaca," *Revista Mexicana de Estudios Antropológicos*, Tomo X, 1948-1949, pp. 5-76.

[33] The list as given by Torquemada includes Cohuaixtlahuacan, Tochtepec, Tepçol, Tzapotla, Tototlan, Tlatlactetelco, Chinantla, and Quauhnochco. Gay judges from the sources that Moteczuma's army was divided at this point in the campaign with one part headed westward for a little way and one part eastward. He thinks the Nahuatl-speaking communities in the nineteenth century were those established at the time of this conquest as garrisons. (Vol. I, pp. 160-169.)

In connection with the campaigns of the hot country it has been most helpful to have the privilege of seeing the maps prepared by Wigberto Jiménez Moreno for his work now in progress on pre-conquest Mexican history. For helpful maps already published see: Barlow, *The Extent of the Empire of the Culhua Mexica*, which relates the *Matrícula de Tributos* to the Millionth Map of the American Geographical Society; Barlow, "Conquistas de los Antiguos Mexicanos"; Isabel Kelly and Angel Palerm, *The Tajín-Totonac*, Part I, pp. 266-272 and 291-295; *Atlas Arqueológico de la República Mexicana;* Cook and Simpson, *The Population of Central Mexico in the Sixteenth Century*. Cook and Simpson place the population of Coaixtlahuaca in 1565, a century after the conquest by Moteczuma, as over 9,000 and believe the figure to represent a considerable decline from the earlier population (pp. 86-87). Their study is based on statistical material available for that decade in many different sources "so varied and independent that their essential agreement cannot be fortuitous" (p. 1) and represents recent reaction against tendencies to discount the basic sources from colonial times: "It seems to us that if the testimony of respectable witnesses can be discarded so easily, then all history would have to be rewritten in the light of later assumptions." (p. 39, note.)

In this connection it might be mentioned parenthetically that the contemporary swing back to respect for the basic sources of Aztec culture is well illustrated by Leslie White's introduction to Bandelier's collected letters, in which he points out the pathos of Bandelier's efforts to convince himself that his friend Morgan was right in seeing Aztec social organization in terms of Iroquois.

[34] Torquemada in his account gives the first explanation; the *Anales de Cuauhtitlan*, Par. 238, the second. The *Códice Mendocino* shows him strangled over the glyph of his city and in front of the burning temple, but does not indicate who did the deed.

[35] Wigberto Jiménez Moreno, *Códice de Yanhuitlán*, p. 11, quoting Herrera, *Historia General de los hechos de los castellanos en las islas y tierra firme del Mar Oceano*, Tomo II (Madrid, 1726) Década III, pp. 99-II.

[36] This is the tribute pictured in the *Matrícula de Tributos*. Besides this list and the items mentioned by Durán and Tezozomoc as part of the treaty, there is an interesting statement in the *Anales de Cuauhtitlan* (Par. 189) that gold, quetzal plumes, rubber, cacao, and other riches began to enter Mexico-Tenochtitlan for the first time with this conquest. The *Anales de Tlatelolco* puts the first entrance of chalchihuites and quetzal plumes earlier in 2 Reed (1455) when Cuauhnauac permitted the Mexica to share in tribute from the Couixca.

This statement is further evidence that the conquest of Cotaxtla had not preceded the conquest of Coaixtlahuaca, because the Cotaxtla tribute, including trade items produced farther south, brought to the Mexica such items as chalchihuites, quetzal plumes, crystal and amber mounted in gold. See Barlow, *Extent of the Empire of the Culhua Mexica*, p. 92, and the *Matrícula de Tributos*.

[37] Durán I, p. 192; Tezozomoc, p. 338.

CHAPTER XV

[1] The ceremony after Coaixtlahuaca is described by Durán I, pp. 192-199, and Tezozomoc, pp. 338-339. It is clearly the Tlacaxipihualiztli, the festival in honor of Xipe-Totec, the Flayed One, described by Sahagún, Lib. II, cap. 21-22 (Ed. Robredo, Vol. I, pp. 123-130; Anderson and Dibble, Book 2, pp. 46-58); by Durán II, pp. 147-155; by Torquemada, Vol. II, pp. 252-253; by Motolinía, *Memoriales*, p. 60; and, as given with the victims from the Huaxteca, by Tezozomoc, pp. 318-323, and Durán I, pp. 174-180. The details which identify it as this fiesta are pointed out in the following notes.

[2] The Cuauhxicalli, or eagle vase, used on this occasion is not identifiable with any presently known stone if the carvings were those described by the Crónica X sources. However, since these sources have a habit of listing conquests according to their own order, we cannot be too sure of the carvings on the stone used on this occasion. See Durán I, p. 194, with Ramírez note, and Tezozomoc, p. 338, with Orozco y Berra note.

[3] For bonnet connections see below.

[4] Tezozomoc, p. 339. The peaked bonnet and the human "skin of gold" are characteristic of Xipe.

[5] Durán I, p. 196, gives this motive for the costume.

[6] Flint knives rather than obsidian belonged to this fiesta. See comparative note on the sources on this point by Anderson and Dibble, *Florentine Codex*, Book 2, p. 47, note 6.

[7] This detail from Sahagún, Anderson and Dibble translation, Book 2, p. 47, where the first part of the Xipe festival is apparently the same as that described as Nahui Ollin (4 Movement) by Durán — on this particular occasion and also as generally done. Sahagún also describes it in Lib. IV, cap. 2 (Ed. Robredo, Vol. I, pp. 308-309; Dibble and Anderson, Book 4, p. 6). The emphasis on the eagle warriors occurs in both. It was given twice a year, says Durán II, p. 155, and in the way he relates the Aztec with the European calendar it would be before the Tlacaxipehualiztli and the Panquetzaliztli. Both 3 Eagle and 4 Movement were date names of Xipe and the glyphs appear in the Xipe 13-day week. See Sheet 14 of the *Codex Borbonicus*.

[8] Durán describes the color of the victim as red on this particular occasion (I, p. 197) but in his general description of this fiesta (II, p. 157) he says that half the face of the victim was painted red and his legs striped white. Both kinds of painting would be typical of Xipe. Sahagún, Lib. X, cap. 29, Par. 9 (Ed. Robredo, Vol. III, p. 133; Dibble and Anderson, Book 10, p. 187), speaking of the Yopimes and Tlapanecas in the area of Yopitzinco, from which this festival apparently came to Mexico-Tenochtitlan, says they are named Tlapanecas because they paint themselves red (*tlapalli* -red) and their idol Totec Tlatlauhqui Tezcatlipoca (Xipe) is red and his clothing and priests red. Jiménez Moreno relates the red to red earth. See also Sahagún, Lib. I, cap. 18 (Ed. Robredo, Vol. I, pp. 40-41; Anderson and Dibble, Book I, pp. 16-17).

[9] Garibay, *Poesía Indígena*, p. 51.

[10] It is to be noted that, though Durán says Cuetlaxtlan, the Huaxteca and Tepeacac were pictured as conquered in the carvings on the sacrificial Vase of the Sun, he does not list them individually among the invited guests, unless he means to include some of them under the "Marquesado" (p. 195), but mentions only the earlier conquests before the famine — a further indication that in spite of his sequence, Cuetlaxtlan had not been conquered before Coaixtlahuaca.

[11] Durán II, p. 148.

[12] Tezozomoc, p. 339, says the gladiatorial combat took place on this occasion. Durán does not mention it. It was a regular part of the Xipe celebration, however. The *Historia de los Mexicanos por sus Pinturas*, p. 231, describing a stone used for the combat, says it was first used for "los de Cuauistrauaca."

[13] The list of the gods represented in this group is given in overlapping but somewhat differing fashion by Tezozomoc, p. 321, Durán I, p. 176 and II, p. 149. The reference Tezozomoc makes to the dress of roses which Toci wore is interesting in connection with the devotion to Tonantzin at Tepeyacac and the succeeding devotion to Our Lady of Guadalupe at the same place. Sahagún identifies both Toci (Our Grandmother) and Tonantzin (Our Mother) with Toteo-innan (Mother of the Gods) and warns his fellow Franciscans to take care that the Indians did not confuse the Christian and pagan devotions. See Sahagún, Lib. I, cap. 8, and Lib. XI, cap. 12, par. 6, Nota, Ed. Robredo, Vol. III, p. 299. The slowness of the Church to permit the new devotion for fear of confusion is treated at length with many quotations from sixteenth century frailes in *La Conquista Espiritual de México*, by Robert Ricard, translated into Spanish by Angel María Garibay K., Mexico, 1947, pp. 346-354.

[14] Tezozomoc, p. 321.

[15] Durán II, pp. 148-149.

[16] This detail is from the direction and color minded Durán (II, pp. 150-151).

[17] Sahagún, Anderson and Dibble, Book 2, p. 52.

[18] Sahagún, Canto XV; Ed. Robredo, Vol. V, p. 150. Seler's commentary on the song (p. 153) relates the skin of gold to the goldsmiths whose patron Xipe was. See also Note 19, below.

The part of Moteczuma the First at this stage of the ceremony seems to be that of gift giver to the sacrificers. There is no implication that he put on the skin of the victim, although he had acted as sacrificing priest at the beginning of the killings and Moteczuma the Second apparently wore the skin and danced in it, according to Motolinía, *Memoriales*, p. 60.

The flaying, an essential part of the Xipe festival, according to all sources, is not mentioned by Tezozomoc and Durán after Coaixtlahuaca. It was, however, included in the ceremony as they describe it in their earlier treatment of the Huaxteca campaign, and Tezozomoc, p. 339, says of the Coaixtlahuaca festival that "it was of the same sort, neither more nor less than what they did in the other sacrifice which we have already described, so that in order not to trouble the reader, I omit narrating the same ceremonies."

[19] Garibay, *Poesía Indígena*, p. 21. The song is also in Sahagún (Ed. Robredo, Vol. V, p. 150; Anderson and Dibble, Book 2, p. 213).

The Fire Snake rite is described by both Tezozomoc and Durán as part of the ceremonies after Coaixtlahuaca, yet it is not included among the Xipe ceremonies by either of these men after the Huaxteca campaign, nor in the general accounts by Durán and Sahagún. It is described, however, in the accounts of the Panquetzaliztli by Sahagún, Lib. II, cap. 34 (Ed. Robredo, Vol. I, p. 198; Anderson and Dibble, Book 2, p. 136) and Lib. IX, cap. 14 (Ed. Robredo, Vol. II, p. 382; Dibble and Anderson, Book 9, p. 65); by Torquemada, Vol. II, p. 282; and by Clavijero I, p. 331, who describes the snake as of wood, and as insigne of the gods of war. This would seem to be a point against considering the festival after Coaixtlahuaca the festival to Xipe. However, the appropriateness of the fire snake in this festival to Xipe is as definite as in the festival to Quezalcoatl, as is clear from the close relationship of the two gods in the song already quoted when the fire snake turns to the plumed snake; and on the Fourteenth Page of the *Codex Borbonicus* where the two gods are companion patrons of the trecena, the Quetzalcoatl is represented by the plumed serpent. Between the two is a twin representation of a snake with two heads. Sahagún makes Xiuhtecutli, the Fire God, the patron of this trecena, Lib. IV, cap. 25 (Ed. Robredo, Vol. I, pp. 343-344; Dibble and Anderson, Book 4, p. 87), and says that his image was carried out of the temple and offerings of plumed paper were made to him — a further tie-up between the fire serpent and the plumed serpent and the god Xipe all in this trecena. There is thus adequate support for considering this the Xipe festival regardless of the presence of the fire snake ritual.

In connection with this symbolism and with the song, light is shed on the earth fire — "The earth rained fire," etc. Such phrases are used by various sources on the years of drought. See Chap. XIII, note 38. Besides referring to the heat they must have had rich ritualistic connotations to the Nahuatl speaking historians.

[20] A phrase from Sahagún, "Relación Breve de las fiestas de los Dioses," traducida por Angel Ma. Garibay K., *Tlalocan* II, No. 4, 1948, p. 294.

[21] Huehue Moteczuma Ilhuicamina introduced this new ceremony in the fifteenth year of his reign, says Tezozomoc, p. 323. This would put it before the Coaixtlahuaca campaign according to the dating of the majority of sources, and before the Huaxteca campaign according to the order which the Crónica X sources employ. However, the cult of Xipe, the skinned god, existed earlier in highland Mexico. Caso in *La Religión de los Aztecas*, p. 27, points out that there is evidence of it in the Teotihuacan culture. Vaillant in *The Aztecs of Mexico*, shows a clay figure of Xipe from the Mazapan horizon wearing his extra skin (Plate 28) and refers to a smaller figure from the same period in which Xipe carries in his hand a little vase of Zapotec type. He adds (p. 79) "This archaeological evidence confirms the traditional origin of Xipe worship in Oaxaca, territory of the Zapotecs and Mixtecs." The *Anales de Cuauhtitlan*, Par. 64, mentions the wearing of the skin in Totec ceremonies in Tula, and the Xipe-Totec relationships in the ornamentation of Edificio B at Tula are referred to by Acosta "La tercera Temporada de Exploraciones Arqueológicas en Tula, Hgo. 1942," *Revista Mexicana de Estudios Antropológicos*, Tomo VI, Núm. 3, Sept., 1942-Dic. 1944, pp. 159-160, quoting Moedano especially. Bertha Dutton in "Tula of the Toltecs," *El Palacio*, Vol. 62, Nos. 7-8, July-August, 1955, p. 222, describes in connection with Edificio B a figure with a pointed cap under a cornice of red, blue, yellow and white snakes.

[22] The Indians who were Sahagún's informants knew about the southern connections of the Xipe festival. They described Xipe as belonging to the Zapotecas and to the Yopimes and Tlapanecas. See notes 8 and 21. Anderson and Dibble, Book 1, p. 17, note 89, refer to Seler on the red people and his two illustrations that indicate that they wore pointed caps. The pointed cap of Xipe is often used to link him to the Huaxteca also. The widespread Xipe complex including the Antilles is worked out by Miguel Acosta Saignes, *Tlacaxipeualiztli: Un Complejo Mesoamericano entre los Caribes.*

[23] This effect of the Xipe festival is described by Durán I, p. 180. However, more distant towns rebelled often.

[24] The collector's name and schedule is given by Durán I, p. 199.

[25] *Anales de Cuauhtitlan*, Par. 238. For earlier fashion notes from Cuauhtitlan and Tenochtitlan see *Anales de Cuauhtitlan*, Par. 158-159, and Chapter IV of this biography.

[26] Description of him in *Códice Mendocino*, Sheet 8 Reverse.

[27] *Crónica Mexicayotl*, Par. 197-201, says that he had seven daughters and a son Iquehuac, with the added comment that some said there were other sons. Iquehuac is also named by Torquemada, Vol. I, p. 170; by the *Anales de Cuauhtitlan*, Par. 186, 218, which mentions four sons; and by Chimalpahin, 3 House (1469) who names two. The *Codex Mendoza* gives two without naming them. The *Códice Ramírez* in commentary on Lám. 13 and 14,

printed as footnotes on pp. 67, 70, makes Moteczuma Ilhuicamina the father of Axayacatl and Tizoc. Durán adds Ahuitzotl (p. 327). The *Historia de los Mexicanos por sus Pinturas*, pp. 229-231, even adds the younger Moteczuma to the list of his sons, in addition to Tizoc, Axayacatl, and Ahuitzotl. They apparently ignore a generation, however, since a daughter, Atototzin, is specifically named as married to Tezozomoc, son of Itzcoatl, and as the mother of Tizoc, Axayacatl and Ahuitzotl, and the grandmother of the younger Moteczuma, by the *Fragment de Généalogie des Princes Mexicains;* Pablo Nazareo, pp. 121-122; and Ixtlilxochitl, *Historia Chichimeca*, pp. 230, 259. She is mentioned, though without her name, by Motolinía, *Memoriales*, pp. 7-8; *Relacíon de Genealogía*, pp. 252-254; *Orígen de los Mexicanos.* p. 274. The three following kings are mentioned by *La Leyenda de los Soles* (p. 128) as grandchildren of Huehue Moteczuma without any mention of the names of their parents. They are mentioned as children of Tezozomoc without mention of their mother by Mengin in the genealogical table worked out from the *Codex Mexicanus;* by Torquemada, Vol. 1, p. 169; by the *Crónica Mexicayotl*, Par. 204-208; and by Veytia, *Historia Antigua de Mexico*, Vol. II, pp. 115, 237; by Chimalpahin, who describes Axayacatl as petit-cousin" of Huehue Moteczuma Ilhuicamina, and by Clavijero, Vol. I, pp. 218, 230. The *Codex Mendoza* makes Axayacac the son of Tezozomoc, and the father of Tizoc, Ahuitzotl, and the second Moteczuma.

Primo Feliciano Velázquez in his notes on the *Leyenda de los Soles*, p. 142, points out that the Nahuatl word used for grandson, the relationship of Axayacatl to Huehue Moteczuma, is also translatable, according to Molina, as "primo, hijo de hermano."

A study of Aztec kinship terms would perhaps clarify some of the confusion in genealogies. It would also be fruitful to study the courtesy terms of relationship used in direct address as they appear in conversations in the chroniclers. Tezozomoc, for instance, ignoring Moteczuma's daughter, has Tlacaelel when urging the election of Tizoc describe him as "Moteczuma's legitimate nephew," (p. 437) and visiting dignitaries address Tizoc referring to "your good father the king Moctezuma." (p. 439) At the funeral of Tizoc reference is made to his uncles Huitzilihuitl and Moteczuma. (p. 434.) Yet Moteczuma has been described as the son of Huitizilihuitl (p. 249). The problem of descriptive and ceremonial kinship terms may lie back of these and similar contradictions in the intricate family connections described in the sources.

[28] See Chapter I and *Crónica Mexicayotl*, Par. 2 and 3.

[29] Garibay, *Poesía Indígena*, p. 21. This episode in which the king fainted is described by the *Anales de Cuauhtitlan*, Par. 189. The compiler of these annals breaks off his three-line summary with an *etc.* The account is obviously influenced by a widespread motif in Indian story telling, but the specifically Aztec symbolism of the chalchihuitl stone gives the story a stratification of meaning which relates it also to the story of Moteczuma's birth in Chapter I. The motif number listed by Thompson in *Motif Index of Folk Literature* is F 547.1.1.

CHAPTER XVI

[1] Torquemada, Vol. I, p. 161, for conquest of Cozamaloapan and Quauhtochco (Huatuxco) and sacrifice of prisoners at dedication of this temple. He gives date as year following conquest of Coaixtlahuaca. The *Anales de Tlatelolco*, Par. 268, give date as 8 House (1461), three years after the conquest of

Coaixtlahuaca, but the next conquest listed. The temple of Yopico was, as is shown by its name, the place of sacrifice to Xipe. It and its skull frame are described by Sahagún, Lib. II, apéndice (Ed. Robredo, Vol. I, pp. 225-226; Anderson and Dibble, Book 2, p. 174-175).

2 The Huaxteca campaign is described by Tezozomoc, pp. 310-317, who mentions the towns of Tzicoac, Tuchpa, and Tamachpa, and the route to them by way of Tulancingo, but who changes Tuchpa to Tuchtepec before he finishes the chapter; also by Durán I, pp. 165-174, who mentions the route by Tulantzinco, and lists the towns of Temapachco, Xochpan and Tzincoac in the chapter heading but not in the text. Neither source gives the exact location of the battle, though the five fortifications are mentioned by both and in Tezozomoc, p. 311, may perhaps refer to the last place in the series of three — Temachpa, presumably the modern Temapache, near Tuxpan, in the state of Vera Cruz. The identification of Tzincoac or Chicoac with the present town of Dr. Montes de Oca as Melgarejo would have it, or with Chicontepec as Meade would have it, is discussed at length by Isabel Kelly and Angel Palerm, *The Tajin-Totonac*, p. 267, note 33, who lean to the Chicontepec identification. In spite of the shift in the name which Tezozomoc makes, I use the usual identification of the Tuchpa of this campaign as the modern Tuxpan in Vera Cruz, rather than as the Tochtepec far to the south, which Torquemada lists as a conquest following that of Coaixtlahuaca, and which Ixtlilxochitl lists as a conquest following that of Tochpan, *Historia Chichimeca*, p. 197.

The Codex *Telleriano-Remensis* shows the conquest of Chicoac in 4 Rabbit (1458), and the first commentator describes this province of the Chicoaque as to the north near the Pánuco; the second commentator describes it as the first province subjugated by the Mexicans. Durán dates the campaign as following the eleventh year of Huehue Moteczuma's rule, which would make it after 1451. Tezozomoc has the following sacrifice take place in the fifteenth year of Moteczuma's reign (1455) after two years of work on the sacrificial stone. The Crónica X dating would therefore put the campaign during the years of famine, though their actual account does not do that.

3 Tezozomoc, pp. 311-312. Even by the Mexican sources the emphasis is put on the Texcocans in this northern campaign. See also above, Chap. XIV, note 1.

4 Tezozomoc, p. 313; Durán I, p. 169.

5 The way of carrying the standard is described by the Conquistador Anónimo, p. 371.

6 *Ibid.*, pp. 371-372.

7 Tezozomoc, p. 317; Durán I, pp. 166, 170. Also see above, Chap. IX, particularly note 13.

8 The material rewards of this campaign are described in detail not only by Durán and Tezozomoc but by other sources. Tziuhcohuac and Tochpan are both mentioned as tributary to Texcoco in the account of the division of tribute in the *Anales de Cuauhtitlan*, Par. 225-227; and by Ixtlilxochitl, *Historia Chichimeca*, pp. 196-197. The name of the tribute collector is given by Ixtlilxochitl, *Historia Chichimeca*, p. 197. The tribute from this area which came into the alliance according to the *Matrícula de Tributos* of the *Códice Mendocino* has been analyzed by Barlow, *Extent of the Empire of the Culhua Mexica*, pp. 54-61, and by N. Molíns Fábrega, "El Códice Mendocino y La Economía de Tenochtitlan," *Revista Mexicana de Estudios Antropológicos*, Tomo XIV, Primera Parte, 1954-55, pp. 303-335. "The Shadows of the King" mentioned by Durán I, p. 173, it will be noticed, did not include a crown. See above, Chap. XIII, note 49.

9 Durán I, p. 180, and Ramírez note.

[10] The campaign against Cuetlaxtlan (Cotaxtla), with its preliminaries, is described by Tezozomoc, pp. 325-333, and Durán I, pp. 180-187. They do not mention the importance of Tlatelolco in the conquest, but it is made clear by Torquemada, Vol. I, pp. 161-162; and by the *Anales de Tlatelolco*, Par. 269. The latter source dates it as 10 Reed (1463); the *Aubin Codex of 1576* as 4 Rabbit (1470) but still within the reign of Moteczuma whose death in this later dating scale is moved up to the next year; the *Historia de los Mexicanos por sus Pinturas* as 141 years after the founding of Tenochtitlan; the *Telleriano-Remensis* and *Vaticanus B* as 1461 (8 House). For sources showing order of the Cotaxtla and Coaixtlahuaca campaigns see above Chap. XIV, note 22.

[11] Tezozomoc, pp. 327-328; Durán I, p. 182.

[12] *Anales de Tlatelolco*, Par. 269.

[13] His name was Chichimecatecuhtli, according to the *Anales de Tlatelolco*, Par. 269.

[14] All three later ruled Tenochtitlan. They are listed by Torquemada, Vol. I, p. 161, as taking part in this battle. The battle is shown with Tizoc on the stone in the Museo Nacional.

[15] Moquiuix was the hero of this campaign according to Torquemada and the *Anales de Tlatelolco;* but in the *Telleriano-Remensis* and the *Vaticanus A* the glyph of Cuauhtlatoa, the ruler of Tlatelolco, Talking Eagle, is shown. Moquiuix would succeed him on his death in 1 Reed (1467).

[16] This participation by the two sons of Nezahualcoyotl in the expedition to "the Cuexteca which is Panuco" is described by Ixtlilxochitl, *Historia Chichimeca*, p. 202, and associated by him with the Huaxteca campaign, pp. 293-294. I follow him in this, though noting Isabel Kelly and Angel Palerm in their opinion (*Tajín-Totonac*, p. 269, note 37) that he was mistaken in identifying it with the Huaxteca instead of with a more southerly town, since the towns listed as gained are in the south. A confusing point in Ixtlilxochitl's account, however, is that Xicotencatl is listed as an ally of Nezahualcoyotl instead of an enemy.

[17] The songs to the two brothers and the rival dances at later festivals are described by Ixtlilxochitl, *Historia Chichimeca*, pp. 293-294. This went on for years until Nezahualpilli, by that time ruler of Texcoco, made the official gesture of going out on the plaza with his own dancers and joining the group of Acapioltzin.

[18] Garibay, *Poesía Indígena*, p. 128. This song is described by the accompanying manuscript inscription as a song of Nezahualpilli, says Garibay's note, p. 199, and "el modo huasteco." Another marginal inscription says it was composed on the arrival of the king of Huexotzinco who was to be killed in the gladiatorial combat. This was initiated with victims from the Huaxteca, according to Durán and Tezozomoc, though as has been seen, we have followed the chronology which puts the Coaixtlahuaca campaign first and has the gladiatorial combat accompany the sacrifice of the prisoners taken then. In the course of the poem Garibay's translation mentions the "Huasteco Tótec," though we have seen his association with more southern areas, also. In any case the Huaxteca connections of the two heroes here help support Ixtlilxochitl on the location of the battle they took part in.

[19] Torquemada, Vol. I, p. 162. Later Moteczuma installed him as king in Tlatelolco. Neither the marriage nor the later relations of Moquiuix with Tenochtitlan were destined to go smoothly.

[20] Torquemada says this dedication was of the Tzompantli or skull frame. Sahagún in his list of parts of the large enclosure of the pyramid area explains its use. See Note 1. The rows of skulls in the skull frame impressed and horrified the Spanish conquerors. The reference to skulls in the following poem is also related to this aspect of Aztec worship.

[21] In this English version of the song I adapt from the Spanish translations of Heinrich Berlin, *Anales de Tlatelolco*, Par. 270-272, and of Angel María Garibay K, *Historia de la Literatura Náhuatl*, I, p. 226.
[22] *Anales de Cuauhtitlan*, Par. 238. See above, Chap. 15, note 25.
[23] From lists given by Tezozomoc and Durán, who also mention Pinotl's appointment.
[24] Something of the complication of receiving the incoming tribute is indicated in Ixtlilxochitl, *Historia Chichimeca*, p. 198, and *Anales de Cuauhtitlan*, Par. 224-233. The extent of it is indicated in the *Matrícula de Tributos*, the account book by quantities and towns. Further account books from the angle perhaps of the taxed towns may be seen in the study by Seler of the "Mexican Picture Writings of Alexander Von Humboldt," *Bureau of American Ethnology*, *Bulletin 28*, Washington, 1904, pp. 123-229, and some additional parts of the *Codex Humboldt I*, discovered by Ortega and identified by Salvador Toscano, "Los Códices Tlapanecas de Azoyú," *Cuadernos Americanos* T.10, No. 4, 1943, pp. 127-136.
[25] The appointment of the Tall Woman, mentioned in the *Anales de Cuauhtitlan*, Par. 189, was unusual but not without parallel in Aztec history. A few years later Azcaxuch, Nezahualcoyotl's daughter, and widow of the ruler of Tepetlaoztoc, succeeded to that administrative position and ruled for nine years until her retirement a year before her own death in 1499, *Códice Kingsborough*, *Memorial de los Indios de Tepetlaoztoc*, p. 4. The role of women in war and in government was important in the Mixteca as shown in the *Codex Nuttall* (Zouche) and pointed out by Zelia Nuttall in her preface. Spinden also comments on it in respect to the life of the lady Six Monkey as she appears in the *Seldon* and in the *Bodley* codices, "Indian Manuscripts of Southern Mexico," *Smithsonian Report for 1933, pp. 429-451.*

CHAPTER XVII

[1] For the sequence of campaigns, *Annales de Chimalpahin*, 3 Stone (1456); 6 Reed (1459); 8 House (1461); 9 Rabbit (1462); 10 Reed (1463).
[2] 6 Reed (1459) for this phrase of Chimalpahin's.
[3] This drought and its results are noted under this date (11 Stone, 1464), by the *Annales de Chimalpahin* and the *Anales Mexicanos: México-Azcapotzalco.*
[4] This episode of Tlacahuepan's capture by the Chalca is described by Tezozomoc, pp. 296-297; Durán I, pp. 145-147. *Códice Ramírez*, pp. 63-64, and Lám. XI. His death is mentioned without any details by Chimalpahin, Relación 3 (Silvia Rendón translation) in the year 11 Stone (1464) and in the same year by the *Anales Mexicanos: Mexico-Azcapotzalco.* His two brothers are named Chahuacue and Quetzalcuauh by all these sources except the *Códice Ramírez*, which does not give the name of any of the three men. Torquemada mentions his death in an earlier phase of the war, and lists him and his brothers and a number of other casualties who were remembered with sorrow at the start of the final campaign. (Torquemada, pp. 158, 163.)

Durán says this happened during the festival of Xocotl uetzi, an identification which fits with the pole and platform. See Sahagún, Lib. II, chap. 10 and 29 (Anderson-Dibble, Book II, pp. 17-18, 104-109; Ed. Robredo, Vol. I, pp. 97-99, 169-174). See also the *Codex Borbonicus* which includes the people singing at the bottom of the pole — a situation remarkably like the Volador, the ceremony still celebrated in the sierra, in which the Santiagos dance at the foot of the pole, and a man dances on the tiny platform at the top, before he comes down, and four or six others climb up, to swing down on ropes in circles to the ground.

The final manner of sacrifice by arrows on this occasion, and the mention of Camaxtli by Tezozomoc, might otherwise identify the fiesta with the feast of Quecholli. However, the variation is explained by Durán's statement that the Chalca had no other manner of sacrificing.

For the raising of an arrow victim on a ladder-like support see the *Códice Fernando Leal* and the *Anales de Quauhtinchan*, Lam. XV.

[5] The owl episode is described by Durán I, p. 148; Tezozomoc, p. 298; Chimalpahin, Relación 3 (Rendón translation) under 11 Stone.

[6] The visit of Coateotl's son is described by Tezozomoc, p. 303; Durán I, pp. 149-150; Chimalpahin, Relación 3 (Rendón translation) 11 Stone. The first two give his name as Teoquizqui, and Durán, in contrast to Tezozomoc, says all three were brothers, as is borne out by the list of Coateotl's sons given by Chimalpahin, Relación VII, 4 Stone, 1444. The three listed by Tezozomoc, though not described as brothers, are the same as in this genealogy.

[7] While Nezahualcoyotl is mentioned by the Tenochtitlan sources as receiving the final surrender along with Moteczuma the part his sons played is recorded by the Texcocan source Ixtlilxochitl in his *Relaciónes*, pp. 248-252, 495-496, and *Historia Chichimeca*, pp. 225-228, and by Torquemada, Vol. I, pp. 152-153. Ixtlilxochitl puts it in the later phase of the war, Torquemada in the earlier. I follow Ixtlilxochitl both because he is the Texcoco source, and because since Acapioltzin's youth was emphasized at Cotaxtla, this campaign in which he was a seasoned warrior at Chalco would appear to be later.

[8] *Annales de Chimalpahin*, 11 Stone (1464).

[9] *Annales de Chimalpahin*, 12 House, 1465. This date in the *Codex Mexicanus*, Sheet LXVIII, shows a hill, the sign of war with shield and spear, and a rising sun. Mengin in his commentary on the basis of Chimalpahin thinks the picture refers to this swift last day's battle. The same date for the victory over Chalco is given by the *Codex of 1576*, *Anales de Cuauhtitlan*, *Telleriano-Remensis*, the *Vaticanus B*, the *Códice en Cruz*, the *Anales de Tula*, the *Anales Mexicanos: México-Azcapotzalco*. The *Anales de Tlatelolco* gives the preceding year, 11 Stone (1464). Durán indicates the 1465 date indirectly, because he says that after Moteczuma was crowned, Tenochtitlan had twelve years of peace (I, p. 132) and immediately following he tells about the war with Chalco which would thus have begun in 1452, 12 Stone, in its final sequence. He refers (I, p. 152) to one of his sources as saying that it lasted thirteen years which would thus bring it to a close in 12 House, 1465. However, in his grouping of events, he includes events, as has been seen, that are dated by other sources as from the early 1440's up to 1465. Torquemada places the final action of the war after the battle of Cuetlaxtlan (Vol. I, p. 162).

[10] In the compilation and repetitive dating of the *Anales de Cuauhtitlan* this episode is placed in 10 Reed (Par. 191), though the final conquest is placed in 1465 in accordance with most of the sources.

[11] Durán I, p. 152, and Tezozomoc, p. 304.

[12] Durán I, p. 152, quotes one of his sources about the honors given to the Chalca by the Mexica.

[13] Torquemada, Vol. I, p. 163, and *Anales de Cuauhtitlan*, Par. 192.

[14] Description of the ceremony including ritual speeches from Tezozomoc, pp. 300-302, and Durán I, pp. 153-156.

CHAPTER XVIII

[1] Garibay, *Poesía Indígena*, p. 46.

[2] *Anales de Cuauhtitlan*, Par. 192; Ixtlilxochitl, *Historia Chichimeca*, pp. 229-230.

[3] Ixtlilxochitl, *Historia Chichimeca*, p. 230.

[4] Estimate of Cook and Simpson, *The Population of Central Mexico in the Sixteenth Century*, p. 27.

[5] Twenty to twenty-five thousand on regular days and forty to fifty thousand every fifth day, says the *Conquistador Anónimo*, p. 392, of the market at Tlatelolco which served also purchasers from Tenochtitlan. The close relation of merchants in the two cities has been noted in connection with Moteczuma's gifts of blankets for trading purposes.

[6] For the planting of the ahuehuete trees in Texcoco see Torquemada, Vol. I, p. 153. The irrigation ditches in the area of Tezcotzinco have been mentioned in Chapter XIII and note 26. Those near the ruins of palace in Texcoco are still visible. The historical sources mentioning them are summarized in Gillmor, "Estructuras en la Zona de Texcoco Durante El Reino de Nezahualcoyotl Según Las Fuentes Históricas," *Revista Mexicana de Estudios Antropológicos*, Tomo XIV, Primera Parte, pp. 363-371. Recent field study of the prehispanic irrigation system of this area is described by Angel Palerm and Eric R. Wolf, "El Desarrollo del Área Clave del Imperio Texcocano," in the same issue of this magazine, pp. 337-349. These authors mention the interesting fact that distribution of water to the farmers in this area today is still on the old basis of a 20-day month.

[7] *Anales de Cuauhtitlan*, Par. 192. The *Otomí Codex of San Mateo Huichapan* also shows public work with a "coa" on the Hill of the Grasshopper, in 1465.

[8] For Nezahualpilli's birth see Gillmor, *Flute of the Smoking Mirror*, p. 170, note 7 to Chap. xiv. For the marriage of the son of Coateotl in Tenochtitlan see Tezozomoc, p. 304; Chimalpahin, Relación 3, 11 Stone (1464) — Rendón translation.

[9] The beginning of the gardens of Huaxtepec in the reign of Moteczuma Ilhuicamina is described by Tezozomoc, pp. 370-372, and Durán I, pp. 252-253. The 1580 "Descripción del Guaxtepeque" by El Alcalde Mayor Juan Gutiérrez de Liévana (Reprinted by Enrique Juan Palacios in *Huaxtepec y sus Reliquias*, Secretaría de Educación Pública, México, 1930, from Boletín Oficial y Revista Eclesiástica del Obispado de Cuernavaca, Tomo IX, Pág. 315-332-350) said that this place recognized the rule of Moteczuma el Viejo — the Old — but never had to pay him tribute. The beauty of the gardens at the time of the conquest in described by Cortés in his Third Letter to the king (Lorenzana, pp. 221-223) who mentions the gentle river and the orchards, fruits and fragrant flowers, as does also Bernal Díaz del Castillo who said it was the most beautiful orchard he had seen in his life (*Historia Verdadera de la Conquista de la Nueva España*, II, p. 198). Clavijero, II, p. 51, mentions the symmetry of the planting, and the imported plants, and says that its medicinal plants were cultivated by the Spaniards after the conquest for a hospital there run by the "admirable anchorite Gregorio López." Torquemada, Vol. I, p. 536, also mentions the gardens here.

The prehispanic irrigation can still be seen. A visit in the lush wet month of August shows the fecundity of this area. The Indian guide cuts a path with a machete to clear the way of blocking shrubs and vines. On a steep overgrown hill one suddenly realizes that he is climbing steps to the top of a pyramid, now called "The Pulpit of the King." The stone inscriptions in the area include date signs carved on the cliff above the river, a coiled stone snake under the water, etc. Among the date signs is 13 Rabbit (1466). For photograph of this date sign see illustration for "Moctezuma's Health Resort" by Laura Álvarez, *Pemex Travel Club Bulletin*, Vol. XV, Núm. 271-A, August 1, 1955, p. 9. A drawing of it is included by Valentín López Gonzáles in *Breve Historia Antigua del Estado de Morelos*, Cuadernos de Cultura Morelense, Departamento de Turismo y Publicidad del Estado de Morelos, 1953.

In connection with the special ceremonies following the planting, it is interesting to note that religious ceremonies now follow the last planting in the annual sequence of crops in Tepoztlan in the Cuernavaca area. A teponaztli is taken to the fields and played. The women and the old men go out from town to meet the farmers returning from the fields and decorate their shovels and hoes with flowers. A church service follows.

[10] The conquest of Tepeaca is set at 13 Rabbit (1466) by the *Annales de Chimalpahin*, *Anales de Tlatelolco*, *Anales de Quauhtinchan*, *Anales de Cuauhtitlan*, *Anales de Tecamachalco*. Torquemada, Tomo I, p. 164, describes it as the year following the conquest of Chalco which would come to the same date. Durán I, p. 156, says specifically that the messengers from Tepeaca came a few days after the mourning for the Chalco dead. Tezozomoc, pp. 306-309, gives no date.

Axayacatl is named by the *Anales de Quauhtinchan* and the *Anales de Tecamachalco* — both records from the conquered area — as their conqueror. The *Anales de Cuauhtitlan* expressly state, however, that this was before he became king. The *Códice Mendocino* and the *Carta de Pablo Nazareo* list it among his conquests — and probably during his reign, if we assume that their grouping so indicates.

See Chap. XIV, note 1, for dating of original conquest of Quauhtinchan.

[11] "Relación de Tepeaca," Paso y Troncoso, *Papeles de Nueva España* Segunda Serie, Tomo V, p. 40.

[12] Tepeaca later moved to the bottom of the hill where it is now. See "Relación de Tepeaca," p. 13.

[13] It is interesting that neither the *Anales de Quauhtinchan* nor the *Anales de Tecamachalco* mention fighting as a part of this conquest. The Tenochtitlan accounts by Tezozomoc and Durán specifically say that there was none, and Durán I, p. 159, referring to his sources, comments on this and puts it down to cowardice. The importance of this area as a market center, however, may have made these towns choose tribute instead of destruction. It should be mentioned that Torquemada, a later source with many basic materials at hand which are now lost, says there was fighting and gives specific figures — more than 700 prisoners taken to Mexico and 204 allied casualties in the battle. I base the account here, however, on the earlier sources, particularly reinforced by Durán's surprised comment as he surveyed a number of them.

[14] Durán I, p. 161, has the speakers refer to the place where the fish fly and Tezozomoc, p. 308, to flying birds caught in nets. I adopt Tezozomoc's interpretation of the lost Crónica X source as fitting with customs still existing on Lake Texcoco. See above Chap. II, note 1, and Chap. VII, note 15, for bird hunting with nets.

[15] Tezozomoc, p. 309, for the king dancing in the market place on this occasion. Durán I, pp. 162-163, limits the dancing groups to the prisoners. Later (II, pp. 215 ff.) in his discussion of market customs he dwells upon the altar and the gods of the market and urges that market days be made not every fifth day as was customary but on a particular day of the week so that the old practices would not get in the way of attendance at Mass on Sundays and would be more quickly forgotten. The god of the tianguis or market is shown in the *Borbonicus* in the merchant fiesta.

[16] *Relación de Tepeaca*, pp. 13 ff. so describes him.

[17] This market treaty is described by Tezozomoc, p. 309, and Durán I, pp. 163-165. Like the treaty with Xochimilco (see above, Chap. VIII, and note 12) its conditions are still being fulfilled centuries after their institution. Tepeaca is still a market town drawing traders and goods on its market day from an area far wider than the ordinary small Mexican market town. The

food section with its steaming cocoa made in many different prehispanic ways, the great cazuelas of meat cooking over the fires, the serapes and other fine craft products make this town on the highway between Puebla and Tehuacan most interesting to visit. Dr. Vincente T. Mendoza and Profa. Virginia Rodríguez Rivera de Mendoza have made an interesting and detailed study of the modern market there on Fridays. It was presented as a paper before the Sociedad Folklorica de México, and is a part of a still unpublished folklore study made by them of the state of Puebla for the Instituto Nacional de Bellas Artes. See Rodríguez Rivera de Mendoza, Virginia, "Los Mercados Tradicionales."

[18] The settlement of disputes in this area by maps is especially mentioned by the *Relación de Tepeaca*, p. 30. The problem of boundaries and the men who came and pointed are described by the *Anales de Quauhtinchan*, Par. 369-382, covering 13 Rabbit (1466) and I Reed (1467). A footnote by Berlin supplies the names of the men from a document in the municipal archive of Quauhtinchan. Par. 396 tells how many of the people by 1486 had moved to the hill of Tollan and then eventually, attracted by the market, to Tepeaca. The town official of Quauhtinchan pointed out to me from the roof of the church the nearby hills, one of which was named Tollan, and showed me in the presidencia old town records written in Nahuatl.

[19] The *Anales de Cuauhtitlan*, Par. 193, and the *Annales de Chimalpahin* date this event as 13 Rabbit (1466) and couple the conquest of Tepeaca with it. The *Anales de Cuauhtitlan* mention the Tepeacan captives going in front of the water. The *Codex Mexicanus* on this date (Sheet LXVIII) shows a drawing of Nezahualcoyotl, standing with a heavy tool in hand, in front of the Hill of the Grasshopper, with the water gushing out toward him. The size of the head of water is described in the *Conquistador Anónimo*, p. 391, and by Cortés in his letter to the king (Lorenzana, pp. 108-109). The good drinking water was sold by canoe in all the canals of the city. The date is put at 12 House (1465) by *Anales Mexicanos No. 2* (No. 8 in *Anales Antiguos de México y sus Contornos* — Ramírez).

CHAPTER XIX

[1] *Annales de Chimalpahin*, 1 Reed, 1467.

[2] Ixtlilxochitl, *Historia Chichimeca*, p. 236; *Anales de Cuauhtitlan*, Par. 194; *Códice en Cruz*, Lám. II.

[3] *Anales de Cuauhtitlan*, Par. 194. The towns which had to supply the victims were Tzompanco (Zumpango), Citlaltepec, and Xilotzinco, all just a little way north of Cuauhtitlan. This employment of foreign troops for a home battle has received surprisingly little attention.

[4] The *Codex Mexicanus*, Sheet LXVIII, under the year 12 House (1465) shows the court and what Mengin interprets as unhewn stone. Where the construction is going on is not clear from the deteriorated drawing, but the emphasis in this codex is often on Texcoco. For reproductions of a number of codex drawings of a ball court see Gillmor, *Flute of the Smoking Mirror*. Pomar, Sahagún and Durán all tell about the high betting, but the particular bet referred to here was between Nezahualpilli and Moteczuma II, and is described by Ixtlilxochitl, *Historia Chichimeca*, p. 314.

[5] *Anales de Tlatelolco*, Par. 273 under 13 Rabbit and *Códice en Cruz*, Lám. II under 1 Reed, and Dibble commentary, pp. 55-56.

[6] *Anales de Cuauhtitlan*, Par. 195, under 1 Reed.

[7] Tezozomoc, pp. 343-349; Durán I, pp. 199-207.

[8] Durán, p. 204, mentions that the rulers hid in the caves. The religious aspects of the caves are described in the 1580 "Relación de Tlacotlalpan y su Partido" in the discussion of Cotaxtla, p. 10 (Francisco del Paso y Troncoso, *Papeles de Nueva España*, Segunda Serie, Tomo V). The report then was that in times past one person was sacrificed a year to a goddess carved in green stone. She was dipped in the river and carried back to her temple. The sacrifice took place with only the old men present. This proceeding was at Tlacotlapan, cabacera of the province. But sacrifices, it is specifically stated, were made in the cave in Cotaxtla.

[9] See end of Chap. XVI.

[10] The Tlaxcala analysis of their attitude toward towns conquered by Tenochtitlan is found in Muñoz Comargo, pp. 108-111, who also emphasizes the salt situation. He describes the encirclement as lasting seventy years. Actually it was close to sixty years before Tlaxcala found an ally in the Spaniards against Tenochtitlan. The situation with emphasis on the salt was described to Cortés by Xicotencatl the Younger (Lorenzana, pp. 56-57). Xicotencatl the Elder, friend of Nezahualcoyotl in his younger days, conspirator against the alliance in his later relationship to it, was still living when Cortés arrived, but so old that the lids of his eyes were lifted so that he could see Cortés whom he welcomed on his entry to Tlaxcala. According to Muñoz Camargo, p. 84, he was the first person to receive Christian baptism after the conquest. According to Bernal Díaz del Castillo, he made a speech to the Spaniards emphasizing encirclement and salt. (*Historia Verdadera de la Conquista de la Nueva España*, Tomo I, p. 253).

It might be noted that salt was available to the highland towns from the lake. Cortés describes to Carlos V the salt gathering and trade in salt (Lorenzana, p. 78). A leaching method is still used in extracting it from the tequezquite earth in the towns around lake Texcoco. I have seen it at Magdalena, and it is described by Ola Apenes, "The Pond in our Backyard," p. 60.

[11] This revolt is described by Durán I, pp. 229-239, and Tezozomoc, pp. 354-361. They both mention the city of Oaxaca, though other sources would indicate that it was not conquered until long after the reign of Moteczuma. Tezozomoc couples Coaixtlahuaca with it (p. 358), probably the more specific location. See Chap. XIII, note 40, for reasons for putting the colonization of the Coaixtlahuaca earlier instead of after this revolt as Durán and Tezozomoc do.

A picture in the *Codex Mendoza* (Folio 67 recto) shows scouts reconnoitering a town with market, house, and temple, and merchants standing by with staff and fan. James Cooper Clark in his commentary (p. 96) refers to the attack on the merchants which led to this campaign as one of many which resemble the situation of the picture, though he thinks the picture refers to a later event.

[12] Durán's emphasis on the conquered coastlands and long marches (I, p. 238) seems to indicate a relation of the war of flowers with the completion of the later conquests in Moteczuma's reign described immediately before it rather than to the earlier years of famine described immediately after it. This does not mean, however, that a war of flowers had not already been resorted to in the years of famine as described by Ixtlilxochitl since such wars had been arranged frequently in Aztec history. See above, Chap. XIII and note 51.

[13] Cholula, Atlixco, Tiliuhquitepec and Tecoac.

[14] Chimalpahin, Relación 6, 1387 (Silvia Rendón translation).

[15] *Anales de Cuauhtitlan*, Par. 131, 132, for earlier wars. The participation of Chalco in this one is indicated by Durán I, p. 242, and also by the *Anales de Cuauhtitlan*, Par. 132.

[16] Muñoz Camargo, the Tlaxcala source, pp. 123-124.

[17] This whole encounter including the speeches of Moteczuma and the priests about the quest to find the mother of Huitzilopochtli is from Durán I, pp. 218-228.

CHAPTER XX

[1] Tezozomoc, p. 370, gives the Nahuatl names of the trees and plants taken to Huaxtepec for transplanting. Sahagún, Lib. XI, cap. 6-7, (Ed. Robredo, Vol. III, pp. 219-277) gives descriptions and uses for them. The *De La Cruz-Badiano Aztec Herbal of 1552* with English translation and commentary by William Gates (Pub. 23, The Maya Society, Baltimore, 1939) gives medicinal uses for them, and Gates identifies species in an appendix.

[2] "La Descripción del Guaxtepeque" of 1580 speaks of the deities worshiped there and mentions the weeping young goddess Ixpachitequicasle. Xochiquetzal, the feminine counterpart of Xochipilli (the god of flowers prayed to after the transplanting, according to Durán), in her variant as Ixnextli, was supposed to go weeping with a rose in her hand, mourning because she had gathered it. Spence describes this (p. 190) quoting the *Codex Vaticanus A* and the *Telleriano-Remensis*. This was also true of Cihuacoatl, Snake Woman, who wailed in the streets at night, and carried a cradle with an obsidian knife within it, symbol of sacrifice. See Sahagún, Lib. I, cap. 6. (Ed. Robredo, Vol. I, pp. 18-19; Anderson and Dibble, Book 1, p. 3) and Durán II, pp. 171, 176-177. Durán in describing Cihuacoatl "by other name Quilaxtly," goddess of the flower fields of Xochimilco, mentions her open mouth, mentioned also by the "Descripción del Guaxtepeque." She is sometimes represented with the face of a skull, as is also the goddess with the serpent skirt Coatlicue, and as is implied by Durán's "snarling teeth."

[3] Tezozomoc, p. 369, and Durán I, p. 251, report this conversation. The comparison to the line of travelers on a road is based on the phrase in Durán.

[4] They were there when the Spaniards came and fought against them, says Durán II, p. 66, referring to the then ruler as son or grandson, and saying that the lords of Yacapichtlan were of Tlacaelel's line.

[5] She did rule, according to one group of sources including *La Relación de le Genealogía*, p. 253, and Mendieta, Lib. II, cap. xxxvi, p. 150. A genealogical drawing, "Fragment de Généalogie des Princes Mexicains," is included in Boban, *Documents pour servir à l'Histoire du Mexique, Atlas*, Planche 72. The interpretation (Vol. II, pp. 151-154) is mistaken in describing the relationships, though the connecting lines in the picture are clearly defined. The suggestion of the commentator that the dotted speech or breath scrolls on the name glyph indicate that Tezozomoc suffered from asthma is an amusing one, apparently based on the still earlier confusion of the tlacuilo, who copied badly, without understanding it, the glyph which could have been familiar to him from the glyph of the earlier Tezozomoc of Azcapotzalco. See *Xolotl*, Sheet 8, for the stone *Te(tl)* surmounted by the smoke-like scroll which meant anger, from *zuma* or *zoma*, to assume a threatening or angry aspect — the same verb, as a matter of fact, which appears in Moteczuma's name but not in his glyph. Alfonso Caso sets the matter straight in his analysis of the drawing. ("Fragmento de Genealogía de los Príncipes Mexicanos," *Journal de la Société des Américanistes*, Nouvelle Serie, t. XLVII, 1958, p. 23.)

[6] He remarked it aloud after Moteczuma's death during the new election, and so presumably had thought it earlier. (Durán I, p. 255).

[7] The relation of the Black House to merchants and to Chantico is analyzed

by Seler, *Fejérváry-Mayer*, p. 67. For their return at night see Sahagún, Lib. IX, cap. 6 (Ed. Robredo, Vol. II, p. 360; Dibble and Anderson, Book 9, p. 27).

The Black House is discussed in connection with Cihuacoatl by Durán II, pp. 171-172, and by Sahagún, Apéndice Lib. II (Ed. Robredo, Vol. I, p. 220; Anderson-Dibble, Book II, p. 168).

[8] Garibay, *Poesía Indígena*, pp. 139-141. This dialogue account of his visit to the dying Moteczuma is probably the only poem accredited to Nezahualcoyotl which may actually be of his composition. The opening of the song says he carried a fan.

[9] Tlatlauhquitepec was the conquest which Durán I, p. 253, says he heard about just before his death. The *Anales de Tula* also say that the conquest was just before his death.

[10] Tezozomoc, p. 372.

[11] Durán, I, p. 254. The elaborate funeral ceremonies described for Azcapotzalco by Ixtlilxochitl and called a Toltec rite did not grow up in the sterner Tenochtitlan until later. See above, Chap. II and note 21.

The date of Moteczuma's death is placed as 2 Stone (1468) by the following sources: *Anales de Tlatelolco*, Par. 275; *Annales de Chimalpahin; Crónica Mexicayotl; Anales de Tecamachalco; Mapa de Tepechpan; Códice de Cuahtlancingo; Códice en Cruz; Mendocino* date signs; *Anales de Cuauhtitlan; Anales Mexicanos: México-Azcapotzalco; Anales Mexicanos No. 2* in *Anales Antiguos de México y sus Contornos* (Ramírez). A death with a somewhat different name glyph in the *Otomí Codex of San Mateo Huichapan* may refer to this also.

It is placed in 3 House (1469) by the *Anales de Tula, Hgo.; Telleriano-Remensis; Mendocino* text; Ixtlilxochitl, *Historia Chichimeca*, p. 230; Durán I, p. 253; The *Codex Mexicanus* puts the Nahuatl statement that Moteczuma died directly above the year-sign 3 House, but it apparently refers to the drawing of him connected with a clear line to the following year 4 Rabbit (1470).

The date is given as 5 Reed (1471) by the *Aubin Codex of 1576; Anales Mexicanos No. 1* in *Anales Antiguos de México y sus Contornos (No. 7 — Ramírez).*

It is put in 1 Reed (1467) by the *Anales de Tlatelolco* (Par. 59-60) contrasting with the other tradition in this source given above in 1468.

Clavijero puts it much earlier in 1464.

The *Historia de México por sus Pinturas* puts it 147 years after founding of the city.

Two stone inscriptions are of particular interest. A stone in Cuernavaca (le piedra chimalli en la barranca de Amanalco) has the date 3 House and is believed to commemorate the death of Moteczuma. A good photograph appears in the *Breve Historia Antigua del Estado de Morelos* by López González with a discussion on p. 38. A stone box in the Museo Nacional de México with the date 11 Stone on the outside and the glyph of Moteczuma inside (crown and noseplug) is believed by some to have held the ashes of the dead ruler. In that case his cremation would have to be added to account given by Durán.

References

I. CODICES

Codices are drawings or paintings made by the Aztecs and other Indians, recounting their history, ceremonies, calendars, etc. Most of those still extant were done immediately after the Spanish conquest though a few have survived from pre-conquest times. After the conquest brief explanatory notes were sometimes written in Nahuatl or in Spanish directly on the manuscripts. Many have been the subject of extensive modern commentaries, some of which are also included in this list.

They were painted on paper made of maguey fiber, or of the pounded bark of the amatl tree, or on skin, or on European paper when that became possible. They were often folded screen-fashion between covers. The craft of the *tlacuilo*, the painter of books, was an important one.

Aubin Codex of 1576 (Histoire de la Nation Mexicaine).

Histoire de la Nation Mexicaine Depuis le Départ d'Aztlan jusqu'a l'arrivée des Conquérants espangols: Reproduction du Codex de 1576. Appartenant à le Collection de M. E. Goupil, Ancienne Collection Aubin. Paris, 1893.

Also translated from Nahuatl by Bernardino de Jesús Quiróz as Vol. 4 of Peñafiel, Dr. Antonio, *Colección de Documentos para la Historia Mexicana.* México, 1902.

Aubin Tonalamatl

The Tonalamatl of the Aubin Collection: An old Mexican Picture Manuscript in the Paris National Library (Manuscrits Mexicains No. 18–19). Commentary by Edward Seler. English translation by A. H. Keane. Published by the Duke of Loubat, Berlin and London, 1900–1901.

Azcatítlan

Roberto Barlow, "El Códice Azcatítlan," *Journal de la Société des Américanistes*, Nouvelle Série, Tome XXXVIII, 1949, pp. 101–135. Separate facsimile reproduction of codex.

Azoyú

Toscano, Salvador, "Los Códices Tlapanecas de Azoyú," *Cuadernos Americanos*, T. 10, No. 4, 1943, pp. 127–136.

Borbonicus

Codex Borbonicus. Photographic reproduction, Museo Nacional de México.

Vaillant, George C., ed. *A Sacred Almanac of the Aztecs (Tonalamatl of the Codex Borbonicus)*. American Museum of Natural History, New York, 1940.

Códice en Cruz

Dibble, Charles E. *Códice en Cruz*, Mexico, 1942. Separate reproduction of the codex.

Fejérváry-Mayer

Codex Fejérváry-Mayer: An Old Mexican Picture Manuscript in the Liverpool Free Public Museums. Commentary by Eduard Seler. English translation, A. H. Keane. Published by the Duke of Loubat, Berlin and London, 1901–1902.

Fernando Leal

Códice Fernando Leal, publicado por el Dr. Antonio Peñafiel. Oficina Tipográfica de la Secretaría de Fomento, México, 1895.

Florentine. See III. Early Chronicles: Sahagún.

Fragment de Généalogie des Princes Mexicains. Les Empereurs Itzcohuatzin et Motecuhzoma Ilhuicamina et leurs descendants. In Boban, Eugene, *Documents pour servir . . .* Planche 72 (Atlas). See IV: Collections. Also Caso, Alfonso. "Fragmento de Genealogía de los Príncipes Mexicanos," *Journal de la Société des Americanistes*, Nouvelle Série, Tome XLVII, 1958, pp. 21–31.

Humboldt

Seler, Eduard, "The Mexican Picture Writings of Alexander Von Humboldt," Bureau of American Ethnology, *Bulletin* No. 28 Washington, 1904, pp. 123–229.

Kingsborough

Códice Kingsborough, *Memorial de los Indios de Tepetlaoztoc*. Francisco del Paso y Troncoso, Madrid, 1912.

Manuscrit Figuratif Circulaire

Reproduced with commentary by M. Le Colonel Doutrelaine, *Archives de la Commision Scientifique du Mexique*, Ministere de l'Instruction Publique, Paris, 1856–1857, Vol. III, pp. 120–133.

Matrícula de Tributos

This is part of the *Codex Mendoza* q.v. It is reproduced separately by Lorenzana. See III. Early Chronicles, etc.

Mendoza (Mendocino)

Codex Mendoza, edited and translated by James Cooper Clark, Waterlow and Sons, Ltd., London, 1938 (3 vols.)

Códice Mendocino. Facsímile Fototipo. Francisco del Paso y

Troncoso. Museo Nacional de Arqueología, Historia y Etnografía, Mexico, 1925.

Paleografía del Códice Mendocino. Ed., Vargas Rea, Mexico, 1951.

Mexicanus

Mengin, Ernest. "Commentaire du Codex Mexicanus Nos. 23–24 de la Bibliothèque Nacional de Paris." *Journal de la Société des Américanistes*, Nouvelle Série, Tome XLI, 1952, pp. 287–498. Separate facsimile reproduction of codex.

Nuttall (Zouche)

Codex Nuttall (Codex Zouche). Introduction by Zelia Nuttall. Peabody Museum of American Archaeology and Ethnology, Cambridge, 1902.

Ordenanza del Señor Cuauhtemoc. Paleografía, Traducción, y Noticia Introductoria de Silvia Rendón. Philological and Documentary Studies, Vol. II, No. 2. Middle American Research Institute. The Tulane University of Louisiana, New Orleans, 1952.

Otomí Codex of San Mateo Huichapan

Unpublished codex in Museo Nacional de México. See also Caso, Alfonso, "Un Códice en Otomí," *Proceedings of the 23rd International Congress of Americanists*, New York, 1928. (Reproduces a few pages.)

Quauhtinchan (See *Anales de Quauhtinchan*)

Quinatzin

"Mapa Quinatzin," *Anales del Museo Nacional de México*, Primera época 1886, III, pp. 305–368.

Barlow, Roberto. "Una Neuva Lámina del Mapa Quinatzin," *Journal de Société des Americanistes*, Nouvelle Série, Tome XXXIX, 1950, pp. 111–124.

Telleriano-Remensis

Codex Telleriano-Remensis, *Manuscrit Mexicain*, du cabinet de Ch. M. Le Tellier, Archevêque de Reims, à la Bibliothèque Nationale (MS. Mexicain No. 385) précédé d'une Introduction contenant la transcription complète des anciens commentaires Hispano-Mexicains, par Le Dr. E. T. Hamy, Paris, 1899.

Teozacoalco

Caso, Alfonso. "El Mapa de Teozacoalco," *Cuadernos Americanos*, Vol. 47, No. 5, 1949.

Tepechpan

"Mapa de Tepechpan: Nota histórica sincrónica y señorial" por Jesús Sánchez. *Anales del Museo Nacional de México*, Primera época, 1886, III, p. 368.

Tlatelolco (See *Anales de Tlatelolco*)

Tovar

George Kubler and Charles Gibson, *The Tovar Calendar.* Memoirs of the Connecticut Academy of Arts and Sciences, Vol. XI, January, 1951. To be obtained also from Yale University Press.

Vaticanus A

Il Manoscritto Messicano Vaticano 3738. Detto Il Códice Rios, Reprodotto in fotocromografia a spese de sua eccellenza il duca di Loubat per cura della Biblioteca Vaticana-Roma 1900.

Vaticanus B

Codex Vaticanus No. 3773. Commentary by Eduard Seler. English translation, A. H. Keane. Published by the Duke of Loubat. Berlin and London, 1902–1903.

Vindobonensis (Vienna)

Caso, Alfonso, "Explicación del Reverso del Codex Vindobonensis," *Memoria de El Colegio Nacional,* Tomo V, Núm. 5, pp. 9–46.

Xolotl

Dibble, Charles. *Códice Xolotl.* Editado en colaboración por las Universidades de Utah y de México. Publicaciones del Instituto de Historia, Primera Serie, No. 22. México, 1951. The *tlacuilos* who drew this codex were Cemilhuitzin and Quauhquechol.

Yanhuitlan

Códice de Yanhuitlán. Edición en Facsímile y con un estudio preliminar por Wigberto Jiménez Moreno y Salvador Mateos Higuera. Museo Nacional, México, 1940. (Instituto Nacional de Antropología e Historia.)

II. ANNALS OF AZTEC TOWNS

These annals with the Aztec dates for each entry were written down, usually in Nahuatl, after the conquest, and often are explanations of dated pictured sequences now lost. In a few cases the pictures are still with the written explanation, and the item has then been included under *I. Codices.*

Anales Antiguos de México y Sus Contornos.

Compiled by José Fernando Ramírez. Two volumes of manuscript material in library of Museo Nacional de México. Of the twenty-six items, those especially useful in connection with the lifetime of Moteczuma Ilhuicamina are as follows:

No. 1. *Anales de Cuauhtitlan.* Published and listed separately. See below.

No. 3. *Historia del Señorío de Teotihuacan.* Published and listed separately. See III. Early Chronicles.
No. 5. Anales Tolteca-Chichimecas. Published and listed as *Historia Tolteca-Chichimeca: Anales de Quautinchan.* See below.
No. 6. Anales Tepanecas. Published and listed as *Anales Mexicanos: México-Azcapotzalco.* See below.
No. 7. Anales Mexicanos No. 1. Published and listed as *Aubin Codex of 1576.* See I. Codices.
No. 8. Anales Mexicanos No. 2 (1168–1546). Listed below as *Códice de Cuantlancingo.* See below.
No. 16. *Anales de Tlaxcala No. 1* (1453–1603). The only date with an entry in the lifetime of Moteczuma Ilhuicamina is 1453 (1 Tochtli).
No. 18. *Anales de Puebla y Tlaxcala No. 1*, Pt. 1. Gives the number of years in reigns of kings of Tenochtitlan.

Anales de Cuauhtitlan. (See *Códice Chimalpopoca* in this section.)

Anales Mexicanos: México-Azcapotzalco (1426–1589). Autor Anónimo. Traducción del mexicano al castellano hecha por don Faustino Galicia Chimalpopoca. *Anales del Museo Nacional de México*, Primera época, 1903, VII, pp. 49–74.

Anales de Quauhtinchan. (See *Historia Tolteca-Chichimeca.*)

"Anales de Tecamachalco." *Colección de Documentos para la Historia Mexicana* No. 5, compilados por Dr. Antonio Peñafiel, México, 1902.

Anales de Tlatelolco: Unos Annales Históricos de la Nación Mexicana y Códice de Tlatelolco. Versión preparada y anotada por Heinrich Berlin, con un resúmen de los anales y una interpretación del códice por Robert N. Barlow. Antigua Librería Robredo de José Porrúa e Hijos, México, 1948. (This is the same as *Unos Annales Históricos de la Nación Mexicana.* Die manuscrits Mexicains NR, 22 und. 22 bis der Bibliotheque Nationale de Paris. Ubersetzt und Erläutert von Ernst Mengin, Kopenhagen. Teill II Der Kommentar, 1939.) The annals were written down in 1528. Facsimile in *Corpus Codicum* . . . q.v. See IV. Collections.

"Anales de Tula, Hidalgo," 1361–1521. Publicados por Roberto Barlow, *Tlalocan*, Vol. III, No. 1, 1949, pp. 2–13.

Annales de San Antón Muñón Chimalpahin Quauhtlehuanitzin: Sixième et septième relationes (1258–1602) Rémi Siméon, Paris, 1889. (Bibliothèque Linguistique Américaine, Tome XII.) Chimalpahin was born the 26th or 27th of May, 1579, in Amecameca, and this is the source for the Chalco region which included his birthplace under its jurisdiction. Citations, unless otherwise stated, are to the 7th Relation in this translation. See also, *Seis Relaciones Históricas de la Antiguëdad de Chalco Amecamecan* escritas en idioma Nahua hacia 1600 por Domingo de San Antón Chimalpahin Quauhtlehuanitzin, Miguel de Quetzalmazatzin, Juan de Sandoval Tecuanxayacatzin, Domingo de Hernández Ayopochtzin, y otros varios autores nativos no identificados. Traducidas al Español por Silvia Rendón, 1952. An unpublished manuscript in library of the Museo Nacional de Antropología, México, D.F.

Códice Chimalpopoca: Anales de Cuauhtitlan y Leyenda de Los Soles. Traducción directa del Náhuatl por Primo Feliciano Velázquez. Universidad Nacional Autónoma de México, Instituto de Historia, México, 1945.

Códice de Cuantlancingo (San Juan). No. 8 in Legajo Num. 7 of first series of Documentos del Museo Nacional de México. Same as Ramírez, *Anales de México y Sus Contornos, No. 8* (1168–1546), entitled in that collection "Anales Mexicanos No. 2." See IV. Collections.

"Historia de los Mexicanos por sus Pinturas" (Sixteenth century work). In García Icazbalceta, J., ed., *Nueva Colección de Documentos Para la Historia de México* q.v., Vol. III, pp. 209–240. See IV. Collections.

Historia Tolteca-Chichimeca: Anales de Quauhtinchan. Versión Preparada y Anotada por Heinrich Berlin en Colaboración con Silvia Rendón. Prólogo de Paul Kirchhoff. México Antigua Librería Robredo, de José Porrúa e Hijos, 1947. This is the same as K. Th. Preuss and E. Mengin, *Die Mexikanische Bilderhandschrift Historia Tolteca Chichimeca*, Baessler Archiv Berlin, 1937. Facsimile in *Corpus Codicum* . . . q.v. under IV. Collections.

Leyenda de los Soles (See *Códice Chimalpopoca*).

"Orígen de Los Mexicanos." In García Icazbalceta, ed., *Nueva Colección de Documentos Para la Historia de México* q.v., Vol. III, pp. 256–280. See IV. Collections.

III. EARLY CHRONICLES, HISTORIES, ETHNOGRAPHIC STUDIES AND GEOGRAPHIC DESCRIPTIONS

These are sometimes from Nahuatl originals. The geographic descriptions of 1580 were in response to the questionnaire from Felipe II. Included in this section are materials of Sixteenth and Seventeenth Century and an occasional Eighteenth Century historian such as Clavijero since he used basic sources now lost.

Acosta, P. Joseph de. *Historia Natural y Moral de las Indias*. Fondo de Cultura Económica, México, 1940. Estudio Preliminar por Edmundo O'Gorman. First published in 1590.

Burgoa, Fr. Francisco de. *Geográfica Descripción*. Publicaciones del Archivo General de la Nación, Vols. XXV y XXVI, 1934. Originally published in 1674.

Clavijero, Francisco Javier. *Historia Antigua de México*. Editorial Delfin, Mexico, 1944. (2 vols.) written between 1770 and 1780.

"Códice Franciscano de Culhuacan." Published by García Icazbalceta, *Nueva Colección de Documentos Para la Historia de México*, Vol. II. q.v. See IV. Collections.

"Códice Ramírez." Published with Tezozomoc, *Crónica Mexicana*, México, 1878. A sixteenth-century manuscript with drawings.

"Conquistador Anónimo," in García Icazbalceta, ed., *Colección de Documentos Para la Historia de México*, q.v., Vol. I, pp. 368–398. Written in sixteenth century. See IV. Collections.

Cortés, Hernán. See Lorenzana.

Cristóbal del Castillo. *Fragmentos de la Obra General Sobre Historia de los Mexicanos*. Escrita en Lengua Náuatl por Cristóbal del Castillo á Fines del Siglo XVI. Los Tradujo al Castellano Francisco del Paso y Troncoso. Florencia, Tipografía de Salvador Landi, 1908.

Crónica Mexicayotl. (See Tezozomoc.)

De La Cruz-Badiano Aztec Herbal of 1552. Translation and Commentary by William Gates. Publication No. 23, The Maya Society, Baltimore, 1939.

"Descripción del Guaxtepeque por el Alcalde Mayor Juan Gutiérrez de Liévana; 24 de setiembre de 1580," *Boletín Oficial y Revista Eclesiástica del Obispado de Cuernavaca*, Tomo IX, pp. 315, 332, 350. Also published as Apéndice to *Huaxtepec y sus Reliquias Arqueológicas* by Enrique Juan Palacios, Sec. de Educ. Pub. Tall. Graf. Nación, México, 1930.

Díaz del Castillo, Bernal. *Historia Verdadera de la Conquista de La Nueva España*. Introduction and notes by Joaquín Ramírez Cabañas. Editorial Pedro Robredo, Mexico, D.F., 1944. (Three Volumes.) Sixteenth Century. The author accompanied Cortes.

———. *The Discovery and Conquest of Mexico 1517–1521*. Translated with an Introduction and Notes by A. P. Maudslay. George Routledge & Sons, Ltd. Broadway House, Carter Lane, London, 1928. (Broadway Travellers.)

Durán, Fr. Diego. *Historia de las Indias de Nueva España.* Mexico, 1867, 1880. Two vols. and Atlas. Written about 1581.

Gómara, Francisco López de. *The Conquest of the Weast India* (1578). With an introduction by Herbert Ingram Priestley. Scholars' Facsimiles & Reprints, New York, N.Y., 1940. The first edition appeared in Zaragoza in 1552.

"Historia del Señorío de Teotihuacan." No. 3 in Ramírez manuscript collection, *Anales Antiguos de México y Sus Contornos.* See below: "Tratado del Principado . . ."

"Huehuetlatolli-" Documento A, Manuscrito de la Biblioteca Bancroft, Universidad de California. *Tlalocan*, Vol. I, Nos. 1 and 2. Reprinted with consecutive pagination, La Casa Editorial de Tlaloc, Sacramento, Calif., 1943.

Ixtlilxochitl, Fernando de Alva. *Obras Históricas.* Publicadas y anotadas por Alfredo Chavero, México, 1891. Vol. 1, *Relaciones;* Vol. II, *Historia Chichimeca.* Written about 1600.

Lorenzana, Francisco Antonio, ed. *Historia de Nueva España Escrita por su Esclarecido Conquistador Hernán Cortés*, Aumentada con otros documentos y notas, por el ilustrissimo Señor, Don Francisco Antonio Lorenzano, Arzobispo de México, México, 1770. Contains Letters of Cortés to Carlos V, and the "Matrícula de Tributos" from the *Mendocino.*

"Manuscrito Americano No. 4, Biblioteca Real de Berlin." See Peñafiel, Antonio, *Colección de Documentos para la Historia Mexicana*, México, 1902, Vol. 1. See IV. Collections.

Mendieta, Fray Gerónimo de. *Historia Eclesiástica Indiana.* México, 1870. Sixteenth Century.

Motolinía, Fr. Toribio de. *Historia de los Indios de la Nueva España*, escrita a mediados del Siglo XVI, por el R. P. Fr. Toribio de Benavente o Motolinía. Sácalos nuevemente a luz el R. P. Fr. Daniel Sánchez García. Barcelona, 1914.

———. *Memoriales.* Manuscrito de la Colección del Señor Don Joaquín García Icazbalceta. Publicado por primera vez por su hijo Luis García Pimentel. México, Paris, Madrid, 1903. Apéndice publicada en 1907.

Muñoz Comargo, Diego. *Historia de Tlaxcala.* Ed. Alfredo Chavero. México, 1892. Sixteenth century.

Nazareo de Xaltocan, Pablo. "Carta al rey don Felipe II de don Pablo Nazareo de Xaltocan, doña María Axayaca, don Juan Axayaca y doña María Atotoz (con genealogía de don Juan Axayaca y don Pablo Nazareo), México a 17 de Marzo de 1566. Paso y Troncoso, Francisco del, *Epistolario de Nueva España* q.v., Tomo X, 1564–

1569. Original Latin, pp. 89–108; Spanish version, pp. 109–129. See IV. Collections.

Pomar, Juan Bautista, "Relación de Texcoco." (1582) García Icazbalceta, ed. *Nueva Colección de Documentos Para la Historia de México*, Vol. III, Salvador Chávez Hayhoe, Mexico, 1941, pp. 1–64. See IV. Collections.

"Los Primeros Señores de Teotihuacan y sus Comarcanos." In "Teotihuacan," *Obras de Lic. Don Alfredo Chavero*, Tomo I, México, 1904 (Biblioteca de Autores Mexicanos, vol. 52), pp. 431–463.

"Relación de Chimalhuacan-Atenco (1579)," In Paso y Troncoso, ed., *Papeles de Nueva España*, Segunda Serie, Vol. VI, pp. 75 ff. See IV. Collections.

"Relación de la Genealogía y Linaje de los Señores que han señoreado esta tierra de la Nueva España." Taken to Spain in 1532. In García Icazbalceta, ed., *Nueva Colección de Documentos Para la Historia de México*, Vol. III, Salvador Chávez Hayhoe, Mexico, 1941, pp. 240–256. See IV. Collections.

"Relación de Ichcateopan y su Partido." (Tzicaputzalco, Alauiztlan, Oztuma, Acapetlauaya, Coatepec, Tlacotepec, Utlatlan, Tetla, Cuezala, Apaztle, Tenepatlan, Teloloapan, Tutultepec) 1579. In Paso y Troncoso, ed., *Papeles de Nueva España*, Tomo VI. Especially Cuetzala, pp. 137–143. See IV. Collections.

"Relación de Tepeaca y su partido." Formado el partido por cuatro poblaciones que son: como cabecera, la ciudad de Tepeaca, y como sujetos, los tres pueblos de Tecamachalco, Cachula o Quechulac y Tecali; hecha la relación de todos en 4 y 20 de Febrero de 1580 por el Alcalde mayor de la provincia, Jorge Cerón Carvajal. In Paso y Troncoso, ed., *Papeles de Nueva España*, Segunda Serie, Tomo V, pp. 12–45. See IV. Collections.

"Relación de Tlacotalpan y su partido." Formado ese partido o acaldía mayor por el pueblo de Tlacotalpan, de la Corona Real como cabecera, y por las villas de Tuztla y Cotastla, del Estado del Marqués del Valle, como sujetos. Hechas las tres relaciones por Juan de Medina, alcalde mayor de la primera población en los días 18, 22, y 20 de Febrero de 1580 respectivamente. In Paso y Troncoso, ed., *Papeles de Nueva España*, Segunda Serie, Tomo V, pp. 1–11. See IV. Collections.

"Relación de la Villa de Tepuztlan." Hecha el 19 de Septiembre de 1580 por el Corregidor de la villa Juan Gutiérrez de Liébana. In Paso y Troncoso, ed., *Papeles de Nueva España*, Segunda Serie, Tomo VI, pp. 237–250. See IV. Collections.

Ruiz de Alarcón, Hernando. "Tratado de las Supersticiones y Costumbres Gentílicas que Oy Viuen Entre Los Indios Naturales Desta Nueva España" (1629), *Anales del Museo Nacional de México*, Primera Época, VI, 1900, pp. 127–223.

Sahagún, Fray Bernardino de. *Códice Florentino*. Edición de Francisco del Paso y Troncoso, Madrid, 1905. (Illustrations for Historia General.) Sixteenth Century.

———. *Florentine Codex: General History of the Things of New Spain*. School of American Research and University of Utah: Monographs of the School of American Research, Santa Fe, N.M. Translated into English from Aztec by Arthur J. O. Anderson and Charles E. Dibble. 13 volumes in process of publication. 1950–. Anderson and Dibble: Books 1 (1950); 2 (1951); 3 (1952); 7 (1953); 8 (1954); 12 (1955). Dibble and Anderson: Books 4 and 5 (1957); 9 (1959); 10 (1961). Books 6 and 11 in press.

———. *Historia General de las Cosas de Nueva España*. Editorial Pedro Robredo, México, 1938. (From Eduard Seler's German translation.) Sixteenth Century. Preliminary study by Wigberto Jiménez Moreno. (Five Volumes.)

[Unless otherwise specified, citations to Sahagún refer to the *Historia General (Florentine Codex)* in the English and Spanish translations and listed in the two preceding items.]

———. *Primeros Memoriales*. Edición de Francisco del Paso y Troncoso. Madrid, 1906-1907. Sixteenth Century.

———. "Relación Breve de las Fiestas de los Dioses." *Tlalocan*, II, No. 4, 1948, pp. 289–320. Traducida por Angel Ma. Garibay K. (MS. de Madrid del Palacio Real, publicado por Del Paso y Troncoso, Madrid, 1904). Sixteenth Century.

Tezozomoc, D. Hernando Alvarado. *Crónica Mexicana*. México, 1878. Written about 1598. This volume also contains the "Códice Ramírez." References in the notes to Tezozomoc are to this work.

———. *Crónica Mexicayotl*. Traducción directa del Nahuatl por Adrián León. Universidad Nacional Autónoma de México, Instituto de Historia, en coloboración con el Instituto Nacional de Antropología e Historia, México, 1949. Date 1609. It is referred to in the notes by title.

"Titles of Tezcotzinco." Edited by Byron McAfee and R. H. Barlow, *Tlalocan*, Vol. II, No. 2, 1946, pp. 110–127.

Torquemada, Fray Juan de. *Monarquía Indiana*. Tercera Edición. Editorial Salvador Chávez Hayhoe, México, 1943. This is a facsimile of the second edition, Madrid, 1723. Completed soon after 1600. Three Volumes.

"Tratado del Principado y Nobleza del Pueblo de San Juan Teotihuacan," in "Teotihuacan," *Obras de Lic. Don Alfredo Chavero*, Tomo I (Biblioteca de Autores Mexicanos, Vol. 52), México, 1904, pp. 431–463. No. 3 in Ramírez, *Anales Antiguos de México y sus Contornos* (q.v.) is part of the "Tratado." See II. Annals.

University of Texas Library — Latin American Manuscripts: Nos. 1169, 1170, 1171, from García Icazbalceta collection.

Veytia, Mariano. *Historia Antigua de México*. Editorial Leyenda S.A. México, D. F., 1944. Two Volumes. Eighteenth Century.

———. Tezcoco en los Últimos Tiempos de Sus Antiguos Reyes, ó sea Relación Tomada de los Manuscritos inéditos de Boturini. Publícalos con Notas y adiciones para estudio de la juventud mexicana Carlos María de Bustamante. México, 1826.

Zurita, Alonso de. "Breve y sumaria Relación de los Señores y maneras y diferencias que había de ellos en la Nueva España," (Sixteenth Century) In García Izcabalceta, ed., *Nueva Colección de Documentos Para la Historia de México*, Vol. III, pp. 65–205. See IV. Collections.

IV. COLLECTIONS OF BASIC DOCUMENTS

Apenes, Ola. *Mapas Antiguos del Valle de México*. Instituto de Historia, Universidad Nacional Autónoma de México, México, 1947.

Boban, Eugene. *Documents pour servir à l'Histoire du Mexique*. Catalogue Raisonné de la Collection de M. E. Eugene Goupil. Paris, 1891. Two volumes and Atlas.

Among items listed elsewhere in this bibliography which are included in Boban are "Fragment de Généalogie des Prince Mexicains," Codex Xolotl, "Mapa Quinatzin," "Mapa de Tepechpan," "Codex en Croix," "Codex Mexicanus," "Histoire Tolteca Chichimèque."

Corpus-Codicum Americanorum Medii Aevi. Editit Ernst Mengin. Copenhagen, 1942–. In this series of facsimiles have appeared the following which relate to times and backgrounds of Moteczuma I:

I. *Historia Tolteca-Chichimeca*.

II. *Unos Annales Históricos de la Nación Mexicana*.

III. *Diferentes Historias Originales de los Reynos de Culhuacan y Mexico y de Otras Provincias* — Chimalpahin Quauhtlehuanitzin.

García Icazbalceta, Joaquín, ed., *Colección de Documentos para la Historia de México*. México, 1858–1866. 2 vol.

———. *Nueva Colección de Documentos Para la Historia de México*.

México, 1886–1892. 5 vol. Vol. III includes the following items listed elsewhere in this bibliography, all sixteenth century documents: Pomar, "Relación de Texcoco"; Zurita, "Breve y Sumaria Relación de los Señores y maneras y diferencias que había de ellos en la Nueva España"; "Historia de los Mexicanos por sus Pinturas"; "Relación de la Genealogía y linaje de los Señores que han señoreado esta tierra de la Nueva España"; "Orígen de los Mexicanos"; "Estas Son Leyes que Tienen Los Indios de la Nueva España"; and two other untitled items. This one volume was republished by Salvador Chávez Hayhoe, México, 1941, and to this new edition all citations refer.

Garibay K., Angel Ma. *Poesía Indígena de la Altiplanicie*. Universidad Nacional Autónoma, México, 1940.

Kingsborough, Edward King, Lord. *Antiquities of Mexico*, London, 1830–1848. Nine volumes. Especially pertinent are Vol. I with the "Codex Mendoza" and the "Telleriano-Remensis"; Vol. II, with "Vaticanus A 3738," "Laud," "Bologna," "Vienna," and "Humboldt"; Vol. III, with "Borgia," "Dresden," "Fejérváry," "Vaticanus B 3773."

Paso y Troncoso, Francisco del, ed. *Epistolario de Nueva España 1505–1818*. Recopilado por Francisco del Paso y Tronosco. 16 volumes. Antigua Librería Robredo de José Porrúa e Hijos, México. 1939–1942. (Vol. 10: 1564–1569 includes "Carta al rey don Felipe II de Don Pablo Nazareo de Xaltocan.")

———. *Papeles de Nueva España*. Segunda Serie. Geografía e Estadística. Manuscritos de la Real Academia de la Historia de Madrid y del Archivo de Indias en Sevilla. Años 1580–1582. Madrid, 1905. (6 vols.)

Especially useful in this biography were: Tomo V: "Relaciones Geográficas de la Diócesis de Tlaxcala" and Tomo VI: "Relaciones Geográficas de la Diócesis de México."

Peñafiel, Antonio, ed. *Colección de Documentos para la Historia Mexicana*. México, 1902.

Vol. 1. "Manuscrito Anónimo," No. 4, Biblioteca Real de Berlin.
Vol. 2. "Cantares."
Vol. 3. "Huehue Tlatolli. Traducción de las antiguas conversaciones o pláticas por Torquemada y Zorita."
Vol. 4. "Códice Aubin (Codex of 1576)." Traducida por Bernardino de Jesús Quiróz.
Vol. 5. "Anales de Tecamachalco."
Vol. 6. "Documento de Texcoco. Lamentaciones de Nezahualcoyotl." De los Manuscritos del Archivo de la Nacion.

Ramírez, José Fernando. *Anales Antiguos de México y sus Contornos.* Compiled by José Fernando Ramírez. Twenty-six documents in the library of the Museo Nacional de México. Unpublished. Those found useful in the preparation of this biography are listed under II. Annals.

Toussaint, Manuel, Federico Gómez de Orozco, y Justino Fernández. *Planos de la Ciudad de México. México,* 1938.

V. GENERAL REFERENCE TOOLS

Atlas Arqueológico de la República Mexicana. Instituto Panamericano de Geografía e Historia, Publicación No. 41, 1939.

Dávila Garibi, José Ignacio. *Del Nahuatl al Español.* Instituto Pan Americano de Geografía e Historia, Publicación Num. 40, Tacubaya, D. F., 1939.

Barlow, Roberto y Byron MacAfee. *Diccionario de Elementos Fonéticos en Escritura Jeroglífica.* Universidad Nacional Autónoma de México: Instituto de Historia, México, 1949. Based on *Mendocino.*

Dibble, Charles. *El Antiguo Sistema de Escritura en México.* Revista Mexicana de Estudios Antropológicos, 1940, Núm. 4. Based on *Xolotl.*

García Granados, Rafael. *Estudio Comparativo de Los Signos Cronográficos en los Códices Prehispánicos de Méjico.* Sobretiro de las Actas de la Primera Sesión Celebrada en la C. de México en 1939, del vigesimoseptimo Congreso Internacional de Americanistas. Instituto Nacional de Antropología e Historia, 1942.

———. *Diccionario Biográfico de Historia Antigua de Méjico.* Instituto de Historia, Méjico, 1952–53. Three volumes.

Garibay K., Angel María. *Llave de Nahuatl,* Otumba, Mex., 1940.

Molina, Alonso de. *Vocabulario en Lengua Castellana y Mexicana.* Colección Americanos, Volúmen IV. Ediciones Cultura Hispánica, Madrid, 1944. (Facsimile of edition of 1571.)

Peñafiel, Antonio. *Nombres Geográficos de México: Estudio Jeroglífico de la Matrícula de los Tributos del Códice Mendocino.* Dibujos de las "Antigüedades Mexicanas" de Lord Kingsborough. Secretaria de Fomento, México, 1885.

Robelo, Cecilio A. *Diccionario de Aztequismos, o sea Catálogo de las palabras del Idioma Nahuatl Azteca ó Mexicano, introducidas al idioma Castellano bajo diversas formas.* Museo Nacional de Arqueología, Historia, y Etnología, México, 1912.

———. *Diccionario de Mitología Nahuatl.* Ediciones Fuente Cultural, México, D.F., 1951.

———. *Nombres Geográficos Mexicanos del Distrito Federal: Estudio Crítico Etimológico.* Publicaciones Hechas Baja Los Auspicios de la Secretaría de Instrucción Pública y Bellas Artes. México, 1910.

Siméon, Rémi. *Dictionnaire de la langue nahuatl ou mexicaine*, rédigé d'après les documents imprimés et manuscrits les plus authentiques et précédé d'une introduction. Paris, 1885.

———. *Estudios Gramaticales del Idioma Nahuatl.* Escritos en francés por Rémi Siméon y traducidos con notas y adiciones, por Lic. Cecilio A. Robelo. Edición del Museo Nacional de México. 1902.

VI. MODERN STUDIES

Acosta, Jorge R. "La Tercera Temporada de Exploraciones Arqueológicas en Tula, Hgo., 1942," *Revista Mexicana de Estudios Antropológicos*, Tomo VI, Núm. 3, Sept. 1942–Diciembre 1944, pp. 125–164.

Acosta Saignes, Miguel. "Los Pochteca: Ubicación de los Mercaderes en la Estructura Social Tenochca. *Acta Antropológica* I:1 México, Junio, 1945.

———. "Los Teopixque," *Revista Mexicana de Estudios Antropológicos*, Tomo VIII, Núms. 1, 2, 3, enero-diciembre, 1946, pp. 147–205.

———. *Tlacaxipeualiztli: Un Complejo Mesoamericano entre los Caribes.* Instituto de Antropología y Geografía, Universidad Central de Venezuela, Caracas, Venezuela, 1950.

Alcocer, Ignacio. *Apuntes Sobre la Antigua México-Tenochtitlan.* Instituto Panamericano de Geografía e Historia, Tacubaya, D. F. 1935.

Álvarez, Laura. "Moctezuma's Health Resort," *Pemex Travel Club Bulletin*, Vol. XV, Num. 271-A, August 1, 1955, pp. 8–12. (With photographs of rock carvings.)

Anderson, Arthur J. O. and Charles E. Dibble. *Florentine Codex.* See III. Early Chronicles: Sahagún, Fray Bernardino de.

Apenes, Ola. *Mapas Antiguos del Valle de México.* See IV. Collections.

———. "The Pond in Our Backyard," *Mexican Life* XIX, No. 3, March 1943, pp. 15–18, 60.

———. "Una Tabla para Cálculo y Correlación del Calendario Mexicano," *Revista Mexicana de Estudios Antropológicos*, Tomo III, Núm. 3, 1939, pp. 185–190.

———. Privately duplicated and distributed table correlating tonalamatl with lords of day hours, lords of night hours, and directions.

Armillas, Pedro. "Tecnología, Formaciones Socio-Económicas y Religión en Mesoamérica." From Sol Tax: *The Civilizations of Ancient America.* Vol. I, *Proceedings of the 29th International Congress of Americanists*, University of Chicago Press, 1951.

Barlow, Robert N. Anales de Tlatelolco: Unos Annales Históricos de la Nación Mexicana y Códice de Tlatelolco. See II. Annals.

———. "Anales de Tula, Hidalgo." See II. Annals.

———. *El Códice Azcatítlan.* See I. Codices: Azcatítlan.

———. "Conquistas de Los Antiguos Mexicanos," *Journal de la Société des Américanistes, Nouvelle Série*, Tome XXXVI, 1947, pp. 215–222.

———. "La Crónica X: Versiones coloniales de la historia de los Mexica Tenochca," *Revista Mexicana de Estudios Antropológicos*, Tomo VII, Núms. 1, 2, 3, 1945, pp. 65–87.

———. *The Extent of the Empire of the Culhua Mexica.* Ibero-Americana: 28, University of California Press, Berkeley and Los Angeles, 1949.

———. "La Fundación de la Triple Alianza," *Anales del Instituto Nacional de Antropología e Historia* III, 1947–48, pp. 147–155.

———. "Materiales Para una Cronología del Imperio de los Mexica," *Revista Mexicana de Estudios Antropológicos*, Tomo VIII, Núms. 1, 2, 3, enero-diciembre, 1946, pp. 207–215.

———. "The Periods of Tribute Collection in Moctezuma's Empire." Carnegie Institution of Washington, Division of Historical Research, *Notes on Middle American Archaeology and Ethnography*, No. 25, 1943.

———. "Un Problema Cronológico: La Conquista de Cuauhtinchan por Tlatelolco," *Tlatelolco a Través de los Tiempos* X, Núm. 4, 1948, pp. 43–47. Sobretiro de *Memorias de la Academia Mexicana de la Historia* VII, No. 2, abril-junio, 1948.

Barlow, Roberto and Byron McAfee. *Diccionario de Elementos* Fonéticos en Escritura Jeroglífica. See V. General Reference Tools.

Berlin, Heinrich. *Anales de Tlatelolco: Unos Annales Históricos de la Nación Mexicana y Códice de Tlatelolco.* See II. Annals.

———. *Historia Tolteca-Chichimeca: Anales de Quauhtinchan.* See II. Annals.

Bernal, Ignacio. *Compendio de Arte Mesoamericano*, México, 1950. Enciclopedia Mexicana de Arte Núm. 7, Ediciones Mexicanas.

______. "Exploraciones en Coixtlahuaca, Oaxaca," *Revista Mexicana de Estudios Antropológicos*, Tomo X, 1948–1949, pp. 5–76.

Beyer, Hermann. "El Jeroglífico de Tlacaelel," *Revista Mexicana de Estudios Antropológicos*, Tomo IV, Núm. 3, Sept.-Dec., 1940, pp. 161–164.

Caso, Alfonso. *The Aztecs: People of the Sun*, University of Oklahoma Press, Norman, Oklahoma, 1958.

______. "Los Barrios Antiguos de Tenochtitlán y Tlatelolco," *Memorias de la Academia Mexicana de la Historia*, Tomo XV, No. 1, México, D. F., 1956, pp. 7–63. With maps.

______. "El Calendario Mexicano," *Memorias de la Academia Mexicana de la Historia*, Tomo XVII, 1958, No. 1, pp. 41–96.

______. "El Calendario Mixteco," *Historia Mexicana*, Vol. V, 4, Núm. 20, 1956, pp. 481–497, México, D. F.

______. "Un Códice en Otomí." See I. Codices: *Otomí Codex of San Mateo Huichapan.*

______. "La Correlación de los Años Azteca y Cristiano," *Revista Mexicana de Estudios Antropológicos*, Tomo III, Núm. 1, enero-abril, 1939, pp. 11–45.

______. "The Eagle and the Nopal," *The Social Sciences in Mexico and News about the Social Sciences in South and Central America.* Vol. 1, No. 1, May, 1947, Mexico, D. F.

______. "Explicación del Reverso del Codex Vindobonensis" See I. Codices: *Vindobonensis.*

______. "Fragmento de Genealogía de los Príncipes Mexicanos. See I. Codices: *Fragment.*

______. *Homenaje al Doctor Alfonso Caso.* México, 1951.

______. "*El Mapa de Teozacoalco.*" See I. Codices: *Teozacoalco.*

______. *La Religión de los Aztecas.* Enciclopedia Illustrada Mexicana, Imprenta Mundial, México, 1936.

______. "Instituciones Indígenas Precortesianas," *La Memoria del* Instítuto Nacional Indigenista, Tomo VI, México, 1954, pp. 15–27.

Cervantes y Cristóbal, Roman. "Los Nahuales en Oaxaca," *Anuario de la Sociedad Folklórica de México*, Vol. VI, 1950, pp. 471–474.

Chavero, Alfredo. *México Atrevés de los Siglos.* Bajo la dirección del General D. Vicente Riva Palacio. Mexico y Barcelona, 1887–1889. 5 vol. Tomo I: "Historia Antigua y de la Conquista," escrita por el Lic. D. Alfredo Chavero.

Christensen, Bodil, "Notas Sobre la Fabricación del Papel Indígena y su Empleo Para 'Brujerías' en la Sierra Norte de Puebla," *Revista Mexicana de Estudios Antropológicos*, Tomo VI, Núms. 1-2, 1942, pp. 109–124.

Clark, James Cooper. *Codex Mendoza.* See I. Codices: *Mendoza.*
Cook, Sherburne F. and Lesley Byrd Simpson. *The Population of Central Mexico in the Sixteenth Century.* Ibero-Americana: 31, University of California Press, Berkeley and Los Angeles, 1948. (With map.)
Dávila Garibi, J. Ignacio. *Arbol Genealógico de los Monarcas Aztecas.* Editorial Cultura, T.G.S.A., México, D. F., 1949.
_______. *Del Nahuatl al Español.* See V. General Reference Tools.
Dibble, Charles E. *El Antiguo Sistema de Escritura en México.* See V. General Reference Tools.
_______. *Códice en Cruz.* See I. Codices: *Códice en Cruz.*
_______. *Códice Xolotl.* See I. Codices: *Xolotl.*
_______ and Arthur J. O. Anderson. *Florentine Codex.* See III. Early Chronicles: Sahagún, Fray Bernadino de.
Doutrelaine, M. Le Colonel. "Manuscrit Figuratif Circulaire." See I. Codices: *Manuscrit Figuratif Circulaire.*
Dutton, Bertha P. "Tula of the Toltecs," *El Palacio*, Vol. 62, No. 7–8, July-August 1955, pp. 195–256.
Esquivel Obregón, T. *Apuntes Para la Historia del Derecho en México.* Trabajos Jurídicos de Homenaje a la Escuela Libre de Derecho en su XXV aniversario. Editorial Polis, México, 1937–1943. 5 vol. (Tomo I: Los Orígenes (1937) and Tomo II: Nueva España (1938).
Fernández, Justino. *Coatlicue: Estética del Arte Indígena Antiguo.* Centro de Estudios Filosóficos, México, 1954.
García Granados, Rafael. *Estudio Comparativo de Los Signos Cronográficos en los Códices Prehispánicos de Méjico.* See V. General Reference Tools.
_______. *Diccionario Biográfico de Historia Antigua de Méjico.* See V. General Reference Tools.
Garibay K., Angel María. *Historia de la Literatura Náhuatl.* Editorial Porrua, S. A., México, 1953–54. Two volumes.
_______.*Llave de Náhuatl.* See V. General Reference Tools.
_______. *La Poesía Lírica Azteca: Espozo de síntesis crítica.* Bajo el signo de "Ábside," México, 1937.
_______. *Poesía Indígena de la Altiplanicie.* See IV. Collections.
_______. "Relación Breve de las Fiestas de los Dioses." See III. Early Chronicles: Sahagún.
Gay, José Antonio. *Historia de Oaxaca*, México, 1881. Two volumes.
Gibson, Charles. *Tlaxcala in the Sixteenth Century.* Yale Historical Publications. Yale University Press, New Haven, 1952.
Gillmor, Frances. "Estructuras en la Zona de Texcoco Durante el

Reino de Nezahualcoyotl según las Fuentes Históricas," *Revista Mexicana de Estudios Antropológicos*, Tomo XIV, Primera Parte, 1954–55, pp. 363–371.

———. *Flute of the Smoking Mirror: A Portrait of Nezahualcoyotl, Poet-King of the Aztecs.* University of New Mexico Press, Albuquerque, N.M., 1949.

Jiménez Moreno, Wigberto. *Códice de Yanhuitlán.* See I. Codices: *Yanhuitlan.*

———. *La Colección Troncoso de Fotocopias de Manuscritos*, Mexico, 1939.

———. "Cronología de la Historia de Veracruz," *Revista Mexicana de Estudios Antropológicos*, Tomo XIII, Núms. 2 y 3, 1952–53, pp. 311–313. Volume entitled also: *Huaxtecos, Totonacos y Sus Vecinos.*

———. *Historia Antigua de México.* Publicaciones de la Sociedad de Alumnos de la Escuela Nacional de Antropología e Historia, Num. 1, México, D. F., noviembre de 1953. (Mimeographed.)

———. "Síntesis de la Historia Precolonial del Valle de México," *Revista Mexicana de Estudios Antropológicos* XIV, Primera Parte, 1954–55, pp. 219–236.

Kelly, Isabel and Angel Palerm. *The Tajín-Totonac:* Part I—History, Subsistence, Shelter and Technology. Smithsonian Institution, Institute of Social Anthropology, Pub. No. 13, Washington, 1952. (Includes chronological tables and maps of conquests in prehispanic period.)

Kirchoff, Paul. "El Autor de la Segunda Parte de la Crónica Mexicayotl," *Homanaje al Doctor Alfonso Caso*, México, 1951, pp. 225–227.

———. "Land Tenure in Ancient Mexico," *Revista Mexicana de Estudios Antropológicos*, Tomo XIV, Primera Parte, 1954–55, pp. 351–361.

Kohler, J. *El Derecho de Los Aztecas.* Traducido del Aleman por Robalo y Fernández. Edición de la Revista Jurídica de la Escuela Libre de Derecho. México, 1924.

Kubler, George and Charles Gibson. The Tovar Calendar. See I. Codices: *Tovar.*

Leal, Luis. "El Códice Ramírez," *Historia Mexicana*, Vol. III, Num. I, Julio-Agosto, 1953, pp. 11–33.

———. *El Cuento y la Leyenda en las Crónicas de la Nueva España.* Doctoral thesis, University of Chicago, 1951. (No. T-894 University of Chicago Library, Dept. of Photographic Reproduction-microfilm.)

León, Adrián. See III. Early Chronicles: *Crónica Mexicayotl.*

León Portilla, Miguel. *La Filosofía Nahuatl.* Estudiada en sus Fuentes. Instituto Indigenista Interamericano, México, 1956.

León y Gama, Antonio. "Descripción de la Ciudad de México antes y después de la llegada de los Conquistadores Españoles," *Revista Mexicana*, Tomo I, 1927.

———. *Descripción Histórica y Cronológica de las Dos Piedras que se Hallaron en el Año 1790 en la Plaza Principal de México*, México, 1832.

Linné, S. *El Valle y La Ciudad de México en 1550:* Relación histórica fundada sobre un mapa geográfico, que se conserva en la biblioteca de la Universidad de Uppsala, Suecia. The Ethnographical Museum of Sweden, Stockholm. New Series, Publication No. 9. Stockholm, Sweden, 1958.

López, González, Valentín. *Breve Historia Antigua del Estado de* Morelos. Cuadernos de Cultura Morelense. Departamento de Turismo y Publicidad, 1953.

McAfee, Byron and R. H. Barlow. "Titles of Tezcotzinco." See III. Early Chronicles.

Melgarejo Vivanco, José Luis. *Historia de Veracruz.* (Tomo I: Época Prehispánica.) Gobierno de Veracruz, Jalapa, 1949.

Mendieta Nuñez, Lucio. *El Derecho Precolonial.* Enciclopedia Ilustrada Mexicana, No. 7. Porrúa Hermanos y Cia., México, D.F., 1937.

Mengin, Ernest. "*Commentaire du Codex Mexicanus* Nos. 23–24 de la Bibliothèque Nacional de Paris." See I. Codices: *Mexicanus.*

———. *Die Mexikanische Bilderhandschrift Historia Tolteca-Chichimeca.* See II. Annals: *Historia Tolteca-Chichimeca: Anales de Quauhtinchan.*

———. *Unos Annales Históricos de la Nación Mexicana.* See II. Annals: *Anales de Tlatelolco.*

Molins Fábrega, N. "El Códice Mendocino y la Economía de Tenochtitlan," *Revista Mexicana de Estudio Antropológicos.* Tomo XIV, Primera Parte, 1954–55, pp. 303–335.

Monzón, Arturo. *El Calpulli en la Organización Social de los Tenochca.* Instituto de Historia, México, 1949.

Muller, Florencia. *Historia Antigua del Valle de Morelos.* Contribución al Primer Congreso de Historiadores de México y Estados Unidos que se celebró en Monterrey, N. L., del 4 al 9 de septiembre de 1949. México, D. F., Julio, 1949. (Acta Antropológica.)

Nicholson, H. B. "The Birth of the Smoking Mirror," *Archaeology*, Vol. 7, No. 3, Autumn 1954, pp. 164–170.

______. "The Chapultepec Cliff Sculpture of Motecuhzoma Xocoyotzin," *El México Antiguo*, Tomo IX, 1959, pp. 379–444.

______. "Native Historical Traditions of Nuclear America and the Problem of their Archaeological Correlation," *American Anthropologist*, Vol. 57, No. 3, June, 1955, pp. 594–613.

Nuttall, Zelia. *Codex Nuttall*. See I. Codices: *Nuttall (Zouche)*.

Orozco y Berra, Manuel. *Historia Antigua y de la Conquista de México*. México, 1880. 4 vols. (Vol. III treats the Aztec period.)

Palacios, Enrique Juan. *Huaxtepec y sus Reliquias Arqueológicas*, Secretaría de Educación Pública, 1930. This contains as an appendix the "Descripción del Guaxtepeque" of 1580. q.v. See III. Early Chronicles.

Palerm, Angel and Eric R. Wolf. "El Desarrollo del Área Clave del Imperio Texcocano," *Revista Mexicana de Estudios Antropológicos*, Tomo XIV, Primera Parte, 1954–55, pp. 337–349.

Paso y Trancoso, Francisco del. *Códice Kingsborough*. See I. Codices: *Kingsborough*.

______. *Códice Mendocino: Facsímile Fototipo*. See I. Codices: *Mendoza*.

______. Cristóbal del Castillo: Fragmentos de la Obra General Sobre Historia de los Mexicanos. See III. Early Chronicles.

Peñafiel, Antonio. *Códice Fernando Leal*. See I: Codices: Fernando *Leal*.

______. *Colección de Documentos para la Historia Mexicana*. See IV. Collections.

______. *Nombres Geográficos de México: Estudio Jeroglífico de la Matrícula de los Tributos del Códice Mendocino*. See V. General Reference Tools.

Radin, Paul. *The Sources and Authenticity of the History of the Ancient Mexicans*. University of California Publications in American Archaeology and Ethnology, Vol. 17, No. 1, pp. 1–150, 1920. Contains English translations of Boturni, "*Tlotzin*," "*Quinatzin*," "*Telleriano, Pt. IV*," "*Mendoza, Pt. II*," "*Historia de los Mexicanos por Sus Pinturas*," "*Codex Ramírez*."

Rendón, Silvia. *Ordenanza del Señor Cuauhtemoc*. See I. Codices.

______. *Historia Tolteca-Chichimeca: Anales de Quauhtinchan* See II. Annals.

______. "Seis Relaciones Históricas de la Antiguëdad de Chalco-Amecamecan." See II. Annals: *Annales de San Antón Muñón Chimalpahin. . . .*

Ricard, Robert. *La Conquista Espiritual le México*. Traducción de Angel María Garibay K., México, 1947.

Robelo, Cecilio A. *Diccionario de Aztequismos*. See V. General Reference Tools.

———. *Diccionario de Mitología Nahuatl*. See V. General Reference Tools.

———. *Nombres Geográficos Mexicanos del Distrito Federal: Estudio Crítico Etimológico*. See V. General Reference Tools.

Robertson, Donald. *Mexican Manuscript Painting of the Early Colonial Period: The Metropolitan Period*. Yale University Press, New Haven, 1959.

Rodríguez Rivera de Mendoza, Virginia. "Los Mercados Tradicionales Indígenas de México," *El Almenaque de Previsión y Seguridad de la Compañia Fundadora de Fierro y Acero de Monterrey de Nuevo León*, 1953, pp. 183–193.

———. "El Nahual en el Folklore de México: Sus Transformaciones," *Anuario de la Sociedad Folklórica de México* VII, 1951, pp. 123–137.

Sánchez, Jesús. "Mapa de Tepechpan: Nota Historica Sincrónica y Señorial." See I. Codices: *Tepechpan*.

Seler, Eduard. *Codex Fejérváry-Mayer*. See I. Codices: Fejérváry-Mayer.

———. *Codex Vaticanus No. 3773*. See I. Codices: *Vaticanus B*.

———. *Gesammelte Abhandlungen sur Amerikanischen Sprach- und Alterthumskunde*, Vols. I-V, Berlin, 1902–1923. English translations of German Papers in the above work made under the supervision of Charles P. Bowditch. Published with permission of Peabody Museum, Harvard University, with slight emendations to Vols. 4 and 5 by J. Eric S. Thompson, Cambridge, Mass., 1939. J. Eric Thompson and Francis B. Richardson, editors, Carnegie Institution of Washington.

———. "The Mexican Picture Writings of Alexander Von Humboldt." See I. Codices: *Humboldt*.

———. *The Tonalamatl of the Aubin Collection: An Old Mexican Picture Manuscript in the Paris National Library*. See I Codices: *Aubin Tonalamatl*.

Siméon, Rémi. *Annales de San Antón Muñón Chimalpahin Quauhtlehuanitzin*. See II. Annals.

———. *Dictionnaire de la Langue Nahuatl ou Mexicaine*. See V. General Reference Tools.

———. *Estudios Gramaticales del Idioma Nahuatl*. See V. General Reference Tools.

Soustelle, Jacques. *La Pensée Cosmologique des Anciens Mexicains (Représentation du Monde et de L'Espace).* Conférences Prononcées au Collège de France (Chaire d'Antiquités Américaines, Fondation Loubat) 1939. Hermann & Cie, Editeurs, Paris, 1940.

———. *La Vie Quotidienne des Aztèques a la Veille de la Conquête Espagnole.* Librairie Hachette, Paris, 1955.

Spence, Lewis. *The Gods of Mexico.* T. Fisher Unwin Ltd., London, 1923.

Spinden, Herbert J., "Indian Manuscripts of Southern Mexico," *Annual Report of Smithsonian Institution for 1933*, Washington, pp. 429–451.

Toscano, Salvador. "Los Códices Tlapanecas de Azoyú." See I. Codices: *Azoyú.*

Toussaint, Manuel, Federico Gómez de Orozco, y Justino Fernández. *Planos de la Ciudad de México.* See IV. Collections.

Vaillant, George. *Aztecs of Mexico.* Doubleday, Doran & Co., Garden City, N.Y., 1941. The American Museum of Natural History, Science Series.

———. A Sacred Almanac of the Aztecs (Tonalamatl of the Codex Borbonicus). See I. Codices: *Borbonicus.*

Velázquez, Primo Feliciano, tr. *Códice Chimalpopoca,* See II. Annals.

White, Leslie, ed. *Pioneers in American Anthropology; the Bandelier Morgan Letters 1873–1883.* 2 vol. University of New Mexico Press, Albuquerque, 1940.

Wonderly, William L. "Textos en Zoque Sobre el Concepto del Nagual," *Tlalocan*, Vol. II, No. 2, 1946, pp. 97–105.

VII. REFERENCES USED IN CONSIDERING PROCESSES OF CHANGE IN TRANSMISSION OF INDIAN-NARRATED MATERIALS.

Hoyt, Nelly Schargo. "The Image of the Leader in Soviet 'Post-October' Folklore" in *The Study of Culture at a Distance*, edited by Margaret Mead and Rhoda Métraux. University of Chicago Press, 1953, pp. 234–242.

El Libro de los Libros de Chilam Balam. Traducción de sus textos paralelos por Alfredo Barrera Vásquez y Silvia Rendón, basada en el estudio, cotejo, y reconstrucción hechos por el primero, con introducciones y notas. Fondo de Cultura Económica. México, 1948.

El Libro del Consejo. Traducción y notas de George Raynaud, J. M. Gonzáles de Mendoza, y Miguel Angel Asturias. Biblioteca del

Estudiante Universitario, Ediciones de la Universidad Nacional Autónoma. México, 1939.

Makemson, Worcester. *The Book of the Jaguar Priest. A translation of the Book of Chilam Balam of Tizimin with commentary.* Henry Schuman, New York, 1951.

Mead, Margaret and Rhoda Métraux, *The Study of Culture at a Distance*, University of Chicago Press, Chicago, 1953. Especially Nelly Schargo Hoyt, "The Image of the Leader in Soviet 'Post-October' Folklore," pp. 234–242.

Métraux, Alfred. "Twin Heroes in South American Mythology," *Journal of American Folklore*, April-June 1946, Vol. 59:114–23.

Oakes, Maud. *Where the Two Came to Their Father: A Navaho War Ceremonial.* Given by Jeff King. Text and paintings recorded by Maud Oakes. Commentary by Joseph Campbell. Bollingen Series I. Pantheon Books Inc., New York, 1943.

Popol Vuh: The Sacred Book of the Ancient Quiché Maya. English version by Delia Goetz and Sylvanus G. Morley from the translation into Spanish by Adrián Recinos. University of Oklahoma Press, 1950.

Reichard, Gladys A. *Navaho Religion: A Study of Symbolism.* Bollingen Series XVIII, Pantheon, New York, 1950. 2 vol.

———. *Navaho Medicine Man.* J. J. Augustin, New York, 1939.

Thompson, Stith. *The Folktale.* The Dryden Press, New York, 1946.

———. *Motif Index of Folk-Literature:* a classification of narrative elements in folktales, ballads, myths, fables, medieval romances, exempla, fabliaux, jest books, and local legends. 6 volumes. Bloomington, Indiana, 1955–58.

———. *Tales of the North American Indians.* Cambridge, Mass. 1929.

Index

The text of this book was set by Morneau Typographers in Linotype Monticello, selected by designer Doug Peck for its charm and readability. This transitional face was first cast about 1796 in Philadelphia by Binny & Ronaldson. Chapter heads are handset in Motto.

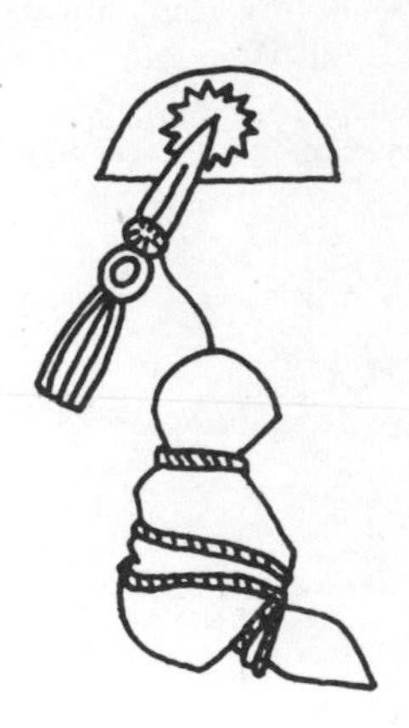